Twenty-Two Cents an Hour

Twenty-Two Cents an Hour

Disability Rights and the Fight to End Subminimum Wages

Doug Crandell

ILR Press

AN IMPRINT OF

Cornell University Press

Ithaca and London

First published 2022 by Cornell University Press

Library of Congress Cataloging-in-Publication Data

Names: Crandell, Doug, author.
Title: Twenty-two cents an hour : disability rights and the fight
  to end subminimum wages / Doug Crandell.
Other titles: 22 cents an hour
Description: Ithaca [New York] : ILR Press, an imprint of Cornell
  University Press, 2022. | Includes bibliographical references
  and index.
Identifiers: LCCN 2021043536 (print) | LCCN 2021043537 (ebook) |
  ISBN 9781501762628 (hardcover) |
  ISBN 9781501763588 (paperback) |
  ISBN 9781501762635 (epub) | ISBN 9781501762642 (pdf)
Subjects: LCSH: Wages—People with disabilities—Law and
  legislation—United States. | People with disabilities—Employment—
  Law and legislation—United States. | Wages—Subminimum wage—
  Law and legislation—United States. | Discrimination against people
  with disabilities—Law and legislation—United States. | People with
  disabilities—Legal status, laws, etc.—United States.
Classification: LCC KF3469 .C73 2022 (print) |
  LCC KF3469 (ebook) | DDC 344.7301/59—dc23/eng/20211029
LC record available at https://lccn.loc.gov/2021043536
LC ebook record available at https://lccn.loc.gov/2021043537

For the millions of Americans past and present who have been segregated and isolated, subjected to the practices of a system designed to keep churning, to keep up the facade of benevolence

Before he was so goddamned special, he was a human being.

—Burton Blatt, *Revolt of the Idiots*

Once you know how hard it is to be looked at, if I'm going to ask someone, can I look at you, I want that to be something that makes their sense of self better.

—Painter and writer Riva Lehrer, in an interview

The problem for many people with disabilities is not that we are not able to work a certain number of hours a week. It's that no one will let us.

—Stella Young, Advocate

CONTENTS

PREFACE

My time in a union shop working with my father at a ceiling-tile factory rife with asbestos, and my grandfather's death from black lung as a coal miner taught me about exploitive labor practices from the inside out. Those experiences would inform my work around disability and employment.

At first, I wasn't certain I could offer much, but gradually I would come to understand how broken the system is, how the tens of billions of dollars spent every year in the United States on vocational rehabilitation didn't produce employment outcomes for workers with the most significant disabilities. In that way I found a purpose. Since then, I've tried for the last thirty years to help reform what can be called the disability industrial complex, where money is difficult to track, and the system itself perpetuates remedies that seem only to create more barriers. I would learn that where someone lives, how they work and are paid, and the nonprofits they depend on, are often mired in unproven interventions. I would come to understand how vulnerable workers with disabilities are inside a maze of confounding human service entities. My initiation into this world brought me to a man living in an institution, and he and others I would meet have fueled my interest and passion in telling this story. I think about him often.

I was only given his name. I stood inside the entrance of Central State Hospital in Indianapolis, Indiana, waiting to get patted down. It was my first visit to the institution, in 1992. I was twenty-four and had been working in the field of disability and mental health for two years. The paperwork was mind-numbing, as were the seemingly endless acronyms rattled off during lengthy treatment-team meetings. My official title was "job coach," and my annual salary was $13,480, less than I had made at the ceiling-tile factory where I'd worked to pay my college tuition and where my dad was still employed.

My type of position had only existed for about a decade. The Americans with Disabilities Act of 1990 had stipulated that workers with disabilities be offered accommodations to help them find real employment, and sometimes that might reasonably include a job coach, someone who can help the worker learn new tasks.[1] Without such assistance people with disabilities were often relegated to workshops where it was common—and legal—for them to earn twenty cents an hour or less. In fact, many of the people I tried to help find jobs were instead whisked up and placed in such workshops, sometimes without their consent. I'd seen weekly paychecks that totaled just three dollars for forty hours of work. I'd grown up in a union family, where the norm was to think in terms of others; to fight for your rights and fair wages was also to stand up for your fellow coworkers. When I tried to explain to my father what my job was, how I was trying to help people with disabilities find good jobs, I also told him about the subminimum wages, the cents on the hour that some workers made. He said, "That's what a union is all about. Oldest trick in the book is when those in charge try to tell those working that they should be happy with what they're getting, no matter how piss poor."

Riley, the person I'd come to the hospital to see, was in the process of being transferred out as part of an effort to reduce the number of people in the institution. Even from the very beginning in the United States, people in institutions worked, in what were usually called workhouses or poorhouses.[2] Riley was one of hundreds of men and women being "transitioned into the community"—which likely meant being sent to a group home where a day program would be attached that would operate much like a workhouse.

The buildings at the hospital sprawled across 150 acres of smooth green turf and sycamore trees. (Most state mental hospitals I visited had gorgeous campuses that belied the grimy stairwells and darkened restraint rooms behind their walls.) I was aware of the irony of my situation: I, who regularly thought of quitting my job, who could barely get to work on time or comprehend the massive paperwork, who was struggling to leave behind the alcohol and drug habits that had gotten me through my shifts at the ceiling-tile factory—I was being paid to help someone else find rewarding work. It was one of many such hypocrisies in the system: Overweight case managers reported that obese clients needed behavior plans to address their eating. A residential director who often invited coworkers to take a dip in his hot tub expressed grave concerns about how his "retarded" male clients ogled female staffers. A van driver with bad breath and body odor shamed people with disabilities for having poor hygiene.

The woman frisking me wore a name tag that read "Supervisor III." She waved a metal-detector wand over me while chatting with a coworker about recipes. After scouring the contents of my book bag, Supervisor III said, "You with that program then?"

I nodded.

She seemed to pity me. "All you're gonna do is rile them up." She handed me my keys without meeting my eye.

I feared she might be right. The first in my family to attend college, I was out of my element in human services and felt more than a little like a phony. I'd grown up on farms and had held only factory, fast-food, and cleaning jobs before this one. There was both disability and mental illness in my family, plus addiction, and we'd lived on the brink of poverty most of our lives. I'd taken this job hoping to use my degree, but I was afraid I didn't have what it took to be valued for my mind and not my strong back. Most of all I worried I'd have to return to the factory in Lagro, Indiana, and become a "lifer"—the term the union men used for a foolish fellow who'd spent money on a college degree and ended up working in the warehouse anyway, too scared to leave. Still, there was a part of me that sensed I was in the right place, doing the work I was supposed to, even if I didn't have much confidence in my skills.

The truth is, I'd had a hard time letting go of the factory. I often drove more than two hours on the weekends—and some weeknights, too—just to sit with my dad and the union men, eat sandwiches, and smoke. Some nights we'd leave the factory at midnight and drive to the Hoosier Point for a pancake "breakfast." Afterward I'd stand in the parking lot with my dad and the other men, feeling anxious and barely able to breathe. I wanted to stay with them, roll up my sleeves, and let sweat and physical effort rule. In college I'd taken a labor-relations class, and the professor was interested in me because I was a member of the United Paper Workers Union. She had introduced me to Asa Randolph, who in 1925 had organized and led the Brotherhood of Sleeping Car Porters, the first predominantly African-American labor union. The professor had assigned the class an essay based on one of Randolph's most iconic quotes: "The labor movement has always been the haven for the dispossessed, the despised, the neglected, the downtrodden, the poor." I had memorized it, and I thought about it as I waited to meet Riley. In fact, I'd worked in the ceiling-tile factory with a few men who would likely be labeled with some type of intellectual disability. Some couldn't write, several others couldn't read, and more than a few had trouble with learning new tasks. They had the union on their side though, and it had aided them in finding and keeping a job with a living wage.

After walking what seemed like a mile in a fog of bleach and Pine-Sol, I finally approached room 203. Riley was one of the last on his wing to go. From his chart, which I'd been handed the Friday before, I knew he was ten years older than I, less than five feet tall, and had been labeled with numerous deficits and problems. I half expected him to be unresponsive and living in squalor, but he sat on his neatly made twin bed, reading an issue of *Prairie Farmer*. When he saw me in the doorway, he smiled a gap-toothed grin, stood up, and placed the magazine on an end table beside a neatly arranged Bible, a yellow comb, and a container of talcum powder. The cinder block room also contained a small writing desk, a single folding chair, and for reasons I never did find out, a large oil drum lined with a trash bag. On a solitary shelf above the bed gleamed a clear plastic Polaroid Sun 600 Instamatic camera and a brown leather carrying case, obviously oiled with care. It was hard to imagine that Riley had lived there for twenty years. I thought of my own apartment, where the bed was unmade, the sheets unwashed, the floor strewn with clothes.

Riley bowed slightly to me and extended his hand. He wore corduroys, a thin gray sweater, white socks, and brown penny loafers with nickels under the straps. His chart said he'd been abandoned by his parents some twenty years earlier and didn't speak. "Deaf and dumb" was how the paperwork put it. It also said he was "easily agitated, prone to fits, stubbornly defiant." I had started to learn that what was written in the official charts rarely fit the person before me.

"My name is Doug," I said. "I'm your job coach."

Riley's dark-brown eyes examined my face closely, as if he might be trying to remember me from somewhere. Then he sat back down on the bed and picked at his cuticles as I pulled up the folding chair and fumbled with my paperwork. I'd been told there was to be a treatment-team meeting where I'd be filled in on Riley's case, but by the looks of things, it would be just Riley and me. Canceling meetings with no warning was so commonplace in the human-service field it had its own acronym: USWN, for unscheduled without notice.

As I arranged my forms, Riley didn't appear defiant or unruly—more like shyly eager. I clicked my pen and read the first question: "What do you like to do with your spare time?" Too late, I recalled that Riley couldn't hear. He stared intently at my face. "Sorry," I said, and Riley waved my apology off as if he'd heard it. I apologized again, and he shook his head as if to say it was nothing to worry over. It dawned on me that he was reading my lips. I asked if that's what he was doing, exaggerating my words the way people do who don't know any better, and he nodded and smiled. "But that's not in your chart," I said. I rifled through the intake forms and handwritten notes going back two years. Riley began to look bored. I excused myself and left.

At an oval island desk in what once must have been a busy central area, I found a lone woman shoving paperwork into boxes labeled storage. I asked if she knew Riley and explained that I was there to help him find a job. She wished me luck, saying Riley never wanted to do his chores.

I asked if he read lips, and she replied, "Not that I know of, no. But he understands just fine; don't let him fool you."

The woman turned to answer the phone, and I hurried back to Riley's room, where he was fiddling with the camera. He offered it to me, and I looked it over. "Very nice," I said, handing it back. "Do you like photography?"

Riley passed the camera to me again. "Do you want me to have it?" I asked.

He grabbed it and furrowed his brow. He was trying to communicate something to me, but I wasn't getting it. He stomped one of his loafers, the nickel gleaming. Finally, he reached for my hand and placed my fingertips where the film was inserted, examining my face as if to see if I understood.

"Film?"

Riley nodded his head with such force I could hear his vertebrae pop. Then he opened the single drawer of the writing desk and extracted a stack of Polaroids. We sat on the bed together and went through them. There must have been a hundred or more pictures—of the staff, of the institutional grounds, of the cafeteria, of the doctors and nurses, their white coats turning ocher on the aging film. Some of the Polaroids near the end clearly dated from the 1970s, showing people in bell-bottoms with long, straight hair and wide shirt collars.

The rest of the afternoon I followed Riley around the state hospital. Other than the woman I'd talked to at the desk, there was only a handful of staff left on his wing. We passed bulletin boards that held everything from current news clippings to yellowing, mimeographed memos. Riley would stop and examine each board, then walk to the next. At dinnertime we entered a nearly silent cafeteria, where we ate chipped beef over toast with green beans and fruit cocktail. I hadn't drunk milk from a tiny carton since grade school. Before long, I returned with Riley to his lonely wing. A new woman was at the island desk. "Hold on," she said when she saw me. "Where's your visitor's pass?"

"I didn't get one," I said, looking around, as if someone might appear with one for me. "I signed in though."

The woman insisted I wasn't allowed on the ward without a pass, and she took hold of Riley's arm and marched him to his room. The setting sun shone through the windows as Riley disappeared. I stood there for a while, not wanting to go home to my unkempt apartment.

I returned to Central State Hospital two days later. Riley was in his room, polishing the camera's lens with a sock. I sat down next to him on his sagging bed and touched his arm. He stopped what he was doing and stared at my mouth.

"I'm not sure I can help you," I said.

Riley went back to cleaning the camera. He was fastidious, sometimes smelling faintly of bleach, his brown hair cut short and combed so purposefully that the lines of it reminded me of a newly planted field. He stood and placed the camera carefully on the shelf, then motioned for me to follow him.

We walked the hospital grounds. I was beginning to understand Riley better: the way he pointed, nodded, cut his eyes to the side. The few words he spoke wore him out, but he seemed to like it when I talked. We passed a fenced-off pond and climbed a green hill dotted with sycamore saplings like candles on a cake.

"What about a job working with cameras?" I asked.

Riley nodded and pretended he was taking pictures.

"I'll see what I can find," I told him. The sun was starting to set, the light turning golden. Riley's digital wristwatch chimed, and he shut off the alarm and started toward the cafeteria. I followed, and I was struck again with how competent he was.

The following Monday I signed Riley out, and we hit the road. He was so short that the bucket seat of my ratty Caprice swallowed him up. He held his Polaroid 600 in his lap like a religious relic.

Our first stop was a pharmacy. Riley knew where the right film would be. He approached the glass case and peered in. I asked the woman behind the counter for ten packs of Insta-Color, enough to take eighty photos. As she started stacking them on the counter, Riley nodded and didn't take his eyes off the film. Afterward we got burgers, shakes, and fries at a drive-through, and I drove to a park. We ate quickly. Riley got out of the car with his camera and a pack of film. At a picnic table Riley ripped open the pack and expertly fitted the film into place. He sat for a moment, looking down at the camera in his lap. He'd had it a long time and had used it to capture images of the people who had come in and out of his life.

Riley took just three carefully chosen pictures that day: a sycamore tree with a crow perched on a limb; a man with a long beard sitting on a bench; and two white poodles that looked exactly alike. After a few hours my beeper started trilling—no doubt someone at the institution had complained that we'd been gone too long. In the car Riley kept arranging the three Polaroids along his thigh, touching their edges lightly, making imperceptible adjustments.

On the hospital's front steps, we were greeted by a staff member with a goatee and kind eyes who put his arm around Riley and asked if he'd seen any pretty ladies. The man introduced himself to me as Sid. Riley handed me the camera, and I snapped a picture of the two of them. After it developed, Sid pointed to Riley's image and asked who that handsome devil was. Then the two of them started using sign language.

"I didn't know Riley signed," I said.

Sid explained that neither of them was fluent; it was a little American Sign Language mixed with gestures they'd devised.

That's when I recognized Sid from the Polaroids in Riley's desk drawer. He was the man in the denim shirt with the black hair past his shoulders—only now it was short and graying.

As I turned to leave, Riley and Sid were on their way back inside the cavernous building. Right before the door closed, Riley stopped Sid and snapped a photo, pulling it from the camera, and blowing on it.

On my last trip to the factory, after the others had fired up their trucks and slowly exited the parking lot, Dad got a squeegee and Windex from his truck and started to clean the windows of my car. He said they were so dirty, he didn't understand how I could see out of the goddamn things. When he was finished, he adjusted his cap, lit a Salem, and exhaled smoke. I'd seen the expression on his face before. He was trying to get the words to come. Crickets chirruped, the power station hummed, and light flickered from the dock doors. After a long moment Dad said, "I like the visits, son. . . ." He looked away toward the dark road in front of the factory. My throat ached as if I'd swallowed a golf ball.

"You got a lot of work there in Indianapolis," Dad said. "You should try hard. Don't think it'll come easy." I think he knew I was stuck between the working life I'd always known and one I still didn't understand. He got in his truck and started the engine. "Be careful on the bypass," he said. I thought I'd heard a quaver in his voice, but I couldn't be certain. I watched as he turned onto the road and disappeared. The factory and my union upbringing would serve me well in my new profession for years to come.

After the drive back to my empty apartment, I tried typing a basic résumé for Riley on my electric typewriter. By morning I'd slept only a couple of hours, and I rushed to make copies at the Kinko's down the street. The resume didn't have much on it, just the few small jobs the institution provided Riley, sweeping, mopping, some landscaping. Under hobbies, I emphasized his photography.

I had work to do for the rest of the people I'd been assigned to help find jobs, but I picked up Riley every other day. I wanted to get to know him better. We had a beer at a pub in Broad Ripple, a little village north of downtown. We played Putt-Putt golf. We jogged in Eagle Creek Park. (Riley wasn't fast, but he loved the running shoes I'd bought him.) We took tours of my friends' workplaces: one worked at a vet; another operated a carpet-cleaning business. We visited the fire station, the library, the fairgrounds, the zoo, the university campuses. We volunteered at a homeless shelter, where Riley took Polaroids of people as they received their paper plates of white bread and meat loaf. He gave them the photos to keep.

On days when I didn't visit, I missed Riley. At night, when I felt tempted to smoke and drink, I pictured him lying alone in his dormitory room, the Polaroid camera on the shelf above him, the nearly abandoned wing deathly quiet. I was trying hard to find him a job. I'd cut back on beer and weed and focused on contacting employers, but none of the fast-food places was interested in hiring someone who didn't speak much or hear. I stayed up late paging through classified ads and picking up my apartment. I cleaned the tub, vacuumed, and put away laundry. I called my dad at the warehouse to talk about the union negotiations, and he seemed relieved that I was phoning him from Indianapolis and not coming to see him in person. In the morning I went to the department of labor office and copied job listings. Most were for landscaping, construction, and telemarketing, but one stood out: Robert's Camera Shop needed a salesperson. I knew Riley wouldn't be a perfect fit—he couldn't talk to customers—but maybe he could do something there, maybe they'd see his passion for photography. I made an appointment with a manager, telling him I was interested in the position myself.

The next day I went to the meeting and explained my real purpose. It was an awkward part of my job: How much should I reveal up front? The manager agreed to meet Riley, and I rushed to the state hospital. On the way, I made a list in my head of what Riley would need: a jacket, a necktie, some cologne.

In the hospital parking lot I noticed news vans lined up along the sidewalk and a fleet of vehicles with government tags. Two more news vans arrived, their back doors opening before they even came to a full stop.

I got out of my car and headed for the front entrance of Riley's building, but a security guard stopped me. "Not today," he said.

I asked what was going on.

"We're on lockdown," he said.

"Why?" I asked, worried about Riley, but the security guard just went back inside and locked the door. On the steps where I'd taken Sid and Riley's picture, a podium had been erected, and folding chairs were arranged at the bottom for the media. My pager was going off over and over: my boss, my coworkers, and other numbers I didn't recognize. I waited around rather than drive back to the office, trying to remember where Riley's room was as I peered up at the third floor.

After an hour or more the hospital administrator and the governor's public-relations staff read prepared statements. Apparently, someone had died overnight: a woman had been found drowned in a bathtub. The administrator announced that he and his staff would cooperate fully with the governor's office to determine what had gone wrong. Then the press conference was over.

I made one last attempt to get inside, but the door was locked. A placard on the window said the hospital would resume normal visiting hours once the situation had been resolved. I walked back to my car, looking over my shoulder as if hoping to see Riley exiting the front doors with Sid and his camera. I stayed in the parking lot until most of the other vehicles had left. By then my beeper had gone dead.

That night at my apartment I watched the news. There was talk of a grand-jury investigation surrounding the bathtub drowning and another case in which a person had frozen to death in bed because a window had been left open. Over the next month more charges of abuse and neglect emerged. There were plans to close the hospital completely. My every attempt at visiting Riley was thwarted. I was no longer on the list and getting back on it seemed impossible. Where once there'd been a paucity of staff, now the place seemed overrun by professionals.

Weeks went by, and I worked with the rest of the people on my *caseload*, the strange term echoing in my head, as if the people I was trying to help were burdens packed in a case. Sitting at my desk one afternoon, I opened a letter that said Riley would no longer need my services. He'd been admitted to a workshop program up north, on the Illinois border. The memo listed the reason for Riley's move as "IS-ADLs for employment." I went in search of someone to explain the acronym and learned that it stood for "insufficient activities of daily living." I thought of Riley's neatly made bed, and how he'd taught himself lip-reading and some sign language. I thought of how he'd survived for decades in the institution—something I did not think I could have done myself.

I called the hospital, pretending I needed Riley to sign something, but the receptionist told me to put it in the mail. Finally, I asked my boss if I could talk to her. She was carrying a load of files, and I followed her into a room lined with filing cabinets.

"I need some help getting to see the guy at Central State," I said. "They won't let me in."

She dropped the stack of files on her desk, sat down, and blew hair out of her eyes. She wished she could help, she said, but with the investigation, there was nothing she could do. "Try focusing on the other people on your caseload." That phrase sounded even more ridiculous.

"But I was so close," I said. I told her I couldn't get his face out of my mind.

My boss handed me a tissue and said, "Look, this work isn't for everyone." She told me there was no way to do it well and not let it get to you.

Back at my desk I pictured Riley riding in a van up north, looking out the window at the flat fields going by. I hoped that Sid would get to ride with him and that there'd be a few stops where Riley could take pictures. Later I sent more packs of film to an address I'd tracked down for him, but I never saw Riley again. I still have some of those Polaroids, including a blurry one that Sid took of Riley and me together, sitting on a bench at the hospital. If I focus hard enough on his face, I can almost make out his expression.

Like so many, though, Riley was lost inside a system that purported to help him, but he and multitudes of others were primarily seen as cheap labor, with added revenue attached in the way of billing state and federal funding sources. As Dr. Amos Wilson, the revered author and professor of psychology, stated so clearly, "If you want to understand any problem in America, you need to focus on who profits from that problem, not who suffers from the problem."

That focus suggested by Dr. Wilson is important as a foundation to understand the issue of paying subminimum wages to workers with disabilities. The legality of doing so is both a symptom of—and a catalyst for—the disability industrial complex, which, like our military industrial complex, is often hidden and sometimes byzantine, and represents tens of billions of dollars of funding each year. With little input from the citizens that pay for it, these systems are lacking in concrete, measurable outcomes. These are the themes of this book, along with a focus on the history of what it means to live in America with a significant disability, specifically those disability labels referred to as intellectual and developmental. I attempt to cover the story of subminimum wages in the light of the battle by advocates to consider disability rights as civil rights. We will go into the details of the Goodwill boycotts related to subminimum wages, and we will meet Anil Lewis, a self-proclaimed "blind, black man from the South." Mr. Lewis was instrumental in conceiving the boycotts. He told me in an interview on the use of subminimum wages, "I know how to deal with racism, but when someone is telling everyone they're doing God's work, that's an insidious benevolence. That's not the God I know, the God I know freed the Hebrews, he didn't give them more straw, he set them free." Lewis was originally labeled *educably mentally retarded*, but eventually he became the first member of his family to graduate from college.[3] He's currently the executive director for blindness initiatives for the National Federation of the Blind—and an outstanding oratorical advocate.

Mr. Lewis and many others represent what is at stake. How does one live and work in America with a significant disability when the systems are soaked in our uniquely peculiar American practices of special-interest lobbying, marginalization, and fundamental resistance to change?

Acknowledgments

I'd like to thank the staff at Cornell University Press for their help and support in bringing this book to life.

Dr. Zo Stoneman at the University of Georgia was supportive of my research and encouraged me to keep going. Brianna Smith was invaluable in making certain the citations were accurate. Dr. Steve Hall, my first boss away from farms and factories, introduced me to Burton Blatt's work and so much more. Thank you, Steve.

I want to thank Nancy Brooks-Lane for her work in this field and also for being a dedicated and gentle first reader.

I'm honored to work with kind and smart people at the Institute on Human Development and Disability and creative colleagues at Griffin-Hammis Associates. Thanks to all of you for helping me with the book.

Lastly, my deepest thanks go to the people who were willing to talk to me about their own experiences. From workers with disabilities to family members and public servants, I've had the great opportunity to learn from them, and I am grateful.

Twenty-Two Cents an Hour

Part I

1

THE STAGE IS SET FOR
BROKEN PROMISES

In 2009 a story about men with intellectual disabilities working on an Iowa turkey farm laid bare to the general public something that professionals, families, and federal and state officials had long been aware of—and for the most part, complicit in. It would also come to light that the exploitation of the men in Iowa had been going on for thirty years, with a major newspaper story documenting the concerns in the 1970s. The long history of exploiting workers with disabilities stretches back to the early days of industrialization.

For decades the men in Iowa, about thirty in all, had been housed in dilapidated bunkhouses and made to work fourteen-hour days, earning less than a dollar an hour.[1] Gutting, butchering, and performing artificial insemination were all part of the daily work routine. Some of the men tried to escape—and many did—only to be rounded up again by the owners of Henry's Turkey Farm and trucked back to the grim lives they endured. "Verbal abuses included frequently referring to the workers as *retarded, dumbass* and *stupid*. The workers reported acts of physical

abuse including hitting, kicking, at least one case of handcuffing, and forcing the disabled workers to carry heavy weights as punishment."[2] The
supervisors at Henry's Turkey Farm, also the workers' purported caretakers, casually ignored injuries or pain. As the details unfolded, and the investigation picked up steam, it became clear that the owners of the turkey
farm were operating as the men's payee, receiving social security checks
in exchange for substandard housing, and paying the men subminimum
wages. It was legal to pay the men far less than the federal minimum wage
under a law ironically titled the Fair Labor Standards Act of 1938, which
included policies that allowed for workers with disabilities to be paid
significantly lower wages, an exception under a certificate from the US
Department of Labor known as 14(c). The men had little choice in how
they spent their days, when they worked, and for how long. All the men
had various types of intellectual disabilities, a new term that has over-
taken the derisive "mental retardation." At the beginning of the twentieth
century, people were clinically categorized as "idiots," "morons," and
"savants." Language—and the terms and phrases used inside the systems
that purport to benevolently care for people—is an insidious tool used to
justify subminimum wages; it also serves to keep the status quo in place.
The practices and systems that often violate a person's civil rights are the
focus of this book, and we will pay special attention to the systematic application of terms within the disability industrial complex, especially how
workers with disabilities are subjected to arbitrary measures of productivity that are used to keep expectations low and lifelong dependence on
human-service systems high.

Without the Fair Labor Standards Act of 1938, the men who were
beaten, made fun of, and often harassed unmercifully would never have
been at Henry's Turkey Farm in the first place; they were there because of
a strong financial incentive for the owners to exploit the men. Labor costs
are the single most expensive part of operating a turkey farm; when the
owners can pay as much as eight times less than the going rate for labor
profitability is a certainty. At the same time the owners can benefit from
the perception that they are "helping the disabled." Along with the status
of being the employees' SSI payee, these owners were raking in hundreds
of thousands of dollars without scrutiny, even though they should have
been reviewed by the Department of Labor. The Equal Employment Opportunity Commission took on the case after a sister of one of the men filed

a formal complaint regarding her brother's paltry pay. The wage claims for each of the thirty-two workers ranged from $28,000 to $45,000 in lost income over the course of just their last two years before Henry's Turkey Farm was shut down in February 2009. The employees should have been compensated at the average wage of $11–12 per hour, reflecting the rate of pay typically earned by workers without intellectual disabilities who performed the same or similar work.[3]

The trial brought by the EEOC was painful and embarrassing for the men, many of whom had been forced to stay on the turkey farm for decades. The descriptions of cruelty and abuse sounded much like indentured servitude. Bureaucrats took the stand and testified to having suspected the abuses and neglect; they insisted they had had a hard time getting anyone in state government to listen to their suspicions because the public believed the owners of the farm were doing a great public service by caring for the men. In the meantime, behind the closed doors of the bunkhouses, and under the secrecy of the paddocks, warehouses, offices and acres of Henry's Turkey Farm, the horrors were numerous.

The men sometimes went into town for some rest and relaxation, eating at restaurants or catching a matinee, and the citizens viewed them as sweet and hardworking. The town had accepted the facade too, but there were cracks. Sometimes there were unexplained bruises, black eyes, a more pronounced limp. Still, it took nearly three decades for someone to blow the whistle. The state systems that oversee programs in the community are bureaucracies, often understaffed, isolated, fragmented, and operating in a manner unconnected to or unaware of the civil-rights legislation they are supposed to understand and implement. In gauging how well state and local programs are run, I sometimes simply mention the laws and court decisions of recent years. From CEOs to board members of nonprofits delivering disability employment services, I'm astounded how little the major players know about the regulatory guidance that pertains to the industry they work in. The 1999 Supreme Court decision in *Olmstead v. LC* was the most important civil-rights decision for people with disabilities in our country's history. In *Olmstead*, the Supreme Court held that people with disabilities have a qualified right to receive state-funded supports and services in the community rather than in institutions. Yet too few people in power inside the disability industrial complex are even aware that the decision exists. The ubiquitous ADA and the Workforce

Innovation and Opportunity Act of 2014, which is supposed to restrict the use of subminimum wages, are also foreign to many who work in the field of disability and employment.

A federal judge in Iowa ordered the company to pay damages totaling $240 million (the largest verdict in the EEOC's history) for disability discrimination and severe abuse to the thirty-two men he referred to as "mentally disabled employees" who had gutted turkeys at the West Liberty processing plant for $65 a month—41 cents an hour—for more than twenty years.[4] US District Judge Harold Vietor issued the partial summary judgment against Hill Country Farms, d/b/a Henry's Turkey Service, and owner Kenneth Henry in the Davenport District Court. Vietor found that Henry's, whose corporate operations were based in Goldthwaite, Texas, had willfully violated federal minimum wage and overtime laws and was liable for unpaid wages and liquidated damages. In other words, it was still legal to pay subminimum wages to workers with disabilities, but Mr. Henry and his henchmen didn't have the records to prove that their employees could be deemed less productive than "normal workers." If they had, the underpayment of wages referenced in the lawsuit likely could have been dismissed. The case brought attention to how some workers with disabilities were paid in the United States, but Judge Vietor did not have the authority to make it illegal to pay workers with disabilities pennies on the hour; that would require legislation and, in the end, a comprehensive civil-rights battle that would take twists and turns to ultimately determine the fate of hundreds of thousands of workers with disabilities.

For professionals like Cary Griffin, the horrible story had a silver lining. "We believed it was the death knell of paying subminimum wages. Here was a decades-long abuse of a legal public law and it was clear to everyone we were finally going to get legislation that would overturn 14(c)." Griffin, along with countless other dedicated reformists, had been trying to change the disability employment system in the United States, a complex configuration of funding that includes Medicaid, Social Security, vocational rehabilitation, and state dollars, all of which are primarily used to segregate and keep workers with disabilities in prevocational day programs or sheltered workshops. It would be a surprise, though, just who would fight the most adamantly against reform.

While the courts dealt with Kenneth Henry, the Iowa men and their estranged families tried to recover and begin anew. There was indeed momentum in the debate around the ethical and moral considerations of allowing some of America's most vulnerable citizens to be paid so horribly. On June 7, 2012, the National Federation of the Blind (NFB), one of the oldest and largest organizations of Americans with disabilities, took an assertive and well-versed lead in calling for a boycott of Goodwill Industries International, Inc., the nonprofit provider of employment services for people with disabilities and retailer, for its payment of subminimum wages to many of its workers with disabilities. It was a bold move, building upon the wage abuses of the men exploited at Henry's Turkey Farm, which had been profiled in a report by the National Disability Rights Network in 2011. With strategic planning and a penchant for muckraking, the NFB went to work, hoping that timing, social media, and an outraged public would help fuel the reform.

Freedom of information requests filed by the NFB confirmed that some Goodwill Industries employees had been paid as little as twenty-two cents an hour. The NFB and more than forty-five other organizations supported legislation, the Fair Wages for Workers with Disabilities Act, H.R. 3086, which would have phased out and then fully repealed the eighty-year-old provision of the Fair Labor Standards Act that permits special 14(c) certificate holders to pay subminimum wages to workers with disabilities. There was hope, and the path forward to a substantial civil-rights win seemed well lit, even as the other side mounted its plans to lobby, counter the cries of reform, and stop any legislation from becoming law.

Dr. Marc Maurer, president of the National Federation of the Blind, took the opportunity to be unflinchingly assertive on the issue:

> Goodwill Industries is one of the most well-known and lucrative charitable organizations in the United States, yet it chooses to pay its workers with disabilities less than the federal minimum wage. While this practice is currently legal and many entities engage in it, many other nonprofit organizations have successfully transitioned to paying their employees the minimum wage or higher. That Goodwill Industries exploits many of its workers in this way is ironic because its president and chief executive officer is blind. Goodwill cannot credibly argue that workers with disabilities

are incapable of doing productive work while paying its blind CEO over half a million dollars a year. Goodwill should be ashamed of such blatant hypocrisy. We are calling upon all Americans to refuse to do business with Goodwill Industries, to refuse to make donations to the subminimum-wage exploiter, and to refuse to shop in its retail stores until it exercises true leadership and sound moral judgment by fairly compensating its workers with disabilities.[5]

Dr. Maurer and the NFB were passionate about using Goodwill as the touchstone in the debate. The cultural timing was right as young people formed the Occupy movement and focused a great deal of their attention on the plight of minimum-wage earners, casting the slogan: "We ARE the 99%." The progressive initiative was related to a global reaction to the deep economic recession triggered by the subprime mortgage crisis. By organizing a movement focused on how some of the least paid US workers were faring after the banking collapse, Occupy protesters and associated supporters were open to the plight of any worker. Dr. Maurer understood that these forces could be harnessed to tell another story of a forgotten and neglected workforce.

Dr. Maurer kept the intensity at high throttle, sensing that the attention and climate were conducive to bring about the change needed to merge what had been largely a disability-rights issue with the larger cultural workplace-rights movements spreading throughout the country. He asked one of his staffers, Anil Lewis, then director of strategic communications, to spearhead a campaign to raise awareness about subminimum wages—and ultimately to find a way to get legislation passed that would eliminate the 14(c) provision. Rose Sloan, one of the NFB's government affairs specialists, had a knack for interviewing people. Ms. Sloan, a microphone in one hand and her cane in the other, approached workers picketing at Johns Hopkins Hospital for raises above the $11 an hour they were receiving. Making her way through the picket lines and the ancillary crowds, tapping her cane on the cement and approaching clusters of people, Ms. Sloan asked them if they knew some workers were paid so little.[6] Worker after worker at Johns Hopkins expressed disbelief that simply having a disability could mean being subjected to subminimum wages. Goodwill sites in several states were boycotted with a succinct flyer that read, "Do you know Goodwill pays some of its workers as little as 22 cents per hour?" The proponents of maintaining subminimum wages for workers with disabilities soon despised Dr. Maurer and the NFB, claiming they were "just trying to stir this up all over again." In Part III of this book, we will take a closer look at the Goodwill boycott, an act of rebellion that ushered in increased scrutiny by the US Department of Labor's (USDOL) Wage and Hour division, the entity charged with overseeing organizations that hold 14(c) certificates.

Since the 1960s there had been numerous attempts to overturn the provisions of 14(c) that allowed for subminimum wages, but those advocating for systems change and the civil rights of workers with disabilities were thwarted at almost every turn. More harm was actually created with amendments to the 14(c) law in 1986, when the absurdly referenced "minimum subminimum" wage floor was removed and workers with disabilities could be paid as little as a few cents an hour. Prior to the 1986 amendments, workers under 14(c) were to be paid at least half the minimum wage, but now that rule had been successfully lobbied against. It became common for working adults with disabilities to bring home checks as miniscule as a few dollars a week for forty hours. This was one of the many ongoing bait-and-switch moves initiated by the professional lobbyists inside the disability industrial complex. In the words of one of the reformers in Georgia, the battle rages on: "I was awestruck when I first understood that organizations that were supposed to be helping people with disabilities had actually lobbied against the very legislation that would have prevented people with disabilities being paid subminimum wages," says Nancy Brooks-Lane, who in the early 2000s led the movement to shutter sheltered workshops in metro Atlanta. She was met with hostility by staff, legislative representatives, and families. "It was as if we were the ones advocating to pay people pennies per hour. That move in '86 to remove the subminimum wage floor set back the civil rights of workers with disabilities by decades. It's still impacting us today. Low expectations have crept into every facet of disability services, from the capacity of a person to learn, to the way families view provider organizations. It's truly a system predicated upon keeping people segregated in buildings so more billing can be amassed. Of course, there are some excellent agencies doing great work, but many aren't even trying."[7]

Both sides saw the developments of 2011, in the aftermath of the exposure of Henry's Turkey Farm, as part of the same push and pull that had occurred over the last forty or more years. Still, the reformers believed they had momentum. Oregon was spending $30 million a year on funding sheltered workshops within the state. By the start of 2012, a young woman named Sparkle Green, living in Beaverton, Oregon, signed onto a class-action lawsuit, claiming that the state had ignored her desires to leave the sheltered workshop and its subminimum pay for a job she knew she could get and keep in the community if she were provided the support she needed. Sparkle and her coplaintiffs asserted they were being denied their civil rights under the Americans with Disabilities Act (ADA) and the Rehabilitation Acts. Sparkle was being paid an average of just thirty-nine cents an hour though she had nearly perfect attendance and followed all the rules and instructions in the sheltered workshop. The other named plaintiffs were Angela Kehler, 48, who had been forced to remain in sheltered workshops since she was laid off from a successful job at a drugstore; Elizabeth Harrah, 32, who previously worked at McDonald's and Safeway and was now at a sheltered workshop while waiting for assistance to return to competitive employment; and Zavier Kinville, 27, who was also at a sheltered workshop, awaiting an opportunity for integrated community employment. Kinville had volunteered in the community, where his favorite job was reading to children. These were not the snapshots of people too disabled to work; because these workers could legally be paid subminimum wages, the easiest thing to provide was just that. Along the way, the sheltered workshops that kept Green, Kehler, Harrah, Kinville, and thousands of others segregated and paid pennies on the dollar could bill for other services too—a common situation inside provider agencies, specifically those that serve people with intellectual and developmental disabilities in sheltered workshops. Perhaps a person doesn't like folding and packaging and begins to slow down, get up from the workstations or simply stop altogether, a scenario most of us could imagine ourselves doing if a job didn't hold our attention, especially if we were paid subminimum wages. This reaction sets in motion a professional verdict on productivity: Workers with disabilities doing these repetitive jobs, most often not by choice, are then labeled with new problems to fix, such as "poor attention," "off task behavior," or "work avoidance." These new diagnoses are then inserted into the worker's record, and a new set of interventions to ameliorate these issues is defined and billed for by the human-service agency. The providers of these services are thus incentivized to identify more and more problems. A bureaucrat at a state Medicaid agency told me, "It's a billing scheme that's been accepted as the norm. Show a person with Down syndrome to a state legislator and talk about how 'these people' need more funding. It's a surefire way to fill the nonprofit agency coffers. There's supposed to be rehabilitation, progress, a lessening of paid supports, but it's actually the complete opposite."

The class-action lawsuit in Oregon and another just beginning in 2013 in Rhode Island gave advocates even more hope that finally a bill would be introduced overturning the ability of United States Department of Labor to issue 14(c) certificates and outlawing subminimum wages for good. The awareness campaign was working, and before long the journalist Harry Smith went behind the scenes at a Montana Goodwill to investigate. The story ran on NBC's *Rock Center* on June 21, 2013, five months after the Fair Wages for Workers with Disabilities Act had been introduced.

Harold and Sheila Leigland, both blind, reported that they had to undergo a "stopwatch test" to check their productivity every six months; inevitably their hourly wage went down. They were making $2.35 an hour hanging and sorting clothes at Goodwill, though both have college degrees. Goodwill records showed that while person after person with a disability was making from seventy-nine cents an hour down to twenty-two cents an hour, the regional Goodwill executives were raking in hundreds of thousands of dollars in pay and bonuses. Goodwill's top executives received more than $53.7 million in total compensation in 2011.[8] The ten-minute piece, titled "Wage War," garnered support from other disability-rights entities that had been working behind the scenes and with congressional members to craft a bill that would stop the exploitation of workers with disabilities. During the segment Ari Ne'eman of the Autistic Self Advocacy Network (ASAN) asked Harry Smith how well he himself would do if someone stood outside his office with a stopwatch to rate his productivity. Smith smiled in agreement, recognizing that workers with disabilities were systematically being subjected to standards most of us couldn't pass.

Indeed, the segment on NBC was the first time many Americans had heard that it was legal to pay less than minimum wage to any worker. One of the "ninety-nine percent" picketers at Johns Hopkins Hospital, interviewed by Ms. Sloan, said, "That can't be true. Is it? We're out here protesting $11 an hour while there are some Americans making twenty-two cents an hour?" Ms. Sloan's interviews and the Harry Smith piece on Goodwill were taking hold, bringing awareness to the issue, while the *New York Times* began an investigation of its own regarding how and why Henry's Turkey Farm could happen. More momentum seemed to be on the side of the activists. Along with many others, I felt that it would only be a matter of time before a legislative fix would be crafted and make it out of the House of Representatives to the Senate.

The stage was set for a real debate around reforming the decades-old law that allowed workers with disabilities to be paid paltry and insulting wages. Reformists felt emboldened with the progress of the Oregon and Rhode Island lawsuits, as lawyers from the Department of Justice continued to find that sheltered workshops like the one where Sparkle Green worked in Beaverton routinely kept poor records, applied erroneous productivity standards, and paid workers with disabilities pennies an hour. The advocacy entities marshaled their resources to tweak the Fair Wages for Workers with Disabilities Act that would overturn the use of subminimum wages after a three-year phaseout and transform the country's disability employment laws to fit a twenty-first-century economic mindset. The language of the bill included some specifics aimed at the nonprofits and their conflicting motivations:

> While some employers possessing special wage certificates claim to provide rehabilitation and training to disabled workers to prepare them for competitive employment, the fact that such employers can pay their workers less than the Federal minimum wage gives them an incentive to exploit the cheap labor provided by their disabled workers rather than to prepare those workers for integrated employment in the mainstream economy. Many employers with a history of paying subminimum wages benefit from philanthropic donations and preferred status when bidding on Federal contracts. Yet they claim that paying minimum wage to their employees with disabilities would result in lack of profitability and forced reduction of their workforces.

These were exciting strides forward because the small crack that had always existed to get the average American's attention regarding this issue was widening, and there seemed to be a fully open door now to walk through, to present legislation that was sorely needed. Everything looked primed and ready. The text of the Fair Wages for Workers with Disabilities Act was simple and direct, a perfect bill for those seeking re-election regardless of party affiliation. The bill emphasized that the practice of paying workers with disabilities less than the federal minimum wage dated back to the 1930s, when there were virtually no employment opportunities for disabled workers in the mainstream workforce. It argued that advancements in vocational rehabilitation, technology, and special education in the last four decades had provided workers with disabilities, especially those with intellectual disabilities, with greater opportunities than in the past. The text of the bill stressed that employees with disabilities, when provided the proper rehabilitation services, training, and tools, could be as productive as nondisabled employees, stating, "Even those individuals that are considered most severely disabled have been able to successfully obtain employment earning minimum wage or higher."

The bill had ninety-seven cosponsors, seventy-three Democrats and twenty-four Republicans. It was the first time a bill had been crafted to overturn the practice of paying subminimum wages to Americans with disabilities. Before long, though, small organizations from all over the country, with benevolent, charitable names like Beloved Acres Rehabilitation, began to mobilize. These "community rehabilitation providers," nonprofit organizations like Goodwill but much smaller, receive funds from federal and state governments to provide rehabilitation and training to workers with disabilities, most of them relying on the use of subminimum wages. Trade groups contacted their legislators, and the industry's largest lobbying group, ACCSES, with the tagline "The Voice of Disability Service Providers," located in Washington, DC, marshaled its membership and substantial political resources to advocate for keeping subminimum wages legal.

As the bill was referred to the Subcommittee on Workforce Protections, the National Federation of the Blind and other advocacy organizations provided information to legislators, including a spreadsheet of the organizations (nearly four thousand nationwide) that held subminimum wage certificates.[9]

The bill calling for fair wages for workers with disabilities and the phasing out of subminimum special wage 14(c) certificates under the Fair Labor Standards Act of 1938 was shelved. The effort by Dr. Maurer to shine a light on the practices of Goodwill would continue, however, with lines being drawn and lobbyists entrenched, each side vowing to stay the course. The battle would include players who would have to rationalize maintaining the public policy that created the abuses at Henry's Turkey Farm and the same labor laws that continued to keep Sparkle Green captive in a sheltered workshop in Beaverton, Oregon, earning forty-eight cents an hour. The reformists were wounded and discouraged but felt they had at least now exposed the special interests that had in the past been mainly cloaked in the faux mission statements that claimed to be helping Americans with disabilities. As one activist put it, "If we can't change this piece of public policy, the idea that workers with disabilities should be treated fairly, then what chance does the country have to fix any social issue?" There would be more proposed legislative proposals and political wrangling, of course, and money would be a central focus for trade groups interested in keeping the status quo.

It would be easy to characterize all people, organizations, and other stakeholder proponents of keeping the legal practice of paying workers with disabilities substandard wages as cruel, greedy, civil-rights violators. Indeed, after working so long inside the systems of these practices, then trying to change them from outside, I'm always reminding myself of my own bias—that anyone who desires to keep the DOL law in place is fundamentally flawed. The truth is there are advocates, parents, lawmakers, and social-service professionals who truly believe that keeping subminimum wages in place for workers with disabilities is best for everyone. I obviously disagree. The issue of disability, intellectual, developmental, and otherwise, instantly comes up against what it means to understand productivity in an economic system of capitalism. The notion that disability is natural, and that neurodiversity is a normal variation in the scope of humanity, are fundamental assumptions if our goal is to best utilize every person's talents, even if it takes significantly changing our biases, practices, and workforce development systems. After all, if we are fortunate to live long enough, every human being develops natural disabilities.

Another truth in this story is what 14(c) represents in the powerful disability industrial complex, which embraces exceedingly low expectations of youth and adults with disabilities to learn, work, and live within typical communities. The history of subminimum wages represents the failure of human service agencies, personnel, and funding administrators to make use of creativity, local economics, problem solving, and community organizing. Paying subminimum wages to workers with disabilities is a symptom of a complex system of state and federal programs, policies, and practices that is woefully steeped in interventions that are unproven and rarely tested. In significant ways the billions of tax dollars spent every year in the United States on disability training and employment programs is similar to our healthcare system. We don't know much about what goes into the costs of the services, or how focusing on more preventive interventions (work early, work often, and don't segregate) can impact the outcomes.[10] Like our healthcare systems, the disability industrial complex has corporate and bureaucratic interests that seem to amass control at the top and end up being the major focus of our elected officials. Senator Tom Cotton from Arkansas in particular has been adamant about his support for keeping sheltered workshops and subminimum wages alive and well.[11] It is very easy to portray 14(c) as a kind of benevolent old law that still makes sense. When trade groups associated with large rehabilitation agencies appeal to their elected officials, it is often through photos and videos of older adults with Down syndrome working in a safe, clean, and respectful shop floor, smiles galore and hugs at the end of the day.

Perhaps the best description of the hazards and special interests related to the use of subminimum wages comes from a manual produced by SourceAmerica. One of the largest players in the disability industrial complex, SourceAmerica had been named NISH or the National Industries for the Severely Handicapped until thirty hours of WikiTapes were exposed, resulting in a scandal in 2015.[12] In 1971 the US Congress passed the Javits-Wagner-O'Day Act (JWOD), a law to create employment for people with significant disabilities who might not otherwise be able to find work. Approximately $2.3 billion a year goes to SourceAmerica, intended to support a mandate that requires its contracts, many of them military-based, to employ workers with "severe disabilities"; these workers are supposed to make up 75 percent of the people hired. SourceAmerica, however, relies on a network of nonprofits that also use 14(c) subminimum wage certificates. SourceAmerica offers training to these organizations, as well as advice on a wide range of topics. The SourceAmerica manual provides information and tips for nonprofit organizations that pay their workers with disabilities subminimum wages, specifically information about how to document "why" the worker should be paid so little. The manual warns that if not correctly documented, the nonprofit could face "potential bad PR or exposure in the press and the community, resulting in possible lawsuits"; it goes on to lay out the most prevalent violations related to paying subminimum wages: improperly conducted time studies, failure to use prevailing wage rates, failure to maintain adequate records, and perhaps most disturbing, failure to adjust wages when a job changes or productivity improves.[13] NISH, now SourceAmerica, cannot use its appropriated federal funds for lobbying, but the contracts they get, intended to employ people with severe disabilities, are not considered appropriated funds, allowing them to spend mightily. From 2008 to 2012, NISH/SourceAmerica reported spending $3.5 million on lobbying. One of the bills it lobbied against was none other than the Fair Wages for Workers with Disabilities Act.[14]

Eddie Glaude, Jr., the university professor of African American studies at Princeton University, reveals in his books our penchant for believing "the American lie." Glaude exposes the undergirding of the American thought process: we adhere to a certain set of egalitarian virtues, only to constantly forsake them in the ways in which marginalized people are treated. That lie permeates the disability industrial complex; we say we love and care about people with disabilities, but we don't legislate or advocate in a way that reflects those same values. This book traces the forces that have come together to create a duplicitous and confusing matrix of nonprofits, sometimes mired in segregation, abuse, and the justification of cheap labor, utilized by the very organizations that most Americans assume are on the side of people with disabilities.

We will hear from people who have worked for subminimum wages, as well as people who have been trapped inside the disability industrial complex. We will profile parents who believe their children have been further disabled by a system that values lifelong dependence in order to keep the agency doors open, through the use of unproven practices that are at odds with the way most young Americans learn to work and contribute to their respective communities. This is a story that includes lobbyists, income inequality between highly paid directors of human-service agencies and their workers, and the powerful narratives of citizens with disabilities as they fight hard for social justice, civil rights, and nothing short of emancipation itself.

2

From Evil Intentions to
Unintended Consequences

The view of disability in American culture is ever changing. While now it's common to see fashion models with Down syndrome and characters with physical disabilities and autism in sitcoms, past generations sometimes held very different opinions about why someone was born with developmental disabilities. There was a common and enduring belief that children with epilepsy were possessed by an evil spirit; some religious families believed a child born with disabilities was punishment for sins, specifically sex out of wedlock. It is impossible to separate the history of the treatment and care (in some instances, the mistreatment and physical and sexual abuse) of people with significant disabilities from the views held by the general public, leaders, and physicians who drove the interventions, often applied without consent. It's a dark and heartbreaking saga, and the bad science and misplaced emphasis can be seen today in the programs and services designed to diagnose, treat, house, and employ people with disabilities. The modern system of disability classification has an insidious connection to one of the world's most shameful and evil periods—and its remnants remain.

In Germany during 1939, a married couple, Richard and Lina Kretschmar had a child they named Gerhard; he had been born missing a leg and an arm. He had severe sensory impairments and likely would have had other developmental disabilities. When he was five months old, the Kretschmars decided to take a drastic and dastardly step. In a letter addressed to the headquarters of the Nazi Party, the couple pleaded for permission to legally kill their son. As Nazi loyalists they believed Gerhard, whom they referred to as "the monster," was an abomination and not in line with the pursuit of Hitler's goal of genetic perfection. Hitler asked one of his doctors to investigate the case. After visiting the Kretschmars at their farm, Dr. Brandt decreed Gerhard an "idiot" and a hopeless case. Several days later, baby Gerhard was given a lethal injection in a hospital near the Kretschmar home in eastern Germany. Just a little over a month later, Hitler ordered the Interior Ministry to make certain that physicians registered all babies born with "forms of mental retardation and deformities." Initially, the seizing of babies was somewhat voluntary, then made mandatory and included "all children under three years of age in whom any of the following serious hereditary diseases were suspected: idiocy and Down syndrome (especially when associated with blindness and deafness); microcephaly; hydrocephaly; malformations of all kinds, of limbs, head, and spinal column; and paralysis, including spastic conditions."[1] Rather than lethal injection, sometimes the infants were simply left to starve.

Soon Hitler created the Aktion T4 project, the Nazi program that slaughtered over a million people with disabilities. A euthanasia program called the Charitable Foundation for Cure and Institutional Care began near the Dachau concentration camp and spread to other geographic areas, also targeting adult "defectives," who were considered through the lens of eugenics as "life not fit for life." Soon there were orders for hospitals and institutions to create lists of patients with "defects," physical, mental, or otherwise. Once identified, these people were rounded up, put on buses (benignly called the Community Patients Transports Service) and sent to one of the six gas chambers that Dr. Brandt had helped orchestrate along with the wartime bureaucracy known as the Führer

Chancellery. Aktion T4 was a precursor and practice for the "Final Solution," but these murderous applications of the pseudoscience of eugenics were imported from the United States, where philanthropic powerhouses like the Rockefeller Foundation and the Carnegie Institute, along with the Ivy League universities Yale, Harvard, and Princeton, funded and conducted propaganda research that espoused the notion that defects, along with talents, were passed through the parents' blood. In the United States even the Supreme Court upheld the forcible sterilization of men and women in institutions. Justice Oliver Wendell Holmes is famously quoted as saying, "Three generations of imbeciles are enough." At the Nuremberg trials, some Nazis quoted Holmes's words as part of their defense, and Hitler himself regarded as his bible the book by the American eugenicist Madison Grant, *The Passing of the Great Race*. What ended the lives of children and adults with disabilities in Germany had all started in the United States. Part of the evaluative process in the Aktion T4 Nazi project to determine whether a person with a disability would live or die was the patient's capacity to work. Those paradigms, diagnostics, and ableist views are alive and well in the modern disability industrial complex.

At nearly the same time the origins of paying reduced wages to some US workers with disabilities first appeared in a law passed in the early years of President Roosevelt's New Deal. While full legislation related to labor conditions would be fleshed out in the Fair Labor Standards Act of 1938, including pay, hours, and breaks, along with worker age limits, the precursor was a law known as NIRA (the National Industrial Recovery Act), which was in place from 1933 to 1935. The act, which sought to assist in the nation's recovery from the Great Depression, covered some industries and attempted to establish regulations related to payment of workers. Labor economist William G. Whittaker, writing for the Congressional Research Service in 2005, described NIRA as "codes of conduct" for industrial businesses. Once in place, the codes seemed to confuse both workers and companies alike, with complaints from both sides related to fairness. Still, on February 17, 1934, President Roosevelt signed an executive order on the treatment of workers with disabilities under the auspices of NIRA. The executive order stated that a worker "whose earning capacity is limited because of age, physical or mental handicap, or other infirmity might (under the DOL guidance) be employed on light work at a wage below the minimum established by the Code." Ironically, most Americans had no idea that Roosevelt himself was significantly impacted by the adult polio he had contracted in 1921. Most citizens simply believed he needed a cane to walk; subsequent stories related to the care with which the media was instructed regarding photographing his wheelchair and leg braces are legendary.

In May 1935 the Supreme Court found NIRA to be unconstitutional because a portion of the legislation included the formation of the NRA (National Recovery Administration) to oversee compliance. NIRA was dead, but many of its tenets would be reenacted under the FLSA of 1938, including the payment of reduced wages to workers with disabilities. In NIRA we can see the origins of the current 14(c) certificates. From the very beginning government officials believed it would be necessary to put safeguards in place through a series of written certifications that specified the worker's disability type, how the impairments impacted production output, both in the past, and in future employment. It seemed from the outset there were concerns that some employers might seek to benefit from low-wage labor under the guise of charity, something that can also be found in today's debates related to subminimum wages.

World War II produced physical and mental disabilities in service members returning home from combat, and the American people were in the mood to address the impact of disability on the lives of veterans back on US soil. Veterans returning home had a broad range of disabilities: bilateral hearing loss, brain injuries, blindness, and various bodily injuries ranging from missing limbs to substantial mobility issues, some of which required the use of a wheelchair. The United States was largely a manufacturing economy at the time, and work typically meant using the body for most if not all the required tasks of a factory worker. While the Fair Labor Standards Act of 1938 had created the forty-hour work week, banned child labor, and designed a minimum wage and overtime pay, it had also codified a system of official certificates that would allow employers to pay workers with disabilities below minimum wage. Section 14(c) is part of the legislation that created the legal use of subminimum wages and was born from a public-policy debate surrounding veterans and productivity. From the beginning, the law seemed to arise from good intentions, but it also was conceived with the same vagueness that still plagues it. Frances Perkins, appointed by President Roosevelt and the first woman to lead the

US Department of Labor, as well as the first female cabinet member, was a worker's rights activist, but she was imprecise about which workers the reduced wages would benefit, stating that the legislation would be used for "persons by who reason of illness or age or something else are not up to normal production." "Something else" and "normal" would shape the inclusion of workers with disabilities under 14(c) for decades to come. For those workers with disabilities returning from war, there was no legal subminimum wage set, but common practice normally kept the wages at 75 percent of the lowest rate paid in the respective industry. Once the 14(c) certificates were applied in human-service settings and not businesses in the community, however, new rules were shaped and put into place that essentially created no statutory minimum for hourly wages. What had started as a tool to assist veterans with disabilities returning to the civilian workforce morphed into a set of practices utilized by advocates for people with other types of disabilities.

NIRA and the subsequent FLSA 14(c) section sought to further classify workers with disabilities into distinct categories, decisions that would have a deep ripple effect over many decades. A classification called "industrial homework" covered shut-in contractual work performed in a residence. The most controversial of the categories was the "sheltered workshop," a term whose functional identity was tied to earlier initiatives dating as far back as 1837 at the Perkins Institution, a school for the blind in Boston. The popular term was simply "workshop," and both the name and the intent were drafted into the FLSA categories in 1938.

John Pringle was the first director at the Perkins Institutions, an energetic man with lots of ideas. He arranged for the blind workers to manufacture mattresses, pillows, cushions, an assortment of flooring products, caning used for chairs, and all manner of brooms and brushes. The initial workers were young blind students living and attending school. Later, when adults were admitted to the school, they too worked in the shop, which also had a residence; this practice of housing and providing employment for workers with disabilities can be seen in the abuses at Henry's Turkey Farm as late as 2009. From 1850 through the early decades of the twentieth century, schools for the blind would adopt the workshop theory for the employment of the handicapped at other schools in New York, Pennsylvania, Maryland, Illinois, and Louisiana. Of course, since there were no wage and hour regulations yet, pay and room and board were synonymous.

The first workshop founded and created in 1874 (without a school component) was the Pennsylvania Working Home for Blind Men. Its mission was stated to provide "a Workshop and a Home for homeless Blind Mechanics, teaching useful trades and giving employment to blind persons."[2] By 1934 more than seventy workshops for the blind were operating in the United States. These places and their practices informed the FLSA legislation in 1938 and the creation of legal payment of subminimum wages to workers with disabilities. In one very real sense the FLSA legislation was inclusive of workers with disabilities since the intent of the Fair Labor Standards Act itself was to establish equitable pay for American workers. To have left out workers with disabilities would have been shortsighted and discriminatory, even if they were included due to faulty thinking from the start. From their beginning in authorizing far-reaching wage and hour regulations, the advocates for the blind urged Congress to do more to help sustain the workshops where blind workers were employed. As part of Roosevelt's New Deal package and consistent with the FLSA, the president signed the Wagner-O'Day Act in June 1938, requiring that all government agencies prioritize the purchasing of products to suppliers that employ the blind. In order to seamlessly facilitate government orders to more than seventy workshops, the National Industries for the Blind was created. By 1961 there were over 120 workshops in operation, and the approach would soon catch the eye of other disability advocacy groups, particularly the National Association for Retarded Children (NARC), which would later become known as the National Association for Retarded Citizens in 1973 and which presently operates under the name of the Arc of the United States.

As the construction of workshops grew, many parents and advocates connected to the ARC preferred the term used in the FLSA regulatory language: sheltered workshop. It would prove to be a phrase that would be debated vigorously and contrasted with the present terms used to describe places where workers with disabilities are paid subminimum wages, almost to the point of absurdity. During the last two decades the language used in the arena of disability services and employment to differentiate intent and funding can sometimes seem like a shell game, something done to constantly move the target and shift the discussion from outcomes to process. It all begins with that seemingly benevolent term, sheltered workshop. In fact, when Goodwill responded in 2013 to the boycotts of its stores and sought to redirect attention away from the twenty-two cents an hour that some workers made, they included a footnote in a report that reads, "Sheltered workshop is a pejorative term." Instead, they preferred "center-based work centers" or "facility-based work centers," a testament to the wordplay and wordsmithing tactics that some nonprofits and charitable organizations have used over the years to describe their missions when previous terms become associated with exploitation. Now, as then, the type of work (and its associated wages) drives where an American worker lives, what he eats, who she knows, and their access to healthcare, regardless of disability or not. The story of paying subminimum wages to workers with disabilities, historically and presently, must be viewed through the lens of the capitalist economy in which we live; we cannot talk about work and wages without also addressing our attitudes and stigmas, our biases regarding disabilities and those who have been systematically removed from regular communities, separated from loved ones and denied access to basic human rights.

People of working age with intellectual and developmental disabilities in the 1950s and 1960s were soon given access to 14(c) waivers pertaining to subminimum wages as the American public and its elected officials grew to comprehend how patients were housed and treated in institutions across the country. First, though, those who in the past had been sent off from their home communities to state-run developmental schools or training centers near larger metropolitan cities would have to be liberated. That would happen slowly, but it would soon produce an entire new generation of workers with disabilities needing somewhere to go during the day. The issue of paying some workers with disabilities substandard and insulting wages over the last eighty-five years has often intersected with various disability-rights movements. The legislation and attempts at oversight related to 14(c) have often been at odds with other pertinent laws, civil-rights initiatives, and the larger social, cultural, and generational changes taking place simultaneously.

In the 1960s there were monumental forces at play that would help propel the issue of institutionalized care to the forefront of the debate related to health and human services and, even more broadly, to the notice of regular Americans. Some of these milestones came in the form of further legislation, but for the most part the groundswell originated from two forces: parents, mostly mothers, and academic muckrakers. This type of exposé was embraced by Dr. Burton Blatt, a reformer and the author of a photographic essay book titled *Christmas in Purgatory*. Although there were other advocates at work, it's difficult to find another person in the mid-1960s who did more to uncover the abuses and atrocities occurring as regular practice in the nation's institutional settings. In 1961 Erving Goffman had published his book *Asylums: Essays on the Condition of the Social Situation of Mental Patients and Other Inmates*. While Goffman's book was significantly impactful in terms of reform, Blatt's exposé was compelling and accessible due to the combination of the words and photos that created in the reader a visceral response through the focus on sights and smells. Blatt had also figured out a method to get *Christmas in Purgatory* into the hands of bureaucrats and elected officials who needed to be aware of the depravity of the system that purported to take care of people. Without his efforts rights for people with significant developmental disabilities congregated in massive state-run facilities would have remained under the control of their superintendents.

Dr. Burton Blatt was a scholar, researcher, and educator. After receiving his bachelor of science degree from NYU, he taught special-education classes for almost a decade before going on to receive his doctorate of education with a concentration in special education from Penn State. He was a voracious reader of the classics and a man with a mind that could easily make links between topics using similes and metaphors. As a public speaker he could hold the attention of an audience by using current headlines to drive home a point, making it salient and modern. He wrote poetry and penned a novel. At Syracuse University he served as centennial professor and director of the division of special education and rehabilitation before he was appointed dean in 1976. Such a cerebral biography does not usually come to mind when one thinks of a civil-rights freedom fighter and an exposer of human abuses. In fact, Dr. Blatt wore three-piece suits, was short, stocky, and stood squarely behind the lectern in the university classrooms in Boston and New York where he taught with precision and honesty. He was also a religious man, as his friend Dr. Seymour Sarason pointed out in an introduction to Blatt's collected papers. At his friend's memorial service in 1985, Sarason re-marked, "Most of us who are Jewish are not religious but rather identify with the cultural-historical traditions that surround Judaism. But Burt was religious in that he believed that what he did, what anyone did, had meaning beyond human comprehension, there was mystery in the world, and that mystery obligated him to revere life and to be intolerant of intolerance."[3]

In December 1965 Blatt and photographer Fred Kaplan undertook a daring and professionally dangerous venture. Together they paid their own way to travel to five institutions in Eastern states to covertly pho-tograph and write about the horrendous conditions that existed there. Even for these men, who knew how awful institutional care was in the United States, what they witnessed shook them to the core. Blatt was al-ready a well-known, respected scholar and could have opted to simply continue his work on the educability of people diagnosed with intellectual and other developmental disabilities. He had been regularly published and was on the tenure track at Boston University. Blatt was trying to dismantle the deeply held beliefs that people with intellectual disabilities could not learn or be trained and were therefore warehoused in terrible conditions because they were not valued in the same way as citizens without dis-abilities. This concept was further applied in Wolf Wolfensberger's work on the idea of normalization (1972) and social role valorization (1983).[4] Without Blatt's activism and study much of the disability-rights work in the following decade would not have been possible. Blatt was a storyteller, and he understood that Americans would need to see up close the horrors going on behind the walls of the buildings they believed were there to help people.

Blatt and Kaplan gave their word to several of the administrators that if they were allowed to see the "back wards" of the massive buildings under the guise of "informational tours" the administrators would be kept anonymous, as would the names and locations of the institutions themselves. True to form, when *Christmas in Purgatory* was published and excerpted in *Look* magazine in 1967, Blatt gave credit to the admin-istrators who were willing to join forces. Writing in the introduction of the book, Blatt said, "If we gained an individual's cooperation, despite the obvious risk he would be assuming with respect to his institutional status, and possible job security, we would be taken on a 'tour' of the parts of the institution that he was most ashamed of." The trust Blatt engendered in the administrators of the institutions speaks to his personal ethics, his ability to get others, even those risking a great deal, to consider the lives that were at stake.

As Kaplan and Blatt spent time inside the five institutions on their "tours," they were sickened by what they saw and recorded. Kaplan utilized a hidden camera attached to his belt, tucked under layers of clothing because the staff and attendants were not to know anything; to them the two visitors were there only to see how the institution was run. Considering the technology of the time, and the covert elements placed upon the photographer, the photos are nothing short of heartbreaking—and breathtaking—first for their content and secondly for the artistry they exude. The two saw men and women completely naked and standing or sitting on metal bleachers in "day rooms" where massive drains in the center of the cement floors were caked with excrement. Some of the spaces didn't have concrete, but rather wooden slats, and Blatt, ever the poet, would recall the stench the most, saying he and Kaplan had to have their clothes dry-cleaned after their visits to get the odors out. As a Jewish man and a scholar, he was well aware of the legacy from twenty-five years earlier that emanated from the Nazi T4 project, and he would go on to view America's pivotal role in creating and spreading the false narrative of eugenics as giving rise to what he called *Souls in Extremis*, the title of his book eight years later in 1973. During one of the "tours," a chief physician (unaware of the real reason for the visit) was excited to show the visitors a strange child with a rare condition, a misshapen body and shorter arms and legs, who also displayed a guttural and deep voice, which according to the physician was a telltale sign of an unspecified condition. Demonstrating to Blatt and Kaplan, the doctor pinched the child's leg, mildly at first, in hopes of eliciting a response from the child. Blatt pointed out with his characteristic truth-telling: "The child did not make any sound." It's easy to recognize in Blatt's numerous writings, in his articles and papers and published books, that today he would be called an empath. One can only imagine how difficult and painful it was for him to stick to his investigative reporting, to not simply push the ridiculous physician aside and pick up the child and offer comfort; after all, Burton Blatt had taught children with disabilities in the classroom. The doctor, shockingly, pinched her again, and again, with more force until his next pinch created a gouge, which finally caused the child "to scream in obvious pain."

Once *Christmas in Purgatory* was completed, after Blatt had written the text, with quotes from Sherwood Anderson, Cervantes, and Dante among others, when the photos Kaplan had secretly snapped were developed under red light in trays of chemicals, there was the question of publication. Blatt desired to have the essays and photos published to incite the most public involvement as possible. He and Kaplan pulled the manuscript together and embarked on enlisting publishers. They started with William Morrow, founded in 1927 and now an imprint of HarperCollins, but the publisher wanted more writing included and believed that some of the photos showing naked patients (and patients in obvious pain and distress) would be offensive to the general reading public. Two other commercial publishers thought the book would be a hard sell and believed the photos would be too costly to produce. Blatt and Kaplan enlisted the Kennedy Foundation to help. The family had a deep connection to disability, and Robert Kennedy had been the one to visit several Massachusetts institutions in the fall of 1965, just months before Kaplan and Blatt launched their undercover "tours." Robert Kennedy's reactions to the visits he embarked upon (which were planned and announced) were picked up with great interest by the news outlets. RFK's exposure of what he witnessed shocked Americans who had not given much thought about the treatment of the "mentally retarded." Local, state, and federal officials were outraged and wanted to know how their own state institutions and training schools were run—all of this, six years before Geraldo Rivera would create the exposé documentary of the Willowbrook State School. Blatt managed to get a meeting with Robert and Ted Kennedy, but the Kennedy Foundation didn't feel it could help, nor did the nonprofit that printed the Special Child Publications series. It was one thing, apparently, to expose what one could witness during a planned visit but quite another when the witnessing was done undercover.

Somehow Blatt and Kaplan were able to pique the interest of the first editor at *Life* magazine named Richard Billings. Blatt writes in his book *Exodus from Pandemonium*, "After viewing our pictures, he remarked he would not be able to have lunch that day." *Life* magazine was enthused and committed to assisting with the publication and dissemination of the photos and text through a two-part series, but doing so would require Blatt to reveal the names and locations of the five institutions portrayed. Blatt had given the administrators of the institutions his word, and he believed that revealing the locations wouldn't help the cause because readers might view them as outliers, anomalies in an otherwise sad but necessary treatment. In his introduction to *Christmas in Purgatory*, he writes: "We have a much more forceful reason for not admitting to where we have been. These pictures are a challenge to all institutions for the mentally retarded in the United States. We are firmly convinced that in many other institutions in America we could have taken the same pictures—some, we are sure, even more frightening."

Eventually, a parent group in Connecticut offered to help finance the first edition, and Blatt and Kaplan assigned all royalties to them. *Christmas in Purgatory* was published without giving up the location of the secret tours or the names of administrators. From the professional's point of view, it created equal measures of outrage in both directions. Some were convinced that Blatt and Kaplan had chosen to focus on the worst of the worst, while others believed they had done the country and the people segregated and locked away a tremendous humanitarian service. This same reaction plays out in our times, whenever someone dares expose the secrets of the disability industrial complex.

Copies of *Christmas in Purgatory* were sent to all 535 members of Congress. When the second edition came out to correspond with an abbreviated exposé in *Look* magazine, a corporate official at Cowles Communications, the owner and publisher of *Look*, objected; he didn't think such a gruesome and inflammatory article should be run in what he believed was a family publication. Still, a year later it did appear in *Look*, and almost immediately Blatt and Kaplan were inundated with requests for interviews on radio and television. President Johnson sent a letter, as did other officials including nearly every governor and many senators. But there were also many detractors from all walks of life. Family members and professionals in both mental health and special education voiced complaints that ranged from disbelief in what the camera captured to claims that the writer and the photographer were socialists. The reaction was one that would reappear over the decades and is alive and well now, especially related to subminimum wages. Still, Blatt and Kaplan's daring work, and their ability to sustain rejection and find a way to get the important stories out, was worth it. A dialogue had been started, and it became permissible for citizens to question what was being done in their name to some of the most vulnerable among us.

In the late summer of 1968, Dr. Blatt was asked to travel to Europe to teach. Along with his wife and three sons he spent three months in Germany. He was convinced that there were direct linkages between the operation of the Nazi concentration camps and the treatment of people with disabilities in the United States, including the notion of evaluation. After the T4 program spread from occupied Poland to eastern Germany and beyond, it entered a new phase of more systematic identification and rounding up of "mental defectives." The health and mental hygiene administrators decreed that it was necessary to establish a method of evaluating which patients with disabilities were allowed to live and which would be killed. The ability to work or join the armed forces was considered, as were communicative abilities, head shape, and other facial features. The evaluative process involved a panel of experts, mostly doctors. After seeing the person's report only, without medical records or examinations, a symbol was assigned. A plus sign (+) meant the person lived, and a minus (-) meant they died; a question mark indicated that a decision had not yet been made. It wasn't hard to see the connection to the American institutional setting, where experts who had never met the person made decisions about their supposed care, and where the IQ of a patient with disabilities fell into one of five classifications: borderline, feebleminded, moron, imbecile, or idiot. These categories sound ridiculous to us today, but they were official, medical terms with associated IQ metrics at the time. The current classifications are mild, moderate, severe and profound, all followed by the phrase "intellectual disability," but the evaluative process remains squarely focused on the IQ score. The concept and process of evaluating and ranking people with disabilities continues today through vocational rehabilitation, state agencies including Medicaid, provider agencies, and special education systems. Until 2014 a person applying for vocational rehabilitation services in the United States could be deemed "unemployable" based on a cursory review of the person's IQ, school records, and reports from other experts; this was sufficient for one to be recommended for placement in a sheltered workshop.

Blatt understood the insidious power of the act of classifying vulnerable people; in 1939 Nazi Germany, influenced greatly by American eugenics, this power meant life or death; in US institutions in the 1960s, it could mean segregation, isolation, and the denial of civil rights. These same classifications would be used to rationalize the use of subminimum wages for millions of people with disabilities. In his next book, *Souls in Extremis*, Dr. Blatt would urge that we shutter all the nation's institutions, believing that no matter the good intentions, grouping people with any type of disability together in buildings for the purpose of treatment, including work, was hazardous. He had pointed out the dire and morally bankrupt practices of large-scale institutions, but that was only a start. An unintended consequence of Blatt's work was a rise in the belief that if programs were made smaller and relocated to local neighborhoods, the care and support would improve. One idea that appeared on the scene was the development of an entity called the intermediate care facility, funded by Medicaid, and seen as a smaller, more personalized institution, often with a day program or work area attached. Even if a person did not need care in a residential setting, many advocates, politicians, parents, and educators put their hopes in local "sheltered workshops," with special buildings set aside where people with sensory disabilities, autism, and intellectual and developmental disabilities could work for subminimum wages and receive other support. Surely if the places people spent their time were smaller and more provincial, they would be safer.

To fully understand the progression of paying workers with disabilities just pennies per hour, it's important to take a closer look at one recent investigation into our notion of disability in American culture and capitalism, specifically the category of disability related to intellect. In his groundbreaking documentary, *Intelligent Lives*, Dan Habib (a filmmaker and father of a child with disabilities) challenges the notion that IQ defines the worth, productivity, and essence of a human being. As he follows three young people with intellectual and developmental disabilities, including autism, he traces our reliance on IQ tests and scores as a way to categorize toddlers, adolescents, and young adults, and we quickly learn the shoddy science and misconceptions of the ubiquitous IQ score. In the 1920s and '30s in America and Nazi Germany, eugenics, classifications, and IQ ruled. However, there were doubts with the IQ measure from the beginning. The French inventor and researcher of the IQ paradigm, Alfred Binet, was commissioned by the government to find a method to identify those children who would have more difficulty in school, presumably to offer additional supports for supervised study and to ensure access to school materials. Binet himself was quick to realize that the IQ test alone was not an adequate tool to measure all types of intelligence. Over eighty years later the writer and Harvard researcher Howard Gardner would explain mankind's seven intelligences as: visual, bodily, interpersonal, intrapersonal, musical, linguistic, and logical. However, Gardner's insightful work would be (and still is) dominated by the application of the IQ score in our military and educational systems. IQ was also the basis for Galton's invention of eugenics, which called for "selecting out" less desirable traits that he associated with race and socioeconomic class and opting for those with high IQ scores, which he used to bolster his racist beliefs. In *Intelligent Lives*, Habib follows one man with the label of autism as he begins to question what his prescribed IQ tells him about his own life. The film is a powerful testament about the ways in which we miss out on talents and contributions by labeling people.

As the application and use of 14(c) wage certificates grew in the burgeoning field of "mental retardation," it became necessary to further categorize people based on their "functioning level." This mindset and process of categorizing and labeling people has been used in evil ways, but it is deemed essential in virtually all our "safety net" bureaucracies, such as social security, special education, Medicaid, and vocational rehabilitation. Perhaps it is inevitable that we rely on labels to appropriate funding and resources. But even today, it's not uncommon to hear staff in provider agencies that support adults with intellectual and developmental disabilities reference an individual's "mental age" or state out loud their IQ score. Dr. Seymour Sarason from Yale University described our compulsion to label people receiving support in our human service systems as "our propensity to segregate people who are or look *different*." We still rely on terms like "low functioning" or "severely autistic and nonverbal" uttered with little understanding of the source of the terms, the harm they've brought about, or the usefulness of such labels. As children in the 1940s and '50s were given the dire diagnoses of "mental retardation," "Downs," and a plethora of other terms, the physicians often blithely stated to parents: "Send them to the state and try and have another baby."

Developmental centers and state institutions for the blind, deaf, and "feeble-minded" had been around since the nineteenth century. While parents wouldn't benefit from Dr. Blatt's work until the mid-1960s, some parents, brave and willing to stand up to a doctor's advice, opted to keep their children at home. In doing so, an alliance between professionals and parent advocates emerged, and their focus became the use of the FLSA 14(c) certificate process to develop a systematic approach to create and operate a series of sheltered workshops, the same configuration first mentioned in the 1938 regulations. It would be almost thirty years later before the FLSA Act was first amended to call for more oversight for the subminimum-wage provision, but the scrutiny over its application would continue to grow, as did the passion of its defenders.

3

SUBMINIMUM WAGES AND
DISABILITY RIGHTS

The FLSA and the practice of paying subminimum wages to workers with disabilities enjoyed a hiatus from oversight as the sheltered-workshop model spread throughout the country. Local chapters of the ARC, then known as the Association of Retarded Citizens sought to bring employment to their loved ones and invested heavily in this pursuit, even if the most abundant commodity at their disposal was time. In Memphis mothers of young adults with developmental disabilities went door to door selling canned beans as part of a fundraiser to garner money for a down payment on construction of a building downtown to house a sheltered workshop.[1] They were not alone. The early and mid-1960s saw a rapid expansion of sheltered workshops designed and operated to serve different disability populations. There were programs for those with cerebral palsy, epilepsy, veterans with disabilities, and people with mental illness. The application of 14(c) grew and was adapted for different settings, which meant new construction of buildings that mirrored the regulations.

One such configuration was designed as a vocational rehabilitation center, replete with a sheltered workshop and ancillary supports including psychological, medical, and social services, perhaps an early variety of what we might today call a health home. The idea that most workers would have multiple well-being issues that could be coordinated in one central place seemed sound, but because of the history of disability in the United States, these developments were rooted in segregation, congregation, and poor pay.

The concerns and lack of oversight regarding subminimum wages persisted, however. In June of 1965, a Democratic senator from Oregon sought to fix the 14(c) certification process by offering amendments that would at the very least create a system that was more equitable to those with fewer barriers to employment. This was the unofficial start to decades of hearings and oversight committees. The efforts would start strong, with purpose and insight, and end up being stalled by players other than the workers with disabilities themselves. Senator Wayne Morse, who had sought his party's nomination for president in 1960, desired to bring attention to a law that by this point had been in operation for two decades. As Blatt and Kaplan, working in separate realms, were conceptualizing their covert entry into some of the country's most horrendous institutions in the summer of 1965, Senator Morse sought to provide economic relief to workers with moderate disabilities, believing they should receive the full minimum wage of $1.25, which in 2020 dollars would be $10.27 per hour. Senator Morse was first a Republican, then an Independent, and finally a Democrat. He opposed the Vietnam war. He had grown up on a farm where his family raised beef, hogs, horses, sheep, poultry, and grain crops. He knew labor and understood that work was essential to one's identity, that fair compensation afforded people the opportunity to move out of poverty. The Morse proposal sought to aid those workers with moderate disabilities in receiving minimum wage over a transitional period of three years; it carried an amendment for those workers with more significant disabilities under 14(c) to be paid at least 50 percent of the minimum wage. This notion of making change gradually, of not upsetting the human-service agencies employing worker with disabilities, would become an ongoing refrain that can be found in current efforts to abolish the practice of paying subminimum wages. At times, the transitional period is referenced in terms of concerns for the workers themselves, with lobby-ists arguing that the change would confuse those being paid subminimum wages or thrust workers into a harsh real world. At other times, when proposals like the one Morse endorsed were presented, the leadership of the sheltered-workshop agencies focused on their need for more time to change their business model. These clichéd complaints stymied change and acted to stall or stop outright progressive moves to ensure that work-ers with disabilities were compensated fairly.

This was the case with the Morse proposal. During the 1965 congres-sional hearings the sheltered-workshop operators testified that Morse's proposal was unrealistic, some arguing that it would be a drain on the economy. Representatives from the National Federation of the Blind (NFB), the same organization that forty-seven years later, in 2012, would urge a national boycott of Goodwill for paying some workers as little as twenty-two cents per hour, also attended the hearings and urged that the proposal be adopted fully. Stating that workers with disabilities should be afforded "the same protection of federal law now available to millions of other workers" in the United States, NFB representatives pointed out that there was just too much opportunity for section 14(c) to be misap-plied. "It permits ready abuse at the expense of handicapped workers." And as in the current debate, uneasiness was raised regarding oversight at the Department of Labor's Wage and Hour Division, "particularly in the absence of a vigorous investigation and enforcement program."[2] The latter concern would prove prescient: the abuses of the men at Henry's Turkey Farm had gone on unabated from the 1970s until they were ex-posed in 2009.

However, the sheltered-workshop leaders prevailed, and the legislation was watered down. The Morse proposal ended up as an inane linguistic configuration in the story of workers with disabilities and pay. In addition to the term "sheltered workshop," a new name was adopted for workers with severe disabilities. The places where they worked under 14(c) cer-tificates awarded by the USDOL would be referred to as "work activity centers." The work performed by these workers was not believed to be substantial enough to warrant minimum wage and could be as low as one penny per hour, since there would be no wage floor. Work-activity cen-ters were defined as "centers planned and designed exclusively to provide therapeutic activities for handicapped clients whose physical or mental impairment is so severe as to make their productive capacity inconsequential." That phrase alone embodies the extent to which low expectations pervade the entire system. In one of the first significant mandates from Congress regarding 14(c) oversight, the Morse proposal set in motion an ongoing request to review the way that "handicapped clients of sheltered workshops" were paid. Notice, the term "client" rather than "worker," a distinction that symbolizes one of the cornerstone issues in the systems that both employ and provide services to people with disabilities. When is one a client, receiving services, and when is a worker with a disability, given the right to form labor unions and negotiate wages, hours, job tasks, and other work site considerations? The mixing of not only the terms and roles but also the approaches and expectations of the sheltered-workshop system would make tracking outcomes and associated oversight requirements a convoluted enterprise at best. Burton Blatt recognized this strange dual role of people with disabilities living in institutions. With his characteristic knack for challenging the ever-present classifications, and possibly to take the power out of an antiquated term, he penned a novel titled *Revolt of the Idiots.*

The USDOL report that Congress directed be created as a result of the Morse proposal and the associated hearings were damning. What is so strange about the history of subminimum wages in the United States is the belief that only in the last decade or so have advocates, politicians, and workers with disabilities spoken up about its inherent flaws and shortcomings. Instead, the 1967 report on the study of 14(c) as a wage structure pointed out several specifics that seemed as though the sheltered-workshop industry had not been completely forthright during public remarks to the Senate Subcommittee on Labor. "Instead of increasing wages, the workshops had reinvented themselves as work activity centers to avoid the statutory minimum wage rate."[3] This issue would only catch on more and more in the coming years, and it's important to understand how a worker employed in a sheltered workshop just a year earlier could be reevaluated and consequently moved to the work activity center operations. It's crucial to understand this development because there is currently an analogous transition of people from subminimum wages to other services that do not include a vocational emphasis.

In the end, the USDOL argued that if wages were increased for workers with disabilities, the likely outcome would be that the sheltered-workshop leaders would simply move people into work activity centers at a faster pace. Reiterating their concerns, professionals from USDOL told Congress that instead of focusing on improving their approaches to training adults with disabilities, especially workers with intellectual disabilities, the agencies using 14(c) would simply reclassify the "sheltered workers" so they could pay as little as possible. It would be easy to assume unscrupulous intent here, but it's more constructive to understand an important divergence in professionals' view of learning. Blatt and others had argued and researched "educability." The premise was that children and adults with the labels of "mental retardation" (an outdated term that has been replaced by "intellectual disability") were not untrainable or uneducable. They were like all human beings in terms of learning. If presented new material aimed at acquiring new skills via an adapted format, and if the focus were on the professional's approach rather than presumed deficits of the learner, progress could be made. This new way of thinking about people born with intellectual disabilities challenged the fields of psychology, psychiatry, health care, special education, and the emerging field of vocational rehabilitation as applied to intellectual disability. The 1967 USDOL report highlighted a fracture in the way two different parts of the employment-and-disability field perceived its primary beneficiaries. If one doesn't believe a worker in a sheltered workshop can learn, improve, and master new tasks, then the idea of paying at least minimum wages seems out of reach. Once more, the fragmentation in research, practice, and policy, along with the general public's understanding of the issues, was clearly on display.

As has been the case over the last eighty-three years of 14(c), the attention and legislative focus on the complex policy issues would be put on hold; in this case not until 1978 would there be substantial hearings in Congress to seek a remedy. In his 2005 report for the Congressional Research Center, titled, "Treatment of Workers with Disabilities Under Section 14(c) of the Fair Labor Standards Act," labor economist William Whitaker summarizes the DOL report from 1967. In his estimation, looking back at those first hearings, there are some implicit questions raised. "Might the very nature of sheltered employment be conducive to exploitation of the worker with disabilities? In the absence of a union, who would speak for such workers?" And the last question continues to be a fundamental quandary as it relates to the primary function of the sheltered workshop: Is it feasible to combine in one entity the roles of caregiver, therapist and employer?

One could add to those roles, advocate, rehabilitation provider and legislative liaison. It's not uncommon for workers being paid subminimum wages to be represented to lawmakers through a trade group whose primary objective is to keep funding coming in to support the continued operation of the provider systems. To understand this fundamental problem of multiple roles, imagine your primary-care doctor also being your employer, or if your boss was also your therapist, seeing you at your most vulnerable and knowing all your shortcomings firsthand. And finally, try to sort through how maddening it might be if someone other than you yourself also served as the main representative for your political concerns, such as voicing your rights regarding something you personally care deeply about, as in LGBTQ rights, gun control, or reproductive rights. The point that Whitaker is making through his proffered question is one that few ponder. How do the voices of people with significant disabilities get heard in this convoluted scenario when so many variables in the design of the system are cloaked in competing roles? The answer is no clearer now than in 1967. In the case of Henry's Turkey Farm and its abuses, add to these roles that of being a person's payee for social security checks and the landlord. Perhaps one of the reasons the abuse went unreported was that the citizens in town believed the operators were first and foremost caretakers, with the best interest of the men as the driving force in their decision making. Recall Anil Lewis telling us about the insidiousness of benevolence; the disability industrial complex benefits from regular citizens believing that all activity related to organizations that appear to be helping people with disabilities must therefore be good and upright, with only the best intentions for those in their care, in their employ, and in the totality of their operations. The terms "nonprofit," "disability service provider," and any name that pulls at our heartstrings, gets a pass on scrutiny. It's a dangerous assumption.

A decade went by, and the numbers of workers with disabilities entering employment under section 14(c) grew at a rapid pace. By 1977 nearly 200,000 workers were earning subminimum wages. More than 3,500 sheltered workshops were in operation, but that number may have been higher, as some workshops operated without bothering to formally obtain a 14(c) certificate to pay subminimum wages from USDOL.[4] The work activity centers where there was no wage floor for work performed by people with severe disabilities were sometimes overlooked when USDOL increased its onsite reviews.

The 1970s saw a more organized and purposeful approach to advocating for the rights of people with disabilities, with a focus on challenging the way that citizens with disabilities were treated in the public domain. The first legal definition of developmental disabilities was granted in 1970; Ed Roberts, who would later go on to become the first commissioner of a state vocational rehabilitation agency with a significant physical disability after that same agency had deemed him "unfeasible for employment," helped found the Physically Disabled Students Program (PDSP) at the University of California in Berkeley. In 1971 the US district court in *Wyatt v. Stickney* decreed that people in residential state schools and institutions (like the ones Blatt and Kaplan had snuck into six years before) have a right to receive quality services, including vocational services, that will actually benefit them, stating, "People should be given a realistic opportunity to be cured or to improve their mental state."[5] This may seem like an obvious statement, but this was one of the first times a court had mandated that the disability industrial complex deliver on its promises and use what would later become known as evidence-based practices in doing so. That same year a public television station in Boston began captioning its programming so that viewers who were deaf could gain information. Groundbreaking court decisions in Washington, DC, and Pennsylvania set the precedent for the passage of the 1975 Education for All Handicapped Children Act, which finally made it illegal to exclude children with disabilities from public schools. These were important milestones toward the active inclusion and equitable treatment of US citizens with disabilities, but the strides were also fragmented, sometimes pursued by or on behalf of specific disability "types": people with sensory barriers, children with disabilities, adults with physical disabilities in university settings, and those held captive by institutional settings. Like so much of social change in America, the approach was messy, with competing interests, including large nonprofits that claimed to be lobbying for people with disabilities.

The year 1973 saw the first handicapped parking stickers introduced in Washington, DC, as well as the passage of capital aid in the way of authorized federal funds for the construction of curb cutouts, a fundamental adaptation to sidewalks. This enabled people who used wheelchairs to navigate community pursuits safely, allowing them to get to and from work without risking death while crossing whatever makeshift path was available. And in 1973 the most far-reaching legislation was passed, which would resonate outward and echo across the decades. Known as the Rehabilitation Act of 1973, the historic language stated in part: "No otherwise qualified handicapped individual in the United States, shall, solely by reason of their handicap, be excluded from participation in, be denied the benefits of, or be subjected to discrimination under any program or activity receiving federal financial assistance." Passage of the legislation required a grueling fight; businesses and government alike declared the Rehab Act would bankrupt their enterprises. It did not. The groundwork laid in the Rehab Act of '73 would go on to serve as the basis for lawsuits filed on behalf of workers with disabilities who were being paid subminimum wages. Some have called the Rehab Act the finest civil-rights legislation ever passed because of its guarantees of equality across a broad range of public services. But would it be enough to carry the changes that subminimum-wage workers needed when their voices were muffled by so many other rival interests? Just the year before in 1972, the Association of Persons with Severe Handicaps (now known as TASH) had been founded by special educators who believed the right to a free and appropriate public education for students with even the most significant intellectual disabilities was still not generally being provided; where it was, there were significant delays from school boards and concerned taxpayers, once again bemoaning the drain that such rights would put on county and state budgets. By 1977 disability-rights activists across ten major US cities orchestrated demonstrations to urge the Carter administration to truly enact section 504 of the Rehabilitation Act of 1973. Section 504 is the key portion of the legislation; it mandates antidiscrimination and emphasizes civil rights to ensure that the needs of students with disabilities are met as adequately as the needs of the nondisabled. Across disabilities, age groups, and rural and urban areas, the idea that people with disabilities, their advocates, and other stakeholders could make a difference by applying pressure politically was starting to gain momentum. It was in this atmosphere that the next major hearings would occur regarding the FLSA 14(c) certificates allowing for subminimum wages. Surely, with the tailwinds in their favor, representatives from USDOL and the sheltered-workshop industry would agree to significant changes to overhaul the antiquated provision. Unlike the cross-disability efforts earlier in the decade, however, these new hearings would focus on just one group, those who were blind or vision impaired.

In May of 1978, Phillip Burton, a representative from California's 6th district (Speaker of the House Nancy Pelosi now occupies the seat) held hearings hosted by the House Subcommittee on Labor Standards. Again, the National Federation of the Blind (NFB) would be pivotal in the hearings, and the leaders were motivated by their past. The NFB had been founded in 1940, just two years after the passage of the Fair Labor Standards Act. NFB articulated its guiding principles clearly: "Blind people have an inalienable right to independence, . . . blind people have equal capacity, and . . . only blind people themselves can legitimately speak for the blind community." The NFB had stated an early version of what would later become known as a self-advocate rallying cry: "Nothing about Us without Us" which gained use in the post-ADA 1990s.

There's a strange irony in what Representative Phillip Burton hoped to accomplish; he intended to make sure that blind and visually impaired workers were paid at least minimum wage, but he also didn't want these same workers to be excluded from the sheltered-workshop setting. This kind of exclusion/inclusion verbal play will dominate the ongoing debates about who (and less artfully, which disabilities as a whole) should be in sheltered workshops or offered jobs in the community with regular wages. While not entirely deliberate, different groups will be favored over others. The notion that disability in all its forms (including old age, mental health, and neurodiversity) is part of the human condition comes in direct conflict with competition for civil resources. For many legislators the messages to government become mired in confusion over priorities. When the layer of nonprofit lobbying activities is added on top of this dynamic, it's not surprising to find drawn out and sometimes incomprehensible attempts to remedy the situation with legislation. Some legislative representatives have stated, "You all need to get on the same page. One group wants equal pay, the other wants to keep sheltered programs."

James Gashel, representing the NFB, was present to testify at the hearings. He had only been part of the NFB since 1974, though he would end up working there for more than thirty years. Visually impaired himself, Gashel was a force of advocacy, wit, and perseverance. At the opening session he announced that he was the "only nonindustry" person at the hearings, meaning most of those in attendance and offering opinions were operators of the subminimum-wage sheltered workshops. Still, if one thought the hearings on the Burton proposal would be fully endorsed by advocacy organizations related to disability, and in this case, associations advocating on behalf of workers with disabilities, they'd be wrong. Mr. Gashel feared the proposal would inaugurate "a far-reaching principle . . . that the blind are not to be considered as handicapped workers." It would also be incorrect to assume that somehow Gashel's fears were driven by anything more than his desire to create a world where blindness was accepted and even embraced. He had been instrumental in legislative issues related to the Social Security Act, the Rehabilitation Act, the Randolph-Sheppard Act, the Individuals with Disabilities Education Act, and twelve years later in 1990, the Americans with Disabilities Act (ADA). The professionals and legal minds backing the Burton proposal, which would have banned paying subminimum wages to workers with visual impairments, believed that these workers were being exploited by the payment of subminimum wages. The backers of the Burton proposal could not see these same factors at play in workers with disabilities other than visual impairments. They were concerned that blind people entering sheltered workshops were at risk of "backsliding" in terms of their skills, both in learning and keeping new skills, impacting these workers' view of themselves. While the phrase "soft skills" was not used much in 1978, there was also concern that workers with visual impairments entering the sheltered workshops would develop decreased abilities in managing emotions and interactions with others and would have lower self-esteem. Decreased social and interactive skill sets are yet another instance of confusion inside the disability industrial complex; rehabilitation provider agencies often cite them to justify a person's inability to work at a real job in the community. Yet, every one of us can recall a coworker, maybe even a supervisor, from the past who did not possess excellent soft skills. The argument is one of the many "readiness traps" set by those who benefit from billing state and federal funds to supposedly ameliorate those so-called deficits. The nonprofits that are supposed to be helping workers with disabilities gain skills are incentivized to continue to find additional problems with the worker so that they can prolong the drawdown of state and federal funds, often times for years. It behooves the nonprofit to keep such a worker in a state of continual need, never ready enough to work in the community for fair wages.

Gashel also found fault with the 14(c) certification process itself, calling it "confusing and cumbersome." While this sounds like an argument against the payment of subminimum wages, Gashel and by proxy, the NFB, were critical of the process, not the outcome. It was the NFB's president in 2013, Marc Maurer, who would take on Goodwill by organizing boycotts of their stores in order to bring attention to the issue of Goodwill workers of all disabilities earning as little as twenty-two cents an hour. Thus, NFB, while always involved in section 14(c) of the FLSA, also changed its position as more information about abuses came to light. The Burton proposal and hearings also brought up another issue that would become mired in the type of economy within which section 14(c) was being implemented. The US economy at the time was at a peak in terms of manufacturing jobs; in June 1977 manufacturing jobs represented 22 percent of all nonfarm payrolls; today it is less than 9 percent.[6] Productivity at the time was understood as how much and how fast a worker could assemble items, and so the criticisms of sheltered workshops not being rooted in good management practices was valid, but it would mean then that the workers earning subminimum wages all favored assembly type jobs instead of tasks the worker preferred and excelled at. Put another way, the poor management of the sheltered workshops should have also focused on the very limited set of tasks that the worker had access to, putting those workers who did not excel at assembly at a disadvantage. This is a critical issue, one that tends to get little attention. Workers under 14(c) are evaluated (using a stopwatch) at least twice a year and on each new job task (usually if a new contract has been secured by management); there is therefore a track record of their "productivity." This means that someone may be rated as being 17 percent as productive as that of a nondisabled worker performing the same task. It sounds reasonable, until you think about it in terms of your own performance. Suppose someone was rating you on how quickly you could do a task that you would normally self-select out of (say, changing the oil or raking leaves). Your productivity level at a task at which you are not proficient would follow you in other endeavors or might even keep you from getting a job because your speed and skill at folding pizza boxes was slow and inexpert. Often, the first "metrics" communicated about a worker trying to leave behind subminimum wages is their productivity level, sometimes qualified in reference to the task, but usually solely based on that productivity number. Some workers on subminimum wages with physical disabilities that would prevent them from assembling and packaging tasks are rated on their productivity without the aid of assistive technology. Choice and dignity then, is having the freedom to not be evaluated on those things we are bad at. Inside the disability industrial complex workers with disabilities don't have that choice, while workers without disabilities use this strategy (self-selecting and focusing on strengths) from their very earliest forays into work as an adolescent.

The Burton proposal brought to the forefront several other considerations, some that echo today. Along with questions regarding the management of the sheltered workshops came the claim that often the work required a team and might include a mixture of speed, accuracy, and other performance indicators within a single work group. The industry argued that this approach led to workers learning from one another. This position is in direct contrast to the pervasive views of the same sheltered-workshop industry, which also propagated and profited from the idea that these same workers need sheltering because their abilities are static, rooted in IQ, and therefore incapable of learning, and that special low wages are therefore necessary. In this portion of the hearing, the sheltered-workshop industry is actually arguing that it embraces the notions of "educable" and "trainable" that led to Blatt's investigations in *Christmas in Purgatory*, and whose research flew in the face of the prolific deficiency-based paradigm active inside the disability industrial complex. One might conclude, then, as is the case now, that those in favor of keeping section 14(c) and its accumulated theories of viewing a worker through the lens of that person's deficits, pick and choose which theory of learning to identify with depending upon the issue at hand. Workers need special places to work with special rules; and workers can learn but only if they are governed by these specialized nonprofits that pay subminimum wages. This fundamental conflict is once again connected to the role of the agency providing the services. If an agency receives funding to "fix" or at the very least ameliorate a person's deficits, it behooves that same agency to focus on the deficits, which if never fixed, will produce more income for that same agency.

The Burton proposal was not adopted. However, it did help to educate some legislators on the stakeholder mix related to employment and disability, especially when it came to which regulations should organize wage structures, and for whom. It was clear that the debate was not purely benevolent, and the testimony surrounding control and accountability could be volatile and fragmented.

However, perhaps the most significant tangible information was uncovered with an analysis of USDOL's enforcement efforts related to the administration of section 14(c). The primary division responsible for this type of oversight is known as the Wage and Hour Division (WHD) of USDOL. The following statement from USDOL attempts to explain what WHD does. "The Wage and Hour Division's mission is to promote and achieve compliance with labor standards to protect and enhance the welfare of the nation's workforce. The Wage and Hour Division (WHD) enforces federal minimum wage, overtime pay, recordkeeping, and child labor requirements of the Fair Labor Standards Act." At the time, the administrator tasked with participating in the Burton proposal hearings was Xavier Vela. Vela had been appointed to head up WHD by President Carter in May 1977. Vela had been instrumental in running housing, credit, and labor cooperatives in six South American countries, and had been a leader in local labor unions in New Mexico and Washington, DC.[7] During the informational portion of the testimony, Vela presented several data points related to the usage and employment of workers earning subminimum wages. Just over 163,000 workers were affected under 14(c), housed in more than 3,500 sheltered workshops that had applied for and been given the status to operate such a facility. Vela reported that a total of 155 onsite investigations had been conducted during 1977, nearly a 70 percent increase from 1976, meaning only 46 of the 3,500 sheltered workshops had been visited, fewer than one per state.[8] Vela also reported on poor management, high turnover, and a lack of cost and pricing skills by administrators. Ironically, the staff who rated the productivity of workers with disabilities were themselves lacking competence on a task (basic production accounting) integral to their job description.

One result of the 1978 Burton proposal was its impact on journalists. Two reporters with the *Wall Street Journal* would take notice of the cause. With their backgrounds in investigative journalism, the story contained echoes of Blatt and Kaplan's work and provided another opportunity for fundamental change.

4

THE FLOOR IS GONE AND MODERN
LOBBYING ARRIVES

In 1979 the *Wall Street Journal* pursued investigations of its own into the way some blind workers were paid. There had been newspaper stories related to sheltered workshops and their workers, but most had been soft news, human-interest pieces reported in a tone that relied less on objective statistics and more on feel-good profiles. One can find lots of these in archives of local newspapers as new sheltered workshops were opened. It's revelatory to note that the efforts of the *Journal* didn't focus on workers with different types of disabilities earning subminimum wages, only blind workers. This approach would be mirrored as the debate entered the early 2000s. It seemed that most people outside the disability systems could rationalize paying workers with intellectual disabilities much less, but for those with sensory disabilities, the argument for at least minimum wage was easier to make. Of course, that conclusion is based on myth and stigma; still the investigative focus was squarely on blind workers who were paid subminimum wages.

As had been the case in most of the federal oversight hearings, the *Wall Street Journal*'s investigation left out other workers under 14(c), those with intellectual and developmental disabilities, people with mental illness working inside asylums, and veterans with significant traumatic brain injuries engaged in therapeutic work and residing in the nation's VA hospitals. The *Journal* published two stories about blind workers in sheltered workshops in New York City. One of the journalists, Jonathan Kwitny, was a prolific author of books on the mafia, the CIA, true crime, and maybe most pertinent, financial swindlers and their scams. The piece that first appeared provided the journalists' point of view succinctly: "Blind people for years have entered the job market through so-called sheltered workshops, sheltered by law, that is, from having to pay the blind workers minimum wages." Along with fellow reporter Jerry Landauer, who had written extensively about judicial ethics and corporate bribery and had had a hand in exposing Spiro Agnew, Kwitny brought to light the side of the 14(c) coin that most had not paid much attention to. The first of the two articles, "Many of the blind workers feel they are working at coolie wages, helping to fatten the profits not only of the charities that run the workshops but also of the big companies that contract with them." Very few Americans at the time were aware of how 14(c) worked or that some workers were being paid pennies for their efforts. Later, in 2009, 2011, and 2013, the public's lack of knowledge related to subminimum wages and the nonprofits charged with advocating for people with disabilities would be highlighted again. But in 1979 and 1980, the *Journal* articles were explosive, setting off alarms that would lead to more congressional interest in understanding the role the US government and more specifically the USDOL played in supporting the practices highlighted in the stories.

Contrary to the 1967–68 and 1978 oversight hearings, the USDOL now focused its attention not only on the oversight issues with 14(c) but the finances of the charity organizations holding the certificates and the companies that subcontracted with them to have menial tasks completed for well under the going rate. To fully appreciate how this issue was exposed and examined, we must consider how a typical contract is procured by the workshop manager.

In order to have tasks for workers to perform, sheltered-workshop managers market their services to companies in the community, sometimes locally owned and operated businesses. For instance, it was very common in the 1990s to see sheltered-workshop workers assembling cable company packages that included a cable box, instructions, a coaxial connector, and a remote intended to be shipped to a new subscriber. The

package would arrive, and the customer could set up their own cable access. Some of these contracts came from locally owned enterprises, while
others were simply subsidiaries of large communications corporations.
A sheltered-workshop manager would meet with a cable company official
and look over a sample of the completed package. The number of units
needed within a specified time would be discussed along with issues such
as transport to and from the warehouse, picking up the raw materials,
and quality control. The meeting would end with the promise of a quote.

Back at the sheltered workshop a time study would be performed.
Using a stopwatch and some knowledge of a worker's bodily movements,
an individual rate (but more likely a team-based average) would be arrived at. Next, the manager would try to arrive at a prevailing wage in
the community. Those numbers would act as the baseline from which
individuals or, more likely, teams, would be paid for their efforts. A quote
would be approved by the executive director of the sheltered workshop
and sent to the cable company representative. Often the quote for packaging for the cable company would be far lower than in the competitive
market. This was theoretically good for the cable company, for the nonprofit, and for the 14(c) workers. The power and the right of denial are
not equal, however. Both the cable company and the nonprofit sheltered
workshop can say no, while the worker with the disability has much less
say in the business arrangement, seeing that he has no labor union or separate advocate acting on his behalf. Such practices spurred an entire subset
of new accreditations, training for staff, and a separate industry born to
help legitimize time studies, prevailing rate calculations, and piece-rate
determinations. There was money to be made in the tools and knowledge
needed to "accurately" rate a worker's productivity. It was common for
a nonprofit to pay for staff to attend training in MODAPTS, described
as a "predetermined motion time system used to perform labor minute
costing."[1]

Kwitny and Landauer attempted to get readers to contemplate the role
of the nonprofits they believed were charitable in nature. They described
the contracting arrangement in their article as "helping to fatten the profit
of charities that run the workshops and the big companies that contract
with them." Until 1979–1980, the focus had only been on USDOL and
the Wage and Hour Division, but readers of these articles saw that what
appeared to be purely a good cause had some complexity, nuances of

consideration that included corporations and some of the best-known nonprofits and charities in the country. The investigative reporters also unearthed the high salaries of the administrators running the 14(c) certificate programs that allowed blind workers to be paid less than the minimum wage.

While these stories were being reported in the *Journal*, significant changes in disability rights law were taking place. In 1979 the United States Supreme Court ruled for the first time on a case related to section 504 of the Rehabilitation Act of 1973, which required that programs receiving federal funds must make reasonable accommodations. In *Southeastern Community College v. Davis*, the Court deemed it too great a financial burden for the college to make the necessary accommodations for Francis Davis, a student with a hearing impairment who was applying to nursing school.[2] The same year the National Alliance for the Mentally Ill was founded in Madison, Wisconsin, by parents of persons (children and adults) with mental illness. The disability rights movement was forging ahead while the issue of paying workers subminimum wages gained momentum and its defenders grew ever more dogmatic.

The *Wall Street Journal* articles quoted administrators defending the low wages on the grounds that blind workers produce less and "that most blind workers also receive SSI benefits." This excuse harkens back to the early days of charitable work provided by religious-based organizations and the theory that those employed should be paying back whatever dole had assisted them. Kwitny and Landauer also pointed out that some blind workers had allegedly been fired for daring to dabble in pro-union talk. The articles were copied and shared with advocates, disability law attorneys, families, elected officials, and some of the same players from earlier congressional hearings, such as the National Federation of the Blind. Readers of the articles had strong opinions. The old complaints about the general public not understanding the central charge of the nonprofits echoed Blatt's work in exposing the conditions in institutions and asylums, and a newer version of the same talking points was born over the course of the 1980s.

It was obvious that these stories were not going to simply disappear. The proponents of subminimum wages believed strongly that they must respond in a more formal way. Thus, the same entities that argued against the formation of unions by workers earning subminimum wages decided to pursue collective organizing in what would now be called a modern trade group association.

While nonprofits serving people with disabilities had organized in the past, most of those efforts had centered around parents forming associations related to a specific disability, such as the national ARC and NAMI organizations. There had been groups dedicated to religious charities and the poor that included disability, but the new trade group took its cue and mandate from similar groups in manufacturing, healthcare, and education. One of the first and largest trade groups was the Association of Rehabilitation Facilities. Many state chapters are still in operation today in Missouri, Illinois, Florida, West Virginia, and elsewhere. In the 1980s the nonprofits that joined such trade groups were just learning how to engage in governmental affairs, set policy priorities, and design lobbying processes. Another national trade group, ANCOR, the American Network of Community Options and Resources, is a national, nonprofit trade association representing more than 1,600 private community providers of services to people with disabilities. Combined, ANCOR supports over one million individuals with disabilities in the United States. Both ANCOR and ARF (mostly through its state chapters) became empowered to act and behave like big business through investing in lobbyists, first in state legislatures and later in Congress. Big names like Goodwill and Easter Seals joined and were active members, as were smaller agencies with similar missions. The introduction of formalized, organized, and staffed trade groups changed the way in which local disability agencies, many of them holding 14(c) certificates, got their messages to state and federal legislatures. Some trade groups formed "disability days" at their state capitals, and national conferences were annually held near Washington, DC. The field of disability training, employment, and rehabilitation had grown up and joined the ranks of professions formally represented by a collective group of like-minded professionals. Of course, there were dues to be paid, and funds raised in other ways to operate state chapters; along with it came power and influence. A professional working in Indiana in the 1980s recalled being summoned by the executive director of one of the state's trade groups. "He had someone come and retrieve me from a bar in the hotel the conference was being held in. I was escorted up to meet the guy and the scene was like something out of *The Godfather*. The room was dark, and the guy said he had heard I was an up-and-comer, and he wanted to know what I wanted, if I wanted to run one of the big, sheltered workshops. I knew then the association had its power brokers." These same groups would become more formally involved as the Government Accountability Office (GAO) started an inquiry into the specifics of 14(c), and they had a voice at the table during the House investigations in 1980 and the Senate's again in 1982. The trade groups would lobby for the 1986 amendments to the law as well. The lessons learned during this formative time would highlight the interconnection of trade groups and subminimum wages; decades later those lessons would become critical, as a more political organization, ACCSES, formed in 2007, an entity that has fought hard against overturning section 14(c).

Because of the *Wall Street Journal* reporting, in the spring of 1980, two days of testimony were scheduled in the House under the auspices of the Subcommittee on Labor Standards. These oversight meetings were known as the Beard hearings, named after the chair, Edward Beard, a Democrat from Rhode Island. The findings were at best conflicted and at worst (as in previous hearings) an alarm sounding quite clearly on the practice of subminimum wages. Representative Patricia Schroeder (D-CO) made her point, though not in line with current views of disability-related language, saying the sheltered workshops were operating within a "schizophrenic" approach, apparently referring to the sheltered workshops' roles as both employer and provider of rehabilitation services. Representative Schroeder believed the natural first step in remedying these conflicting roles was to reorganize the system itself; she called on the sheltered workshops and work activity centers to conceive of their "clients" only as bona fide employees. This distinction would change everything—from pay, the right to organize, and most importantly, the nonprofit's ability to bill state and federal funders for rehabilitation services for the same workers for whom they were determining productivity levels. In other words, there was an incentive inherent in the setup of the sheltered workshops to label workers as unemployable outside the building. These hearings made that fact public.

In these hearings, as in the past, a representative from USDOL responsible for the operational oversight of section 14(c) provided remarks, mentioning the disability severity of some 180,000 sheltered-workshop workers in more than 4,000 locations nationwide and stating that the program had essentially been neglected by other administrations. Assistant

Secretary for Employment Standards Donald Elisburg was candid, if somewhat nonchalant, in citing the many problems. He stated for the congressional record that the primary purpose of USDOL's oversight was to monitor wage payments to ensure that handicapped workers were paid wages that accurately reflected their assessed productivity levels. USDOL "bears a particular responsibility to see that this program is vigorously enforced since these workers are largely unorganized and often hesitate to question their pay," he said.[3] Without the benefit of what came fully into light at Henry's Turkey Farm thirty-one years later, Elisburg added, "To the extent there has been exploitation, it should never have been allowed. We are simply not going to allow it in the future."[4] He would return to testify as a citizen and lawyer nearly fifteen years later, in 1994.

In the room that day in May 1980 was a representative from NISH, the National Industries for the Severely Handicapped. NISH had spent $3.5 million in lobbying between 2008 and 2012. In 2013 NISH would relaunch under a new branding called SourceAmerica, following the release of some damning WikiLeaks tapes. Jerry Daugherty from NISH found fault in the 1980 hearings and was critical of the articles by Kwitny and Landauer, believing that it would be ill advised to take the *Wall Street Journal* reports as the only version of the story. In fact, Mr. Daugherty felt the need to contrast the views of NISH and his own with the *Journal* articles. "More important," he said, referring to the conditions unearthed by Kwitny and Landauer, "is the opportunity to work." Today we see his claim as problematic since he is speaking as a professional for workers with disabilities but painting the employment landscape of a marginalized group as an outsider as one whose organization also benefits from keeping wages low. Daugherty further testified, "To the handicapped individual, work means much more than therapy or wages. It means that there is a place to go where people are friendly, understanding and accepting. A place where the person has the chance to make a real contribution, to be appreciated as a valuable member of a team effort, and to participate in a meaningful and stimulating environment."[5] This language of apparent benevolence saturates the disability industrial complex and attempts to justify the billions of dollars of taxpayer funding expended on its operations.

Daugherty tried to explain that a sheltered workshop is run almost identically to a small, for-profit business, but a private business needs to pay minimum wage and can't also bill state and federal rehabilitation funders for training their workers. The argument of Daugherty on behalf of NISH sidesteps their other streams of revenue, something a for-profit business simply could not overlook. In the end, he advised Congress that paying these workers minimum wage would be "disastrous."

Daugherty was followed by testimony from one of the largest nonprofit members benefiting from NISH's lobbying. Dean Phillips from Goodwill Industries attempted to explain the same conflicted roles emphasized in earlier Congressional hearings in 1967 and 1978. "Sheltered workshops are a very special kind of enterprise with a special type of employee or client." Once again the roles are unclear—"special" describes both the place and the person, and the worker is both "employee" and "client." Outside the disability industrial complex it's difficult to find workers who consider themselves clients of their place of employment, and this obfuscation lead to even more confusion and game playing on behalf of the organizations using 14(c) certificates.

The blind workers were represented by Kenneth Jernigan of the National Federation of the Blind. While the organization had done stellar work over the decades advocating for its primary constituents, it had waffled and sometimes contradicted itself on the issue of subminimum wages—but not this time around. Jernigan was adamant as he testified. "Agencies which serve the blind and the workshops which employ the blind have often assumed the status of self-appointed spokesman for the blind." Perhaps we see here what will end up thirty years later in the efforts by the NFB to bring attention to subminimum wages by calling for a boycott of Goodwill. Jernigan's comments were an indictment of the entire industry of shelter workshops. "It unfairly discriminates . . . then forces the members of this class to justify every penny of their paychecks by means of productivity ratings." Jernigan addressed the operation of some of the sheltered-workshops' productions lines, belying the industry's claim that they must run like any other business. "There is poor job layout and deliberate work-stretching by management during periods when contracts are slow." This work stretching is one of the many inanities of the sheltered workshop industry: I have seen teams of workers earning subminimum wages seated at a table, one side of the team assembling an item, only to have it disassembled by workers on the other side of the table before being once again assembled by the original workers.

Perhaps most damning was Jernigan's observation of an industry at odds with itself. The sheltered workshops, he stated, "have covered their business activities with a veil of social services," addressing the "worker" versus "client" issue raised by Goodwill's Dean Phillips. Finally, Jernigan described the workshops as conducting "very little rehabilitation and a whole lot of business and industrial activity." Here Jernigan is on much more solid advocacy grounds than NISH or Goodwill, having actual experience with disability. He was born totally blind in Detroit and learned to work on a farm in Tennessee. After high school Jernigan managed a furniture shop in Beech Grove, Tennessee, making all the furniture and operating the business. From 1958 until 1978, he served as director of the Iowa State Commission for the Blind. In this capacity he was responsible for administering state programs of rehabilitation, home teaching, home industries, and library services for the blind and those with physical disabilities. The improvements made in services to the blind of Iowa under the Jernigan administration were groundbreaking: he believed that professionals relied on the medical-model approach to disabilities, which spent too much time on labels, deficits, and treatment. He challenged the notion that disability meant less capability.

In 1960 the NFB presented Jernigan with its Newel Perry Award for outstanding accomplishment in services for the blind. In 1968 Jernigan was given a special citation by President Johnson. Harold Russell, chairman of the President's Committee on Employment of the Handicapped, came to Des Moines to present the award, noting, "If a person must be blind, it is better to be blind in Iowa than anywhere else in the nation or in the world." The citation continued, "This statement sums up the story of the Iowa Commission for the Blind during the Jernigan years and more pertinently of its Director, Kenneth Jernigan. That narrative is much more than a success story. It is the story of high aspiration magnificently accomplished—of an impossible dream become reality."[6] Kenneth Jernigan used his voice and experience and moved well beyond the boundaries of the typical avenues of advocacy. His Press Club address was broadcast on National Public Radio, and he appeared on the *Today Show* and the *Larry King Show*. Jernigan's testimony was respected and held considerable weight; his gravitas was not lost on the hearing's committee, but in the 1980 hearings it wasn't enough.

The beginning of the 1980s saw Congress pass the Civil Rights of Institutionalized Persons Act, which authorized the US Justice Department to file civil suits on behalf of residents of institutions whose essential human rights were being violated. Burton Blatt's work to free people from the horrid conditions of spending another "Christmas in purgatory" had taken a significant step forward. Despite people with disabilities in the United States advocating, and in some cases risking their lives, for their inherent inalienable rights, however, their efforts would not be reflected in the most basic of workers' rights, i.e., that of a protected and mandated minimum wage. The 1979 *Wall Street Journal* articles along with the 1980 Congressional hearings kicked off a decade that would see more contradictory changes in the FLSA law pertaining to section 14(c). The issues that had come up back in 1966 related to the separation and delineation between sheltered workshops and work activity centers reemerged. In 1966 legislators and the USDOL had sought to provide some guidance related to workers earning subminimum wages in the sheltered workshop versus workers whose output, according to evaluators, was more a therapeutic benefit in a work activity center. Many nonprofits had already embraced this distinction and had tried to delineate areas of the sheltered workshop from what would be the work activity center, but this too was problematic. While positions were raised on both sides, such as penalizing less productive workers, now increasingly referred to as "clients," the discussion didn't seem to focus on the most salient issue: if a person couldn't move his hands quickly, why insist that same person perform a task that didn't at least nominally correlate with his strengths? The arguments remained squarely on combining two programs (sheltered workshop and work activity center) with associated requirements into one. It was inevitable that the central concern of how a worker was paid would be revisited. The notion of determining a prevailing wage for a task by surveying similar businesses in the local area, and then rating an individual worker's commensurate wage based on that person's productivity level had its weaknesses. The accuracy of the sheltered-workshop's assessment of prevailing wage was fairly loose and arbitrary; while some staff in the sheltered workshops and WACs received training in evaluating a person's level of productivity, the evidence behind such findings was not established. Even if both the prevailing wage and the individual's productivity could be measured with fidelity, the tasks offered to a worker were limited in choice. The disability industrial complex has an obvious incentive to label people as having low productivity, although we know that productivity can be enhanced with the right type of tasks, supports, and accommodations.

In September of 1981, the Government Accountability Office, spurred on by the *Wall Street Journal* articles and the Congressional hearings at which Jernigan had testified, issued a report finding that less than 17 percent of workers in sheltered workshops earned the federal subminimum wage rate, in other words, were paid at least half the federal minimum wage. The report also found that 60 percent of workers had been underpaid. The physical divider between some sheltered workshops and WACs in the same space was sometimes just a curtain or other temporary barrier. The GAO also reported widespread issues with the programs visited, citing "problems computing hourly rates" to be paid to workers. None of the report sounded a firm and confident endorsement in the official oversight systems that had only grown more inept as the sheltered-workshop system grew. An important finding criticized the level of productivity that might follow a person from job to job within the sheltered workshop: "Workers may switch jobs but retain the same hourly rate even though the individual's ability and level of productivity will likely vary for different jobs." Despite these concerns, industry lobbying efforts ultimately won out, and the sections of the FLSA requiring a wage floor for workers with disabilities were eliminated. By 1982 legislation was introduced to eliminate the separation of the WACs (which could essentially pay pennies on the hour because of their supposed therapeutic mission) from the sheltered workshops. The NFB suggested these two moves would "effectively repeal the 50% minimum wage rate." Several more hearings and investigations by House members were conducted, but in 1986 there was no longer a floor to the subminimum wages that could be paid to a worker with disabilities. As in decades to come, the lobbyists managed to insert language that supposedly offered more protections by giving workers the opportunity to appeal their wage rates, but this was purposefully misleading window dressing. By all appearances, instead of updating and modernizing FLSA's section 14(c), Congress had walked back protections, informed by the same nonprofit disability and employment agencies that would most benefit. Under the guise that the previous wage floor inadvertently discriminated against the most severely disabled workers, and to decrease red tape and burdensome oversight, President Reagan signed the bill into law.

The removal of the statutory subminimum wage would allow organizations like Goodwill to pay some of its workers just pennies. The 1980s saw more coordinated efforts in the way of advocacy while the issue of fair pay lagged behind. In 1983 the National Council on the Handicapped (NCH) made an urgent call to Congress to "act forthwith to include persons with disabilities in the Civil Rights Act of 1964, along with voting rights legislation." The NCH would later become the National Council on Disability and played a pivotal role in researching the detrimental nature of section 14(c).

In 1985 the US Supreme Court ruled in *City of Cleburne v. Cleburne Living Center* that municipalities cannot use zoning laws to prohibit community-based group homes for people with intellectual and developmental disabilities from opening in a residential area simply because the residents were labeled as disabled.[7] The Protection and Advocacy for Mentally Ill Individuals Act was passed, and another significant stride had been made on behalf of residents of mental health facilities, including institutions, treatment centers, and other types of segregated programs. By 1988 the students at Gallaudet University, "the world's only university designed to be barrier-free for deaf and hard of hearing students," would demand that the university appoint a deaf president in Irving King Jordan (he went by I. King Jordan) through their protest "Deaf President Now." I. King Jordan had been in a motorcycle accident at age twenty-one that fractured his skull in two places, shattered his jaw, and severed the nerves in his ears. Jordan took the mantel on March 13, 1988, and the changes related to disability policy in the closing years of the decade did indeed seem biblical in name and nature. The reformation of the FLSA, however, continued to be mired in a potent mixture of lobbying, poor oversight, and competing interests.

As the late 1980s gave way to a new decade, a powerful piece of legislation, which would be referenced in the DOJ lawsuits regarding subminimum wages, was signed into law. On July 26, 1990, the landmark Americans with Disabilities Act was officially the law of the land. Three months later, after having completed my undergraduate work, I took my first job trying to help workers with disabilities in sheltered workshops leave for jobs in the community where they would be fairly compensated. Like many advocates, my employer was also the same nonprofit that ran the sheltered workshop, a common situation, I would later find out, and a pivotal issue in the DOJ lawsuits that would later arise. Just a year later, in 1991, Jerry's Orphans would stage its first annual protest of the *Jerry Lewis Muscular Dystrophy Association Telethon*, which dismayed the host, as the self-advocates fought back against the pity and stereotypes they felt his efforts had trafficked in. Jerry's Orphans was founded by Mark Ervin and his sister Cris, both former poster children, who, along with others, protested the Chicago MDA telethon events, and made a searing documentary called *The Kids Are All Right.*

In 1992 I met Riley in the institution in Indianapolis, and he was whisked off to a program before I could help him find a job. The subminimum-wage issue was reopened by Congress again just two years later, an occurrence that repeated for decades; while the issues remained roughly the same in 1994, the parties in disagreement had sharpened their skills of influence.

In March of 1994, the House Subcommittee on Labor Standards, Occupational Health and Safety took up the issue, led by Representative Austin Murphy, a Democrat from Pennsylvania. The panel heard from the NFB again. James Gashel argued that the so-called protections put in place in 1986 to afford workers with disabilities the right to challenge their assessed level of productivity and the subminimum wage assigned to their efforts was not working. Goodwill countered, with Admiral Cooney, the president and CEO from 1981 to 1995, stating that the protections "allow workers with disabilities or their guardians to appeal wage determinations to the Secretary of Labor." It's hard to imagine how a subminimum wage worker with disabilities would have easy access to a cabinet member. Admiral Cooney had been a supporter of Reaganomics and was quoted in the *New York Times* in his first year of running Goodwill, when it was a $ 264 million organization: "We're a nonprofit corporation founded on the principles of capitalism. We've always believed it's better to make people work for what they get than to just give it away." Admiral Cooney also believed that imputations regarding the habitual exploitation of workers under section 14(c) were simply "unsubstantiated allegations."

When the 1994 hearings took place, I was a professional working inside the behemoth disability industrial complex. At conferences and through newsletters, I met people who were trying to overturn the practices of section 14(c), and I learned that there were leaders of sheltered workshops who were trying to shut down the very buildings they worked in. It was a revelation, first because it seemed righteously covert, and secondly, because I recognized in these people something missing from my union upbringing—a sense of camaraderie, of working together on something bigger than myself, a way to keep solidarity alive by putting another worker's well-being if not above my own, then side by side. I started hearing that there were people who'd been fired from the nonprofit sheltered workshops for pointing out the oversight problems, the inherent injustice of subminimum wages. The idea that this wasn't more widespread was a shock. Still, I tried hard to understand how the hearings were going. Since email wasn't yet ubiquitous in the nonprofit world, that meant poring over reports and listening in on mammoth teleconference calls where people from all over the country were trying to find a way to overturn the 14(c) practice.

Donald Elisburg had left the Department of Labor in 1981 where he'd been assistant secretary and was now employed as an attorney in a private law firm. In 1978 and again in 1980 while still at the USDOL, he had been one of the first bureaucrats to provide facts and figures during the Beard hearings that followed the *Wall Street Journal* exposés. He had been blunt about how little oversight related to 14(c) was being done by the Wage and Hour Division at the USDOL nearly fifteen years earlier. He had vowed that exploitation would not go unnoticed and that the department would significantly step up its enforcement obligations. By all accounts, his testimony and reassurances seemed sincere and earnest. Indeed, Elisburg is still active within a broad range of labor issues; he's spent his entire career advocating for worker rights. Elisburg's testimony in 1994 was nothing short of astounding. Since 1981 he had been in private practice in Washington, DC, representing organizations on environmental, occupational health, training, worker disability, and labor standards issues, as well as legislative and regulatory matters. From 1986 to 1991, he was the executive director of the Occupational Health Foundation, an organization assisting five departments of the AFL-CIO on worker safety and health issues; from 1990 to 1992, he was the principal investigator and project director for the Center to Protect Workers' Rights, a nonprofit organization supported by the Building and Construction Trades Department of the AFL-CIO to conduct and sponsor research concerning the quality of working conditions in the construction industry. Mr. Elisburg served on the governing council of the American Bar Association's Labor and Employment Law section and was a former cochair of the section's OSHA committee as well as its workers' compensation committee. During the Carter administration he served as assistant secretary of labor for employment standards, which addresses the enforcement of protective labor standards laws such as minimum and prevailing wages, child labor and farmworker rights, equal employment in government contracts, and several worker compensation programs administered by the federal government. For seven years prior to that he was on the staff of the US Senate Committee on Labor and Human Resources, including three years as the committee's general counsel and staff director.[8] With this impressive background he found time to appear, as a private citizen, testifying in 1994. He was no longer optimistic that the FLSA section 14(c) standards could be brought under the control of deeper and more judicious oversight. As a bureaucrat, attorney, and citizen, he explained why the entire system was broken.

Elisburg's experience had shown him that "the present system for challenging workshop abuses is a study in futility."[9] The protocols laid out in the 1986 amendments (especially related to a subminimum-wage worker's appeal to the secretary of labor) along with other so-called oversight measures didn't make sense. Elisburg argued they were "not only unhelpful, they are useless."[10] He believed the very structure of the system related to the law was woefully misconceived and lacking serious thought on the part of the party with the most power, once again not the worker with disabilities. For instance, how and who would pay attorney's fees if subminimum wages were challenged was not specified, a basic legal consideration. As Elisburg pointed out, "Basically, the individual workers who are required to sign a complaint are put at tremendous risk of conflict with their employers under difficult employment circumstances." The 1986 amendments allowed the subminimum-wage worker to have a complaint filed by a parent, a not-so-subtle reference to one of the enduring stereotypes of people with developmental disabilities, known as "the eternal child." In sum, the entire process was fraught with provisions typical of the disability industrial complex, where the goal is to not afford basic civil rights but to maintain the status quo.

Elisburg also exposed the unrealistic enforcement of the timelines associated with a worker's complaint, which gave the secretary ten days to assign a case to an administrative law judge, who was then supposed to hear the case within thirty days. He had recently been involved with a case in Texas that had taken over fifteen months to resolve, roughly more than ten times the amount of time written into the amendments. From this experience Mr. Elisburg noted that for the worker with the disability and their guardians to proceed with a complaint, they would need "expert economists and others in time and motion studies."[11] Elisberg's testimony is rife with passion and a desire to make sense of a law that seemed only to get worse each time it was brought before Congress. Adamant, he pointed out that "the sheltered workshop personnel and management had little understanding of the rules, . . . the records they had were virtually non-existent to support the exemption" (that is, to pay subminimum wages). He added, "And they had little economic justification for the wage scales they set."[12]

In closing, Elisberg asked, "How in good conscience can we ask these workers to also foot the legal bill?" He did not believe any amount of oversight could remedy the essential flaws in the outdated system, adding that "to suggest a worker earning $2.05 an hour can afford legal counsel is ludicrous."

One might expect that Elisburg's testimony, as a USDOL insider, an attorney, and a concerned citizen, would have prompted the overhaul that the law needed, especially since the 1986 amendment had removed the wage floor and the reporting of abuses was essentially void or at the very least defunct, but it was not to be. Perhaps the lobbying by the sheltered-workshop industry had achieved its end, or maybe, since few subminimum-wage workers with disabilities were seen as constituents, the political will just was not there. As it turned out, no changes were made during 1994, in oversight, complaint processes, or reinstatement of the wage floor. Instead, the practice of paying subminimum wages to workers with disabilities went untouched and would remain that way for two more decades. It would take three women from Georgia, two with intellectual disabilities, to take their cases to the Supreme Court in order to win a decision that would set them free and create the basis for a real challenge to section 14(c), the sheltered-workshop system, and its lobbyists. The path would be a winding one, and justice would come only in short spurts. There had been oversight hearings for decades, and civil-rights wins too, but subminimum wages for workers with disabilities seemed cocooned in a time capsule.

Part II

5

THE *OLMSTEAD* SUPREME COURT
DECISION AND FREEDOM FIGHTERS

It is difficult to overstate the resilience required to fight back against imprisonment in an institution. We have confidence in physicians and believe medical professionals know best. Over 90 percent of Americans in a 2019 survey stated that they trust doctors.[1] American institutions have been run by physicians and nurses since their inception, and many families in the early decades of the twentieth century were encouraged to give up babies born with disabilities to be cared for in such institutions, which required large amounts of capital and human resources to fully function. On May 23, 1974, two men who had been in Indiana state institutions, Leo Sonnenburg and Gerald Hartnett, filed a class action lawsuit seeking compensation for labor performed while they were patients. The complaint contended that the plaintiffs were entitled to payment under the minimum-wage and overtime provisions of the Fair Labor Standards Act. Their lawyers also saw another legal angle, a violation of the Thirteenth Amendment to the United States Constitution, which prohibits slavery and indentured servitude. The appellate-court judge defined the class members as "all patient workers who have labored in the State of Indiana Institutions for the Mentally Handicapped or Mentally Retarded from May 23, 1970 to December 31, 1974." The appellate court found in favor of the 7,400 "patient workers" and awarded $ 28 million in back pay for jobs performed in the institution, ranging from working in a hair salon cutting other patients' hair, preparing meals, cleaning, working on vehicles, doing landscape work, providing nursing care, and even working in the institution's bowling alley. Most of these were found to be full-time jobs. In June 1991, however, the appellate court was overruled by the Indiana Supreme Court in *Bayh v. Sonnenburg*, where the court found that the labor fit within the civic-duty exception to forced labor.[2] "The court looks to whether mental patients' work had ever been compensated throughout history, because the constitutional convention records make clear the framers did not intend to create new rights to compensation. The 1816 constitution makes clear that the institutionalized may be made to work when they're institutionalized." There was only one dissenting opinion; Justice Dickson found exceptions with the concept of involuntary servitude: "Other jurisdictions have found that patient labor does not fit squarely into the civic duty exception. The requirements of the extended full-time work go way beyond the civic duty requirement." And Dickson argued that the right to compensation was not applied across the board. "Working at the state's mental institutions was not required of all citizens. The labor of patient/workers was not demanded for merely a few days each year. It was required full-time during their confinement."[3] That Dickson used the term "citizen" rather than "patient," even if only once, was promising. There would be no $ 28 million in back pay for the 7,400 citizens held captive in Indiana institutions, but others would take up the fight in just a few years.

For most professionals embroiled in the legislative back-and-forth related to subminimum wages, the years from 1994 to 1999 were spent like so many others, living in their own homes, working, enjoying life in freedom, but for Lois Curtis, those five years, plus many before, had been spent in an institution where among other tedious tasks, she performed work for subminimum wages, ate food not of her choosing, and spent her days isolated, uncommunicative, and trapped behind cinder block walls and razor wire. She would end up in the Oval Office meeting President

Barack Obama in the fall of 2014, but before that day arrived she would endure more isolation, segregation, and neglect.

Diane Cobb was a nurse at Georgia Regional Hospital in the 1980s. She clearly remembers Lois as a teenage patient: "Lackluster and isolated. She did what many of the patients did—walk about the hospital grounds unkempt and uncared for. Her hygiene was horrible. Lois was sullen and depressed. She was withdrawn into herself and rarely smiled. That's how she survived that environment. She didn't look forward to something she couldn't keep, like a friendship with someone or a rapport with a staff person. There wasn't any nurturing within the psychiatric unit, only more meds and endless monotony."[4] Since Burton Blatt had exposed America's treatment of its citizens with disabilities in *Christmas in Purgatory*, the entanglement of residential and vocational settings was still common, if not fully residential, then in the form of day centers, which looked like the day rooms in Blatt's institutions.

Georgia Regional Hospital–Atlanta (GRHA) sits on 174 acres of real estate in Dekalb County. Nearby is a facility run by the Georgia Bureau of Investigation, along with Georgia State University's Perimeter College, and an area called Rovena Acres. South River and Blue Lake are nearby. GRHA, one of the sites run by Georgia's Department of Behavioral Health and Developmental Disabilities (DBHDD), was still viewed by most as an institution. As we've stated earlier, human services, especially disability services, tends to alter language to make the programs and services sound more palatable. Hospital sounds normative, while institution reminds us of *One Flew Over the Cuckoo's Nest*. Lois Curtis was admitted into Georgia's disability and mental-health systems at age eleven for various dubious reasons. Lois was considered unruly, lacking judgment, possessing a defiant personality, and the list goes on and on. Lois was finally able to leave the institution for good at the age of twenty-nine. From a poor family, without means for even modest private care, Lois struggled in school. Then, as today, the understanding of the interplay between intellectual and behavioral health disabilities is minimal.[5] There are clinical assessments and research, but most of the work in this area fails to consider how those diagnostic labels impact a specific human being, like Lois Curtis. However, the outcomes are usually predictable, with poverty, lack of opportunity, and abuse being the trifecta that produces the most trauma.[6]

Elaine Wilson had been homeless and in and out of institutions nearly forty times. "Elaine was shunted among institutions and shelters from age 15 and subjected to shock treatment and psychotropic drugs 'that knocked her out and ruined her kidneys,'" said her mother, Jackie Edelstein.[7] Lois and Elaine were provided essentially what the state of Georgia had the most faith in—institutional settings replete with vocational programs that included sheltered work in the form of janitorial jobs. Neither Lois nor Elaine had been sentenced for criminal charges, but they had been involuntarily committed to what most would consider imprisonment. Georgia's Department of Behavioral Health and Developmental Disabilities system was subsequently sued by the Department of Justice, but for now it would take another strong woman to help Lois and Elaine experience self-determination, to take on their cause and stick with it.

Sue Jamieson met Lois and Elaine in 1995 in her role working for the Atlanta Legal Aid Society, which was founded by the Atlanta Bar Association in 1924 to assist the poorest of the poor with legal issues and advocacy they could not afford—specifically, protection against neglect, abuse, and exploitation. Sue Jamieson had started her legal career assisting poor people in Florida, but by the early 1980s she was in Atlanta and eager to begin a project that would focus on people confined to the grounds of Georgia's institutional system. Like Burton Blatt before her, Jamieson found the treatment and living conditions in these places isolating, inhumane, and wasteful of human potential. Deinstitutionalization in the United States had begun in the 1970s. Many people living inside institutions had left, but it would be erroneous to characterize the country's investment in institutions as a bygone, historical fact.

Today the number of people living in institutions is far lower, but there are new terms used now. As of 2018, there were 11,682 registered mental-health treatment facilities in the United States. Within those, 8,956 were less than twenty-four-hour outpatient facilities while 1,920 facilities were twenty-four-hour inpatient facilities.[8] The phrase "twenty-four-hour residential setting" is a way of saying "institution" inside the disability industrial complex, and in 2018 there were 1,932 twenty-four-hour residential settings.[9] Almost 130,000 people labeled with intellectual and developmental disabilities still live in places called "intermediate care facilities."[10] The names change, but the conditions rarely do.

Once Sue Jamieson had met Lois and Elaine, she went about advocating for them to have the appropriate supports to live in the community through a Medicaid waiver, known as a Home and Community Based Services (HCBS) waiver. Essentially, states can create their own HCBS waivers, providing they meet the guidelines and parameters set in place by the Centers for Medicare and Medicaid (CMS), part of the federal Health and Human Services (HHS). HCBS waivers are designed to "meet the needs of people who prefer to get long-term care services and supports in their home or community, rather than in an institutional setting." It's a strange way to describe a set of funding and policy tools specific to each state's budget and political leadership, since it's hard to imagine anyone preferring to live in an institution. For Lois and Elaine, that question had been settled; both women, along with their remaining family members, had tried over and over to leave the institution behind, but poor funding and a lack of coordination returned Lois and Elaine back inside the chain-link fences again and again. Both women had been warned by institution staff that if they were discharged, they would have at their disposal only homeless shelters. Still they persisted.

Life in institutional settings had changed some since the 1960s when Blatt and Kaplan took their covert pictures of naked patients, cowering in corners. There was more oversight now, and one might find people fully clothed, but it would be overly optimistic to concede that Lois and Elaine's care in the 1980s and 1990s was completely sound. There were long days with little but the janitorial chores that never seemed to end. They were prescribed multiple pills, swallowing them after taking a cluster from a nurse's hand along with a paper cup of water. Incidents of misconduct among unrelated people living in any institution is common, and both women had infractions, arguments, and what the disability industrial complex likes to call "behaviors," as in "she's having behaviors." The phrase is intended to communicate something, but even those who use it can't define it. Still, the phrase "she's having behaviors," can be heard in nearly any setting related to disability— certainly in sheltered workshops and work activity centers. Lois and Elaine had both been labeled as "having behaviors."

Mostly the days were monotonous for Lois and Elaine, with few visitors and even fewer variations in schedule, activities, or food. The Civil

Rights of Institutionalized Persons Act (CRIPA) of 1980 had been passed to protect confined people, those with intellectual disabilities and mental-health disabilities in institutions, as well as people living in nursing homes. CRIPA is enforced through the special litigation section of the Department of Justice's Civil Rights Division. The focus in determining the application of CRIPA is narrow and must fall within one of the following six areas: 1) the rights of people in state or local institutions, including: jails, prisons, juvenile detention facilities, and health care facilities for persons with disabilities; 2) the rights of individuals with disabilities to receive services in their communities, rather than in institutions; 3) the rights of people with disabilities who interact with state or local police or sheriffs' departments; 4) the rights of youth involved in the juvenile justice system; 5) the rights of people to have safe access to reproductive health care clinics while confined; and 6) the rights of people to practice their religion while confined to state and local institutions.[11] People who may be at risk in these scenarios may also merit an investigation, meaning that there are conditions present that could allow for abuse. CRIPA can be enforced under this "at risk" guideline too. People in institutions, their family members or advocates, and current or former employees can initiate a complaint. Many times local newspaper reports have tipped off the DOJ about CRIPA violations, and an investigation is started. The law allows other concerned citizens to act on behalf of someone with much less power.

By the mid-1990s CRIPA was in full effect. Lois and Elaine were asking the state of Georgia to assist them in moving out of the institution because that was their preference; they preferred to have their supports and care provided in the community, not within the grounds of an isolating institution like GRHA. The basis of their claim was the Americans with Disabilities Act, not yet even a decade old at the time. These women, fighting for their rights, were embarking on the first bold steps that would lead to taking on the state of Georgia. It's important to understand how terrifying this would be for Lois and Elaine. The state seal was prominent within the institutional grounds; they had tried to leave before but had either ended up homeless or back inside the institution. It was a brave endeavor.

Sue Jamieson recalls the logic of the *Olmstead* case. "Our theory was that Lois and Elaine were confined in a state hospital and that professionals believed they didn't need to be there (in the institution) but they also felt that they would need appropriate services in the community.

The ADA says exactly that: if you are providing services to a person with a disability, those services must be provided in the most integrated setting appropriate to the individual."[12]

For the "most integrated setting" to be the community, though, the state of Georgia, specifically its Department of Behavioral Health and Developmental Disabilities, named the Department of Human Resources in the 1990s, would have to develop individual budgets for Lois and Elaine and allow the two women access to the HCBS waivers. While the institutions are certified by the Centers for Medicare and Medicaid, the funding is entirely different, much more of a group rate/bed reimbursement model than the highly individualized HCBS waivers it would take to make sure that Lois and Elaine were getting the right supports in the most integrated setting. Inside the disability industrial complex, access to these waivers is often fraught with competition, making the situation susceptible to pressure. The proverbial squeaky wheel gets the grease. Sue Jamieson helped Lois and Elaine harness their voices to make noise.

Tommy Olmstead was born in Macon, Georgia, and attended Mercer University there. He was the CEO of an office equipment company for more than forty years. His political life started on the Bibb County Commissioners Board, but by 1986 he had been elected to the Georgia state senate for three consecutive terms, where he chaired the Health and Human Services Committee that, among other issues, focused on disabilities and mental health. In 1995 Governor Zell Miller appointed Olmstead as the commissioner of the Department of Human Resources, where the HCBS waivers and the institutional funding and operations were administered. The state's Medicaid agency was a necessary collaborator in setting up the HCBS waivers. Olmstead would end up as one of the defendants in Lois and Elaine's legal fight for freedom.

In early 1996 Sue Jamieson and the Atlanta Legal Aid Society filed their case on behalf of Lois Curtis and soon added Elaine Wilson. The plaintiffs won considerable legal points related to the ADA in front of United States District Court Judge Marvin Shoob and in the Eleventh Circuit Court of Appeals. Both courts confirmed that Georgia was required under the ADA to serve Lois and Elaine in the community rather than confining them in an institution. The state of Georgia, concerned that the case would set a precedent, appealed to the United States Supreme Court. Olmstead and the state of Georgia argued that although the women were cleared (medically and psychologically) for a more integrated setting to receive their services, the state's funding constraints and the obligation to restructure existing models of treatment and care prevented the option for community living.[13] But just because a state's human-service bureaucracy can't innovate and provide support consistent with the ADA does not mean it has no legal responsibility to do so. This fact would echo across the ensuing decades as the lawsuits pertaining to sheltered workshops and subminimum wages proceeded.

On December 14, 1998, the United States Supreme Court agreed to hear the appeal of Georgia and Olmstead after their loss in the Eleventh Circuit, presided over by Judge Elbert P. Tuttle, who had been a hero of the desegregation movement. The attorneys and advocates for Lois and Elaine believed that Tuttle's background in civil rights was a good sign. Oral arguments at the Supreme Court took place on April 21, 1999. There would be a focus on the ADA but also several citations to the Rehabilitation Act of 1973, specifically Section 504. In this way, one can now see how the Rehab Acts of 1973, the ADA, and the *Olmstead* decision create a through-thread, a kind of line woven from one to the other, such that a violation in one part of a person's life (where they live) is connected to others, such as where and how they work.

The oral argument before the Supreme Court lasted a little over an hour, but the efforts behind the scenes, the endless trail of legal paperwork, and the toll on everyone involved was intense. More than four years had passed since Sue Jamieson helped Lois and Elaine take the first tentative steps toward reclaiming their lives. Inside the institution at GRHA, both women had been essentially labeled as "unemployable," based on erroneous assessments like the IQ test and a battery of vocational and social instruments that were supposed to predict a person's ability to work and live in the community. During the time they waited for their case to make its way through the legal process, they had been assisted by other advocates, people who were trying to help the two women determine what their futures might look like, including how they would spend their days working.

Gillian Grable was one of those advocates who routinely picked up Lois at the institution for forays into the community, brief trips to help with the transition, but she and Lois had a history that dated back to when Lois was just twelve years old. As part of a family visiting program,

Grable had met Lois and her mother in public housing as part of an initiative known as Family Visitors. The idea was to provide friendly services that could help connect people to needed resources but with a basis of engagement squarely centered on citizenship, rather than professional intervention. Gillian recalled Lois's early interest in art. "She was already a person who needed to create. Earrings, drawings, Lois was a creative child."

Their relationship would span decades, but it wasn't easy for either of them, especially when Lois became a young adult and her civil rights were violated. At one point, Lois spent a stretch of over 700 days in Georgia state-run institutions. "When I'd take her back, after I'd somehow gotten permission for a day pass, she'd plead with me, 'Can I come home with you?'" Both women, highly emotionally intelligent, would weep. However, they were also strong human beings who wouldn't stop hoping for something different. Gillian Grable convinced a bureaucrat with a big heart to listen to how Lois could be supported to live outside the walls of the institution, using a planning technique that would allow for both paid staff and a dedicated inner circle of unpaid citizens who would help Lois find an inclusive, productive life. It was at this stage that Grable introduced Lois to Sue Jamieson.

"That place was something else," Grable recalled. "I'd been to many institutions before, and while it certainly wasn't the worst, there didn't seem to be much logic surrounding the rules about trips off the campus. I got the feeling things were handled from just whatever popped up day-to-day." The trips Grable took Lois on were also to help with planning for what life would be like after leaving GRHA. Freedom after such long stints in institutional settings can be traumatic. It was clear from the start that Lois liked to draw; she had small notebooks with penciled portraits and salvaged cardboard with little caricatures sketched in ink. Lois had stories too, things that had happened to her, that had happened to others she knew in the different places where she had been placed. "She told me lots of things on the car rides, many of them too sad to recount, but she also had dreams of having her own place, friends, choosing what she wanted to wear and eat. It was astonishing she hadn't had control of those things. She's so smart." Gillian and Lois worked on quilts together too, along with daily routine activities that most of us take for granted, like shopping, going to the hair salon, and choosing a movie to watch.

Gillian Grable and her husband, a judge, traveled to Washington, DC, to witness the Supreme Court oral arguments. Grable often cites a phrase that is moving in its simplicity: "Lois led us all." After the court heard oral arguments in April 1999, it took another two months before a judgment was announced. Justice Ruth Bader Ginsburg announced the Court's decision, a "qualified yes" on the question of whether the ADA's prohibition of discrimination by a public entity required the "placement of persons with mental disabilities in community settings rather than in institutions."[14] The Supreme Court created three requirements for such action: (1) treatment professionals determine that community placement is appropriate; (2) the individual does not oppose being served in the community; and (3) the placement is a reasonable accommodation when balanced with the needs of others with mental disabilities.[15]

That qualified "yes" was a victory, but not a complete repudiation of keeping people warehoused and segregated in institutions, including being subject to subminimum wages. And who would speak for someone in an institution? Their parent and/or guardian? What if someone doesn't speak and doesn't have a loved one to speak for them? Isn't it logical to assume then that any human being stuck inside an institution would prefer freedom to choose their food, clothes, home and friends?[16]

While Lois and Elaine, and for that matter the lawyers involved, may not have envisioned it, the outcome of the arguments before the Supreme Court would go on to be referenced as the "Brown v. Board of Education for disability rights," especially in lawsuits pertaining to subminimum wages. In 2000 the *Olmstead* settlement agreement was signed. The agreement provided that the state of Georgia would guarantee the two women were provided community-based housing, training supports, and employment services. After hearing both Lois and Elaine speak, Judge Shoob said, "I was amazed. They were both so articulate. At a party after the hearing, they gave a talk about how it felt to take care of themselves and what a wonderful life they were leading. I went up on the podium and hugged each one of them. I'd never done that before."[17]

Of course, there was still a great deal of work to be done, and healing was needed. For Lois, the start wasn't exactly clear cut. At first, since she often sketched little girls in portraits, the team supporting her thought she might like hanging baby clothes at Target, but that was not her passion. Several people who knew Lois well helped her pick out and purchase high-quality art supplies, resources she had not had access to in the institutions. Her artwork was transformed. She preferred pastels and watercolors, sometimes just an ink pen. She created art for hours at a time, taking only small breaks between sessions. The members of her circle of support bought her pieces, and through word of mouth so did others. There were art shows in local galleries and pieces bought through the mail. In 2007 Lois received the Harriet Tubman Act of Courage Award, an aptly named honor for Lois's fight to find freedom, purpose, and the opportunity to showcase her talents while making it possible for others to do the same. In 2011 she was invited to meet President Barack Obama and his family in the Oval Office where she presented the president with an original piece of her art.[18] According to one person in attendance, she was thrilled, and on the way out, broke into singing the song "We are Family" by the group Sister Sledge.

In 2015, in an interview conducted by Lee Sanders, one of her support staff, Lois talked about meeting President Obama, how she and Elaine were the "first ones out," and how she spends her time, with art, going out to eat, cooking grits and sausage in her home, and her love for others still trapped inside institutions.[19]

Elaine Wilson went on to find her voice presenting to advocacy groups. She was often photographed wearing pearl earrings with a matching necklace. While she was the less familiar woman in the *Olmstead* case, that did not stop her from doing her part to spread the word of her life experiences in and out of the institution, with and without suitable employment. She became a public speaker at conferences and "Disability Days at the Capitol." She used PowerPoint presentations to highlight the differences before and after the Supreme Court heard her case. "She blossomed," said her attorney Sue Jamieson. "She took an interest in cooking and church and her personal appearance. She developed a PowerPoint presentation that described her life. When I heard it, I was extremely moved. I had no idea that Elaine had acquired that level of sophistication. She had exploited her natural skills and abilities to a degree I would never have believed possible. It makes you wonder how many other people like Elaine are out there."[20] Jamieson's astute observation points to the central misconception in how we evaluate and assess someone's potential for employment and contribution inside the disability industrial complex. It's a deception that keeps citizens duped. What are we missing out on by cordoning off people with disabilities from working in our country's economic land-scape? There are losses related to tax revenue, but much more important is the forfeiture of an array of human expressions, of unique insights, robust experiences, and diversity that our communities desperately need. We lose because we've been tricked to believe that so-called normality is the only economically beneficial commodity.

Elaine died on December 4th, 2010. According to records she had been admitted thirty-six times into institutions during her life. Elaine fought for and obtained the right to live her life the way she felt best suited her; she used her experiences as both a means to employment and to help change a severely broken system, even if she lived only a handful of years after winning her right to do so. Ironically, the institution that she and Lois left (Georgia Regional Hospital–Atlanta) would be sued under the same ADA integration mandate that had propelled their case to the Supreme Court. Among other abuses, the DOJ asserted that the institution did not protect its patients from harm and used restraints and seclusions in a manner not consistent with appropriate standards. Other areas of concern cited were nutrition, healthcare, and physical therapy, all denied to the very people whom the state deemed must be institutionalized.

In 2019 disability advocacy organizations across America celebrated the twenty-year anniversary of the Supreme Court decision that Lois, Elaine, and Sue had initiated. A slogan was adopted in their honor: "I am Olmstead!" A strand of StoryCorp recordings exists of people who have been impacted and saved by the landmark court case, with video recordings and writings on the intersection of civil and disability rights.[21] And the *Olmstead* precedent was the partial basis for sheltered-workshop lawsuits in Oregon, Rhode Island, and elsewhere.

It's instructive to look at the work of advocates for ending sheltered work and subminimum wages before *Olmstead* (1999) and even before the ADA (1990). Like other civil-rights movements, this is not a narrative arc that starts and ends with legislation, court decisions, or class action lawsuits; instead, it is a mixture of those elements with a specific person's devotion to justice and fair treatment, often at their own personal and pro-fessional risk. For a full picture of the ongoing battle to end subminimum wages, we need to consider those who read and learned from Burton Blatt, Wolf Wolfensberger, and others, and who believed that people with dis-abilities, specifically those considered intellectually and developmentally disabled, could learn. Recall Blatt's research and writings regarding those stored away in institutions as being "educable and trainable." In a very real sense, the early adopters of these sets of beliefs were on a track toward a head-on collision with the parties that believed people with disabilities needed special places to live and work, including special wage provisions. Those entities would enshrine their efforts to keep people segregated and exploited in supposed benevolence, while there was plenty of money involved. What would happen to the disability industrial complex if it was discovered that subminimum wages were the linchpin that held together a faulty and dangerous set of practices?

6

EARLY ADOPTERS AND TEARING
DOWN ASSUMPTIONS

Marc Gold wore a ponytail pulled tightly back and a thick, black mustache in Fu Manchu style. He'd grown up the son of a bicycle shop owner in San Francisco but had become a special educator in Los Angeles by the late 1960s. He found that the way teachers and administrators viewed their students with disabilities had little regard for possibilities. By the time he left for graduate school in Illinois, where among other things he studied psychology, disability, and adult learning, Gold had formulated what would later become his major contribution to the field. As a teacher he saw that students with disabilities had much more potential than many believed and that given the right supports and offered equitable opportunities, these students could learn, grow, and hone skills to work. Always the one to question dogma, especially when those doctrines were used to keep people down, devalued, and destitute, Gold began to study the way in which people who were labeled "mentally retarded" in the 1970s were treated, educated, and trained. Like Blatt, he found very few professionals held the belief that all human beings are capable of growth, learning, and value. Also like Blatt and others, Marc Gold set out to explore and understand the institutions in which many people had been warehoused after they been removed from their regular communities.

Why mention he was the son of a man who owned and operated a bicycle shop? Because it was the Bendix bicycle brake that Gold used to test his central hypothesis: Perhaps it's not the learner who is deficient or lacking in skills and intelligence, but the other way around. He would call this notion, the "Try Another Way" approach, a technique he honed and eventually used to train others in the United States and Canada. It was nothing short of revolutionary, and like all rebels regardless of their field of study, he would evoke the wrath of professionals who had invested their lives in that most dangerous of dogmas, we've always done it this way, and you're only stirring things up.

The basis of the "Try Another Way" approach to teaching complex tasks rested largely on a series of techniques that can be categorized as systematic instruction (SI). SI is a method of teaching tasks and skills that focuses on breaking learning down into specific steps such that mastering each one will lead to the acquisition of the whole. SI relies heavily on data collection but even more on the belief that if a learner is not learning, it is not their misstep but the teacher's, hence the name Gold gave to his approach. Of course, Gold himself was working within a certain tradition, at least partially, with B. F. Skinner's early papers on what would later be called the field of instructional design, specifically the basics that Skinner highlighted in *The Science of Learning and the Art of Teaching* in 1954. Obviously, Skinner would have viewed people with intellectual disabilities, and certainly the people Gold chose to teach, as needing reinforcement strategies that could be focused on more punishment than reward. Skinner's idea that environments shape people's actions, however, was one that Gold could see at work in the institutions he visited, both with the paid staff and those forced to live and work there. Robert Glaser's research study on forgoing the standard norm-referenced test in 1962 and Robert Gagne's 1965 contribution surrounding "Conditions of Learning" are also at play in how Marc Gold developed his "Try Another Way" technique. With roots in industrial-organizational psychology and what today might be categorized as positive psychology (i.e., what is right with you is just as important to focus on as what is wrong with you), systematic instruction in the hands of Marc Gold became not only a new way to think about people previously deemed unteachable but also a method to shatter the low-expectations of the disability systems (special education, vocational rehabilitation, and symptom management), systems that were addicted to treating the very problems they had helped to create, which in turn provided a never-ending loop of diagnosis, treatment, side effects, diagnosis, treatment—and more side effects.

By the mid-1970s Gold and others were taking their work inside the same type of places that Burton Blatt had infiltrated. While some things had improved, much of the country's population of institutionalized people suffered from the same neglect and assumptions by administrators that people could not learn or benefit from training. Some institutions had rebranded themselves as "training and developmental schools" or similar monikers, but their programs were still about warehousing people, and the abuse remained rampant.

With a large box containing the Bendix bicycle brakes, Gold and his colleagues entered these facilities, sometimes by invitation, even if most were half-hearted. Gold asked to meet the people who were labeled as having low IQs, a concept he believed was flawed. After chatting a bit with the person, a workstation would be set up, containing all the pieces, that when assembled, would become a bicycle brake. Gold admitted that the task in and of itself was somewhat meaningless (in the 1970s there were not many jobs solely dedicated to putting bicycle brakes together by hand), but he was comfortable with the task and understood that to most observers it would appear complex. Nearly twenty parts were needed to build a Bendix bicycle brake; and the parts were intricate and fit together like a puzzle. The task was also a perfect example of something that could be broken down into many steps, each one teachable. For the most part, Gold's work was just as much about convincing professionals that their minds had to change if they wanted people to learn. It was a tough sell. Most of the staff was trained in addressing behaviors (in a vacuum) and held firm to their beliefs that what they needed to know could be found in the *Diagnostic and Statistical Manual of Mental Disorders* (DSM).[1] That is not to say that Gold and his colleagues didn't have their fans and followers, but the "Try Another Way" approach and its associated humanistic principles were competing with the heavy history of otherness, labels of deficit, and a medical model that the field embraced from diagnosis to treatment. The application of the deficit-minded approach meant that the "cure" could take decades— maybe even a lifetime spent in an institution or sheltered workshop without any improvement, and probably more detriment.

Gold's work stirred the true advocates, however. They took his bicycle brake task to heart and started to try in their own ways to wrest the people they knew and worked with every day from the clutches of the disability industrial complex's hyperfocus on fixing people.[2] They would be an important part of trying to reform the systems that were most rooted in subminimum wages. Interestingly, some of their efforts were stymied by the very places where they worked themselves.

Back in 1990, when I took my first job in the disability employment field, there were stories told about people who were essentially trying to close down the sheltered workshops they worked for, to end subminimum wages by getting a job for anyone who wanted to leave. The phrase "a job on-the-outside" or "a real job" is how workers with disabilities inside the 14(c) work centers referred to them. These mavericks (both the staff and the workers trying to leave) and their associated stories were usually bathed in the light of rebellion and civil rights. I'd heard of professionals who stood up to their boards of directors and paid the price by losing their jobs. There were tales of other states trying to stop new entrants into sheltered workshops, not unlike the recommendations from the congressional hearings of the 1970s and '80s.

The catalyst for these individuals was something called Supported Employment (SE), developed and researched by Dr. Paul Wehman at Virginia Commonwealth University, and first established in every state through Title III, Part C of the Rehabilitation Act Amendments of 1986.[3] Growing out of the work of deinstitutionalization, community inclusion, and systematic instruction, and the notion that people with intellectual and developmental disabilities could learn and be trained, SE was a direct affront to professionals who believed otherwise, who desired to keep sheltered workshops as the primary mode of service delivery. The basic premise behind Supported Employment was simple: people who are relegated to sheltered workshops and work activity centers can learn to do jobs that pay minimum wage in the community if given the right supports in the right environment. Under federal law SE is defined as competitive work in an integrated work setting for persons with the most severe disabilities; for whom competitive employment has not traditionally occurred; or for whom competitive employment has been interrupted or intermittent as a result of a severe disability: and who, because of the severity of their disability, need intensive support services; or extended services in order to perform such work. This term also includes transitional employment for persons with the most severe disabilities due to mental illness.[4] It was clear that the powerful tools associated with SE intervention (a job coach, sometimes known as an "employment specialist," being the most radical) would assist the eligible recipients of the supports in all aspects of the job by working side-by-side with the worker with a disability to learn a real job for real pay outside the sheltered workshop or work activity center. It was the alternative to warehousing people and paying them trivial sums, and claiming that was all they could do. Like many new approaches inside the disability industrial complex, the application and implementation of Supported Employment services would be slow—and sometimes deliberately impeded.

Much of the impetus to expand the application of SE came out of the nation's developmental disabilities network, which was fully established when the Developmental Disabilities Act was amended in the Senate in June 1975, although several iterations of the law go back to the Kennedy administration, when funding was first set aside to support research, training, and outreach in 1961 and 1963.[5] The DD Act, among other things, established three major components that make up the Developmental Disabilities Network in each state: State Developmental Disability Councils, Protection and Advocacy entities, and university centers related to developmental disabilities. These components are overseen and funded at the Administration on Community Living (ACL) at the US Department of Health and Human Services, a cabinet-level federal agency. As defined by the ACL, the entities operate with several important charges, all related to employment and disability. To understand how this network has and has not supported the rights of workers under 14(c), we must understand their respective and collective charges.

> State Councils on Developmental Disabilities work to address identified needs by conducting advocacy, systems change, and capacity building efforts that promote self-determination, integration, and inclusion. Key activities include conducting outreach, providing training and technical assistance, removing barriers, developing coalitions, encouraging citizen participation, and keeping policymakers informed about disability issues.

State Protection & Advocacy Systems (P&As) are dedicated to the on-going fight for the personal and civil rights of individuals with developmental disabilities. P&As are independent of service-providing agencies within their states and work at the state level to protect individuals with developmental disabilities by empowering them and advocating on their behalf. P&As provide legal support to traditionally unserved or underserved populations to help them navigate the legal system to achieve resolution and encourage systems change.

University Centers for Excellence in Developmental Disabilities Education, Research & Service (UCEDDs) are unique in that they are affiliated with universities, allowing them to serve as liaisons between academia and the community. UCEDDs are a nationwide network of independent but interlinked centers, representing an expansive national resource for addressing issues, finding solutions, and advancing research related to the needs of individuals with developmental disabilities and their families.[6]

These three types of organizations had mostly focused on dissemination until the late 1980s and into the 1990s when they began to collaborate around employment for people with the labels of ID/DD. The UCEDDs were instrumental in taking the new idea of Supported Employment into much broader practice and implementation, conducting studies, training parents on alternatives to sheltered workshops, and helping people tell their own stories of leaving sheltered, subminimum-wage work for regular jobs in the community. The Protection and Advocacy entities in each state often handled issues related to being underpaid in a sheltered workshop, among many other civil rights. It was the trade association of these Protection and Advocacy organizations that broke the news regarding Henry's Turkey Farm; the National Disability Rights Network (NDRN) issued the report in 2011, titled "Segregated and Exploited: The Failure of the Disability Service System to Provide Quality Work."

The DD Councils took on the charge of advocating with state legislatures about the benefits of putting valuable and flexible state dollars into matching funds with the Rehabilitation Services Administration at the Department of Education so that more funding could enter a state to actually support workers with disabilities in finding competitive integrated employment. As states tried to ramp up their ability to provide more access to Supported Employment, it seemed natural that the nonprofit agencies, many of whom operated sheltered workshops and work activity centers, would receive funding to grow their agencies' capacity to offer support to workers with disabilities who wished to leave the buildings for a job in the community. As with much of the 14(c) story, the unintended consequences would be detrimental. One advocate said in hindsight, "Giving the sheltered workshops and day programs funds to help find people real jobs in the community was like a vegetarian wearing a full buckskin outfit. It didn't make sense."[7] In other words, the organization that could step outside its embrace of subminimum wages and low expectations was rare. When that did happen, it usually was because the leadership of the organization had a strong vision of inclusion and fairness, along with a view that people could rise to the expectations set for them. If the leadership saw possibilities with the advent of Supported Employment to close a sheltered workshop, then action was taken. But many of these early adopters found themselves isolated and sometimes attacked for believing that workers with disabilities could leave 14(c) subminimum wages behind.

Some states were working hard to implement Supported Employment services in place of sheltered workshops. Most of these initiatives came from the state agencies responsible for funding and overseeing intellectual and developmental disabilities services and supports. Low-vision and blind advocacy groups like the NFB kept up their focus too, but at the state agencies the people behind the focus on real jobs in place of sheltered, subminimum, segregated jobs were usually commissioners like Dr. Steve Hall. Hall had completed his doctorate degree at Virginia Commonwealth University, where Dr. Paul Wehman carried out studies on Supported Employment and trained people like Hall to go out into the field and make a difference. Hall first led the effort in Indiana by delivering training and technical assistance to programs under a Supported Employment demonstration grant funded by the Rehabilitation Service Administration. In this capacity Hall toured sheltered workshops around the state and gave talks, including data, on the outcomes of subminimum wages versus Supported Employment. "It was tough work," he told me. "There were lots of small programs that had been started by local families that had begun to take on much more of a facility type operation. It was nothing to see thirty people all huddled around a table doing packaging work. I remember someone showed me their check at one of the programs. It was for a week's work and it didn't total ten dollars."

Hall would go on to become the executive director at Sycamore Services in Danville, Indiana. I was one of the first job coaches he hired for the Supported Employment program he was trying to build up there, even while the sheltered workshop held nearly a hundred people. Hall, like many others, felt he could make needed changes by leading with strong values and focusing on doing things in a different way. It would prove daunting. Hall faced resistance from the board of directors, families, and local funders. As Hall brought in grants and new sources of funding, the local vocational rehabilitation counselor was invited to use office space at Sycamore Services, where he could do intakes and drink free coffee. The trick, though, was to get the counselor to begin opening Supported Employment cases for people who wanted to leave the sheltered workshop. Since the Rehab Act of 1973 had been amended in 1992 to focus more on jobs in the community through the use of Supported Employment, it was a new idea to open cases for workers with disabilities who had been relegated to sheltered, subminimum wages. The counselor in the sheltered workshop at Sycamore Services was not convinced that would work, stating that he didn't want to bother with the "sheltered shop." So, to open cases for workers wishing to leave, we walked people out the back door (the facility was new and had lots of access points) and brought them in through the front door as if they had just arrived. The case would be opened, and the services were begun that would help people get and keep jobs of their choosing.

These stories illustrate a phase little known outside the disability employment complex and those knowledgeable about the system. It could perhaps be called "closing the shop from the inside out." All over the country were examples of sincere, hardworking people trying to eliminate subminimum wages by building the capacity to offer more services directly linked to helping a person get a job outside the sheltered workshops and work activity centers. Some began to call it "changeover" and later "provider transformation," both terms meaning that the organization holding the 14(c) certificate could develop a plan, including a budget, and with the right focus on Human Resources and solid training, including a focus on disability rights as civil rights, it could make the necessary changes. This would prove to be an approach with limited success. A potent mixture of resistance as seen in the decades-long 14(c) congressional hearings was alive and well in local communities. Still, people kept trying.

KFI is a nonprofit provider of services located in Maine. According to the agency's executive director, Gail Fanjoy, KFI engaged in the "planned systematic abandonment of the old."[8] In 1974 the organization received a 14(c) certificate for the Katahdin Workshop in Millinocket. The Katahdin Workshop obtained subcontracts to make leather utility-knife cases, wooden seedling racks, and other products from recycled materials. In 1986, however, the organization's leaders became passionate about changing their services, phasing out subminimum wages, and replacing them with the powerful tools of Supported Employment. KFI abolished subminimum wages in 1986. It was the same year that officials in Washington held hearings to remove the floor on subminimum wages. Fanjoy and others across the country were doing what representatives from the sheltered-workshop industry had said couldn't be done; that fact alone is a prime example of how disability and employment policy is out of synch between those who believe in change and those who have lobbied to keep things as they are.

Gail Fanjoy credits the organization's ability to sustain change with the energy created when people formerly considered only productive enough to work in a subminimum-wage setting began getting real jobs for real pay. When staff, families, and workers with disabilities saw others succeed outside the walls of the sheltered workshop, the momentum for change was created. Fanjoy said, "The early successes caused staff to question the efficacy of vocational training provided in segregated spaces. They reflected that the sheltered workshop taught few of the skills that people were using in their competitive jobs, and that people were better able to learn these skills on the job." Fanjoy noted that they just decided to support people, and not groups, and work with one person at a time with a focus on real homes, real jobs, and valued social roles.[9] The early adoption of better practices in lieu of sheltered workshops was happening, but far too slowly; it was easier for states to fund provider agencies to use a group model rather than an individual one. The change was difficult; since it was still perfectly legal to keep people segregated and offer only subminimum wages, that's what happened most often.

Still, there were practitioners and researchers following the work of people like Fanjoy. Susie Rinne had worked on a process called "conversion," an early term for organizational transformation from sheltered work to jobs in the community.

"Several community rehabilitation providers discontinued use of subminimum wage during that time," said Rinne. "It looked like we might be on a path to making a dent." The subsequent surveys by Rogan, Held, and Rinne in 2001 found those same agencies that had eliminated their reliance on 14(c) and switched their services to focus on real jobs at minimum wage or above continued to be financially viable. "In fact, many of the agencies reported improvements of their fiscal health resulting from the changeover."[10]

By 1994 Dr. David Mank and others were trying to study agencies in the throes of making systems change. In an article for the *Journal of the Association for Severe Handicaps*, he and his fellow researchers laid out the requirements to fully embrace the true spirit of the 1973 Rehabilitation Act as amended in 1992. The title, "Realigning Organizational Culture, Resources, and Community Roles: Changeover to Community Employment," itself describes the effort necessary to get organizations conceived and built around the unfair practice of paying workers subminimum wages to change their essential processes. As Mank pointed out, different financing and radically different mindsets on behalf of the agency's staff, board, family members, and workers with disabilities themselves would be required. Nothing short of something radical would create the desired change, but for some, "change over" was too slow. In a reader's response to the Mank article, a husband-and-wife team from California, the Zivolichs, argued that progress was stymied by talk of "planning to plan to change," a phrase that certainly has weight inside the disability industrial complex, where change is yet another reason to lobby, hold conferences, or author a white paper. Their reaction was published in 1995, titled "If Not Now, When? The Case Against Waiting for Sheltered Workshop Changeover." The article was brief but passionate and reflected the feelings of thousands of professionals and family members regarding the lack of responsiveness from a system that had been the heart of congressional hearings for decades and fifteen years after the *Wall Street Journal* exposés. As so often: the alarm is sounded, studies and hearings are conducted, recommendations are made, and still more stalling, more phasing out ensues, and more time is requested to fix the problems and abuses.

The study of organizations wasn't a new concept twenty-five years ago, but it was a novel idea when directed toward the kind of sheltered-workshop settings that had gone relatively unchanged for decades. When the principles of systems change were levied against the settings where subminimum wages were the norm, a predictable set of outcomes often rose to the surface. Research related specifically to human services and change demonstrates why most sheltered workshops run by nonprofits didn't respond more rapidly. Gordon Shen and Lonnie Snowden have studied how change does or does not occur in mental health systems. The authors state, "The pattern of policy diffusion reflects readiness for change and propensity to take political risks. Tracing the sigma-curve of innovation diffusion, a few early-adopters ("innovators") are followed by a critical mass of late-adopters ("laggards") and non-adopters ("resisters"). The phase of policy adoption lends itself as a predictor of mental health system change."[11] There's a satisfying labeling role reversal going on here, whereby the penchant of the disability industrial complex for labeling people with disabilities is turned back on itself with the Shen and Snowden labels of "laggards" and "resisters" applied to organizations. Using the descriptors above as related to sheltered workshops shifting to a model of supported employment, many late-adopters (laggards) simply added onto their services instead of making a complete changeover. As for resisters, or nonadopters, their voices were amplified by state and national trade organizations so that the expectations from the funders of their programs were less formal and permitted a dual system in which significant investments in buildings and segregated, subminimum wages, with a much smaller investment or concern with offering supported employment.

A national advocacy organization, unlike the ones representing the sheltered-workshop industry, had come into its own as well. APSE, first known as the Association of Persons in Supported Employment, was the brainchild of two of Dr. Paul Wehman's graduate students. It was still a fledgling organization in 1995, but because it sought out people—both with and without disabilities—who believed everyone could work in the community for regular wages, it was the essence of the very best of grassroots associations: subversive, disruptive, creative, committed, passionate, and irreverent. Also in 1995 Pat Rogan and Stephen Murphy published one of the first manuals related to organizational change, a book that would have a somewhat underground existence, *Closing the Shop: Conversion from Sheltered to Integrated Work*. The authors profiled four agencies embroiled in a changeover; like the papers by Mank and responses like that of the Zivoliches, they spent time on the organizational dynamics at play to make such a shift. The early adopters of replacing subminimum wages with regular jobs in the community included individuals with disabilities, families, organizations, researchers, and practitioners, but when Congress again chose to take up the issue at the start of the new millennium, there was no concerted effort regarding what should govern the billions of dollars spent each year on the pursuit of vocational rehabilitation, training, and support for workers with intellectual and developmental disabilities. An alternative approach existed now, however, in the tools and practices of Supported Employment, which had been substantiated by federal authorization. Would its availability be expanded? Who would benefit from such developments, workers with disabilities or the structures that purported to serve their best interests? Those sheltered workshops labeled as laggards and resisters had the upper hand because the disability industrial complex helped keep wholesale change at bay. The resisters had passion, but as the writer and academic Eddie Glaude has pointed out, what we believe to be true is a stronger motivator than what we know, what we can observe and measure. The lie that subminimum wages were, for some, for their own good would require a whole lot of speaking truth to power.

Federal Policy as Catalyst, Barrier, and Duality

The federal approach to employment and disability, specifically toward those considered to have the most severe impact from disabilities, has shifted both in name and policy over the decades. In addition to the issues related to subminimum wages, lawmakers and regulators have struggled with everything from employer inducements to something known broadly as "work incentives," a phrase geared toward helping workers with disabilities make choices about going to work or changing jobs.

On the employer side, it's a story of lapsed legislation and what could be characterized as only mild incentives for businesses to hire workers with disabilities. The Work Opportunity Tax Credit (WOTC) is made available to employers to hire individuals from certain targeted groups that have consistently faced significant barriers to employment; two of those categories encompass workers with disabilities who have been earning subminimum wages. The US Department of Labor (USDOL) and the US Department of the Treasury, through the Internal Revenue Service, jointly administer the implementation of the WOTC program, which was passed by Congress in 1997. The WOTC provides for a tax credit if a worker is part of a vocational rehabilitation program with a state plan written under the guidelines of the Rehabilitation Act of 1973 as amended or if the applicant is a recipient of SSI, Supplemental Security Income.[1] A person can qualify for SSI if she is blind or has a disability; the cash payment generally allows one to access Medicaid through his state agency. The employer of someone who falls into either of these two categories (part of a VR program or SSI recipient) can claim a tax credit that averages $2,400 per person, but the employer must make sure that the new hire is certified as part of the targeted group. Often, WOTC is not reauthorized consistently by Congress, and typically there are backlogs. There is not much incentive. In contrast to Germany, where companies are required to fill 5 percent of their workforce with workers with disabilities, the United States is woefully behind in policies related to the role that private business plays in employing people with disabilities, although Germany's companies have been impacted by the Nazi eugenics of the past and often struggle to meet the mandate.[2]

For workers with disabilities receiving SSI and/or SSDI (Social Security Disability Insurance), Congress passed the Ticket to Work and Work Incentives Improvement Act (TWWIIA) of 1999, creating special rules that would incentivize going to work by reducing the risk of income loss, improving access to rehabilitation, and providing access to new entities, "employment networks," whereby SSI and SSDI beneficiaries could assign their ticket to a new set of community rehabilitation providers and thereby create choice.

By the beginning of 2000, we had the *Olmstead* decision, the ADA, and incentives for employers to hire people with disabilities (WOTC), who now had their own new set of incentives to go to work in the form of TWWIIA. But in 2001 Congress once again held hearings on subminimum wages, and once again nothing changed in relation to the rules that applied to section 14(c) of the Fair Labor Standards Act. As introduced, House Resolution 881 would have made it impermissible for the secretary of labor to issue approval for any further payment of subminimum wages to workers whose only disability was low vision or blindness, generally referred to in advocacy circles as "turning off the pipeline." Under H.R. 881 workers with all other types of disabilities, intellectual and developmental, including autism, cerebral palsy, and brain injuries, would have continued being paid subminimum wages. The bill was not acted upon, mostly due to previous lobbying efforts by the same players in the earlier debates who had wanted to keep subminimum wages legal and widespread. The federal point of view related to disability policy, especially concerning employment, was at odds with itself again, but even more so in 2001 since the Supreme Court, as well as the IRS, Social Security, and the USDOL itself, had weighed in.

As part of the remedy for a perpetually discombobulated set of policies, the federal government acted by creating a specific entity at the Department of Labor known as the Office of Disability Employment Policy (ODEP). It was authorized by Congress in the Department of Labor's FY 2001 appropriation, an outgrowth of the Presidential Task Force on Employment of Adults with Disabilities and the President's Committee on Employment of People with Disabilities. The USDOL's press release strove to establish a forward-thinking set of values for the new entity, stating, "Recognizing the need for a national policy to ensure that people with disabilities are fully integrated into the 21st-century workforce, the Secretary of Labor delegated authority and assigned responsibility to the Assistant Secretary for Disability Employment Policy. ODEP is a sub-cabinet level policy agency in the Department of Labor."[3]

One of the first priorities at the newly minted ODEP was related to workers with disabilities who had spent most of their adult lives in sheltered workshops and work activity centers laboring under subminimum wages. While the development and utilization of Supported Employment had been beneficial, the values and implementation principles associated with the service had been watered down once it moved from the demonstration phase funded by grants in the 1980s to common use. Funders at the state level had taken a powerful tool and embedded it inside bureaucracies, which are notoriously risk avoidant. The reauthorization of the Rehabilitation Act in 1992 had set the stage by using language that was to reinforce the notion of presumption of ability. Recognizing the systems that were designed to assist workers with all types of disabilities had become infected with a persistent belief in low expectations, the amendments instead insisted that vocational rehabilitation professionals assume that people with disabilities can work. While that seemed an odd declaration to have to make, especially to those who did not have much knowledge of the disability industrial complex, it was absolutely necessary.

Supported Employment (SE) had been designed to find jobs in the community, not in sheltered programs, and was specifically recommended for persons with the most severe impact from disabilities who had not worked before and who needed intensive supports to do so. The SE approach was effective and replicable, but for many workers with disabilities stuck inside sheltered workshops, the service was not available to them. In the Shen and Snowden approximation regarding readiness for change, either the agency supporting the workers with disabilities were "resisters" and hadn't started offering SE, or the agency fell into the category of "laggards," slow to build skills and capacity and ramp up availability. In addition, the implementation of Supported Employment tended to focus on those job seekers with fewer impacts of disability, who may not have been the recipient of subminimum wages. ODEP's leadership decided to challenge this issue head-on by robustly funding grants related to an emerging best practice known as "Customized Employment." ODEP funded its first grants cycle that included multiyear initiatives to validate Customized Employment as an effective workplace practice for employing people with significant disabilities previously perceived as "not employable."[4]

By 2001 I was working for an organization in Georgia called the Cobb and Douglas Community Services Boards (CSB). The state of Georgia created CSBs in 1994 as a public safety net for intellectual and developmental-disabilities services as well as programs for mental health and substance use. CSBs are public corporations and instruments of the state. I'd been hired to run a Supported Employment program that was connected to four sheltered workshops in the metro Atlanta area. My experience in Indiana had taught me how to write grants and seeing that I needed to infuse some much needed creativity into the nonprofit agency, I began looking through lists on grants.gov. The ODEP request for proposals (RFP) caught my eye because it focused on workers with disabilities who had been labeled unemployable and who had spent time in segregated programs paying subminimum wages—but even more intriguing, the funding was linked to the *Olmstead* Supreme Court decision regarding employment in a way that had not been fully realized. I buckled down and began writing.

Creating a response to a federal grant can be a maddening process. It takes the ability to imagine what the infusion of funding can do to assist with changing a specific system, often one that is resistive. Like most

RFPs, only a limited number of grantees can be awarded and it's competitive. There are collaborators to enlist, which includes stakeholders, the traditional systems already engaged (sometimes theoretically) in the pursuit of the same improvements. For instance, when the Clinton administration along with Congress acted to revamp the welfare program, the systems in states and localities would have to change as well. For the disability industrial complex, that meant Georgia's vocational rehabilitation program and the state agency that Tommy Olmstead had led, now known as DBHDD. All states have these same programs, albeit named differently. In the end, I wrote for a grant from ODEP in 2001, 2002, and from its sister agency, the Employment and Training Administration (ETA) in 2003, securing funding each time. It was exciting to be on the forefront of bringing change to the organization I was employed by, but these were demonstration grants, meaning that the funding was to be used to investigate promising practices (such as Customized Employment) in order to determine how the practice, sometimes referred to as an "intervention," could be taken to scale, developed in such a way to infuse those stakeholder agencies with better services that would help create employment opportunities for what the grant funding called "the focus population." But for the people I'd met in the sheltered workshops, this meant I might find a little redemption, maybe even right some wrongs created by the four sheltered workshops, and of course, help unleash the talent and perseverance of workers who had had to endure subminimum wages and segregation.

The funding from these initiatives helped to hire new staff, provided for additional state-of-the-art training and technical assistance from subject matter experts, and just as important, allowed for a reason to convene. As a burgeoning community of practice (CoP) there were opportunities for open discussion, to gather data that could be analyzed and to make changes in the focus systems. These were five-year grants that offered occasions to attend nationwide convenings in Washington, DC, where the other grantees (from over twenty states) shared the barriers they had encountered, as well as the elements of the demonstration projects that were working well and could be incorporated into the work of other states.

For the first time since the inception of the FLSA and section 14(c), the nation had a lead agency taking on the awesome task of trying to unite other vested federal agencies to create a more cohesive approach to employment and disability policy. For ODEP's part, it didn't sit idle after Congress created it in 2001. Year after year new plans were developed, and the staff at ODEP kept at it, putting out new grant opportunities and taking its convening role seriously. In a flurry of work, the first decade of 2000 saw the creation and launch of DisabilityInfo.gov, the first federal interagency website for disability-related information and resources. ODEP collaborated with USDOL's Employment and Training Administration (ETA) and the Social Security Administration to launch the Disability Program Navigator initiative to increase the capacity of the general workforce development system to serve people with disabilities so that the endless referrals from one program to another would cease.[5] There were grants to help identify and reproduce best-practice approaches to supporting youth with disabilities in working during school to avoid segregation and subminimum wages, resulting in a set of principles known now as "Work Early, Work Often."[6]

By 2003 ODEP had created a national project via a cooperative agreement to implement Training and Technical Assistance to Providers (T-TAP), a national effort to increase the capacity of community rehabilitation programs and other community-based service providers to promote integrated, competitive employment for people with disabilities through customized employment strategies and forgoing time spent in subminimum-wage sheltered workshops and work activity centers. T-TAP ran from 2002 to 2007 and resulted in several dissemination products, including a mentor guide that was developed based on the experiences of the T-TAP mentors and project staff as they provided technical assistance and training to provider agencies that applied for and were awarded assistance from ODEP. The purpose was to provide information to community rehabilitation providers about organizational change designed to improve employment outcomes. The T-TAP project was a collaborative effort between ODEP, Virginia Commonwealth University, and the Institute for Community Inclusion at the University of Massachusetts–Boston. As the new subagency at the USDOL, ODEP was trying to make a dent in the foregone conclusion by the disability industrial complex that subminimum wages and segregation were the best options for workers with intellectual and developmental disabilities.

Back in suburban Atlanta the grant work at the Cobb and Douglas CSB went on as well. By 2003 it seemed a direct contradiction of the grant funding to keep the four sheltered workshops and the associated 14(c) certificates. Nancy Brooks-Lane was the director and responsible for administering large budgets and programs that supported hundreds of people and their families. Brooks-Lane was trained as a psychologist but had also spent time in the civil-rights movement in Mississippi. She was perfectly suited to change how things had been done, to spot within the system the points where people were not being heard, treated fairly, or provided opportunities for growth. As people with disabilities in the programs received Customized and Supported Employment services and left the sheltered workshops for community jobs, the decision to take on the arduous task of ceasing to pay subminimum wages was complex. It meant angry parents, confused funders, disgruntled staff, and impatient board members who preferred to not be bothered with large-scale systems change. Yet, she persisted. The special 14(c) certificates were not renewed, which meant the four sheltered workshops would need to reevaluate their mission, including how to arrange programmatic supports moving forward. Brooks-Lane and her colleagues ordered several copies of the book *Closing the Shop*. It would be the first in many books, manuals, and reports that would be incorporated into the systems change, but one of the internal staff who did not believe that subminimum wages should have been ceased, alerted family members that a case of *Closing the Shop* had been delivered.

Systems change in any type of industry is difficult; people resist, hunker down, and take things personally, but when that change is connected to a specific worldview—for instance, where and how people with the most significant disabilities should spend their days—the resistance is amplified.[7] For the next eighteen months Brooks-Lane worked with families and board members, often in the evenings and on weekends. The influx of the grant funds helped, and it was decided that dissemination of the stories of workers with disabilities leaving the sheltered workshop would support the sustained momentum needed for further change. The connections with the federal grant partners at ODEP as well as Georgia's Council on Developmental Disabilities helped; several profiles were written and photos shared of the stories.[8]

Storytelling became a critical tool in communicating the changes, and with those successes came additional opportunities for more grant applications. Brooks-Lane was asked to serve as a mentor on the ODEP project

(T-TAP) that assisted other provider agencies in the country to implement systems change as well. In 2007 a research article was authored by Brooks-Lane and others (including myself) for publication in the *Journal of Vocational Rehabilitation*. The editor-in-chief at the journal was Dr. Paul Wehman, who had been such an early influence on the idea of using Supported Employment services to help workers with disabilities leave subminimum wages for jobs of their choosing in the community, working alongside nondisabled coworkers and making the same pay. Wehman had argued for the Rehabilitation Act as amended in 1992, "These Amendments pull together the best of what we know about how to assist people with disabilities and their families. The rest is up to us." As editor-in-chief at *JVR*, Wehman endeavored to keep that spirit alive. Our article, "A Revolution in the Employment Process of Individuals with Disabilities: Customized Employment as the Catalyst for System Change," was published in 2008, and the title explains how our nonprofit rehabilitation agency strove to offer more real employment to people who had been traditionally supported in sheltered workshops or day programs. By using case studies and qualitative data, the path to real and effective organizational improvement in the area of customized employment outcomes was explored. Seven points of analysis in the systematic organizational development emerged from the data review: (1) staff development; (2) community partnerships and diversified funding; (3) sustainability; (4) a shift in managerial approaches and supervision; (5) changes in human resource processes; and (6) expanding customized employment to diverse populations, i.e., those leaving justice systems, foster youth, and welfare-to-work recipients. The examination illustrated the need for best-practice staff training, person-centered and community-based vocational assessments, customer-directed personal budgets, flexible funding, a focus on evidence-based customized employment outcomes as performance indicators, values-based human-resource processes, and executive leadership involvement with staff and customers to break down barriers and achieve organizational momentum for outcome-driven change.[9]

Customized Employment (CE) was an emerging best practice for people who had not been given the opportunity to leave the arena of subminimum wages. In 2007 CE was defined in the *Federal Register*[10] as: "Individualizing the relationship between job seekers and employers in ways that meet the needs of both. It is based on an individualized determination of the strengths, requirements, and interests of a person and matching those to the needs of the employer." Customization was not a new concept; all job descriptions are created by a business to address unmet needs. All job seekers, whether subject to a disability or not, routinely consider the work environment, job characteristics, and other conditions that they prefer in a job. Customized employment starts this process with up-front negotiations between the job seeker and the employer. The methodologies of customizing a job include a process called "job carving," which can be thought of as creating a job from one or more but not all of the tasks of the original job; "job negotiation," as in creating a new job from various tasks from parts of several jobs; "job creation," which is creating a new job based on unmet workplace needs; "job sharing," which consists of two or more people sharing the same job and performing different tasks at different times; and "self-employment," which includes the use of a micro enterprise. In an effort to address the *Olmstead* decision, the project in Cobb and Douglas Counties, Georgia, focused on moving twenty persons per year from the day program into customized employment (the subminimum wage 14(c) certificates were not renewed). The project was successful in substantially exceeding these goals. Project Exceed served 198 individuals through accessing Individualized Accounts (IA). These dollars were set up as funds specific to a person's employment goals. The IA dollars helped purchase equipment (i.e., a digital embroidery machine), tools (i.e., two hydraulic pet grooming tables), and other necessary items that could be leveraged in negotiation with an employer.[11] One technique used in Customized Employment is to capitalize the job seeker with disabilities with equipment and tools that they own and use to perform job tasks; this process is known as "resource ownership." It can be a powerful way to assist workers with disabilities who have been in sheltered workshops and work activity centers to compete in the marketplace, and it helps a small business benefit from capital resources attached to a specific job seeker.[12] The worker with the disability retains ownership of the resources; if they decide to leave for another job, the resources go with them. This can also offset in some instances any additional supervision or accommodations related to productivity that the employer might make. Of the persons served, 105 individuals were female, 93 were male. The predominant age range for persons served was 18–29. However, the age range extended through the full working-age population, including twenty-one individuals who were age fifty and over, meaning that these job seekers had spent a great deal of their time in segregated programs earning subminimum wages—or in other types of day programs aimed at training prevocational skills, another phrase in human-service speak that means "getting ready to work" and that rarely ends up producing such an outcome. It is a term so fraught with ambiguity in the disability industrial complex that the Centers for Medicare and Medicaid (through its guidance to state agencies tasked with implementing the Home- and Community-Based waivers related to employment) had to reiterate that prevocational skills could not continue for years and years. It's not uncommon to see workers with disabilities who have plans for ten years or more that involve billing related to prevocational services. One might question how an organization can claim to provide vocational rehabilitation that takes decades to achieve or whether the services are lacking in effectiveness to the degree that perhaps it is the very services themselves that are the problem. Perhaps it behooves a provider agency to keep people with disabilities in prevocational services so it can continue to bill, rather than supporting a person to become employed. The guidance from CMS states, "Segregated *pre-vocational* or habilitative programs that have a poor track record of placing people in competitive integrated employment may not be considered to provide adequate opportunities."[13] In other words, the nonprofits that purport to be "readying" people for employment outside the sheltered workshop or work activity center cannot just simply keep billing Medicaid year after year under the auspices of "prevocational" services if there's never any intention of transitioning services for the person with a disability to "postvocational," which, to the taxpayer who doesn't know the disability industrial complex's lingo, means—a job!

The five-year grant in Cobb and Douglas Counties helped workers with disabilities leave these types of settings. The predominant, primary disabilities of the persons served were mental illness (77) and developmental disability (85). By the project's conclusion a total of 141 project participants had achieved employment outcomes. The average hourly earnings in 2007 wages was just over $8 per hour, and the average hours worked per week was 22. Self-employment earnings fluctuated more and were difficult to quantify in an hourly format, but on the average self-employed participants earned higher wages for their services. For instance, a person with his own computer repair business billed $40 per hour. Project participants worked in a variety of jobs, such as car detailer, pet groomer, receptionist, teacher's assistant, data entry technician, childcare worker, bookstore employee, hair salon personnel, chef, embroiderer, lab technician, arcade attendant, vending machine owner-operator, and home inspector and fields, such as catering, pest extermination, flea market, sales, computer technology, motivational speaking, dry cleaning, jewelry sales, and lawn care, a stark contrast to what the disability industrial complex usually provided, which was only fast-food and grocery bagging jobs.

The grant initiative was a major undertaking for an agency that had been acutely immersed and invested in delivering the outdated subminimum-wage services that kept people perpetually lacking in work skills. Because the agency was part of Georgia state government, it also took on an early pledge to consider hiring workers with disabilities when posting job vacancies, which ran the gamut from mail room clerks, maintenance positions, data entry jobs, and transportation positions, as well as the traditional human-service jobs. This idea of government's putting its proverbial money where its mouth is would later be more formally adopted by the leadership at the Office of Disability Employment Policy at the US Department of Labor and given the moniker State Government as a Model Employer. The intention was that in order to be good stewards of both financing and federal legal mandates, both the federal and state governments should become role models, making accommodations and utilizing the same customized-employment techniques that were being used with local employers.[14]

By 2008 the programs in Cobb and Douglas Counties were considered leaders in the country for their efforts to systematically change, with intense efforts to build capacity to support workers with disabilities in real jobs in the community. There was still resistance, however, and daily there were discussions with the budget office about how the good work done under the grant initiatives would continue after the funding sunset. It wasn't a problem with a good answer. All over the country states grappled with how to increase the incentive so that sheltered workshops would opt for providing Customized and Supported Employment in the community, but the rates from state Medicaid and vocational rehabilitation agencies varied widely.[15] This funding discrepancy and the notion that nonprofit programs like the sheltered workshops and work activity centers could have more predictable revenue by keeping workers with disabilities in the buildings doing contract work, created confusion. While some states had made strides in realigning their funding, the result wasn't easily laid over another state's dissimilar structure. It didn't take a historian to see that the roots from the problems with section 14 (c) dating back to 1938 were bringing forth new iterations of the same old model of segregation, with more trade associations, an increase in providers of disability services deeply committed to organizing their programs around subminimum wages, and families buying into the low expectations that these groups held of people with disabilities and work.

In the end, while the grant initiatives helped 141 workers with disabilities in obtaining employment, they did not create long-term change, as in transforming the agency away from segregated day services. The 14(c) subminimum wage certificates were gone, but like so many other organizations around the country, the future didn't hold more employment for others. The systems related to disability and rehabilitation primarily charged with funding services, and the inherent nature of the agency itself to routinely rely mostly on state funds returned to the old ways of doing business. The number of people in facility-based and nonwork services grew and has continued to do so nationwide, suggesting that employment services remain an add-on, rather than a systemic change.[16]

This trend of seeding demonstration grants to help the sheltered workshops and activity centers switch over to providing supports for real jobs for fair wages in the community can be seen in many of the suggested fixes at the federal level. While there are some examples of this change happening, it's rare, and more often, as in the Cobb and Douglas CSB example, it occurs only for a brief time before resorting to previous ways of organizing services. This tendency is deeply ingrained in leadership and its vision—or lack—for change and innovation. In 2009 Dr. Katy Inge and others at Virginia Commonwealth University surveyed disability and employment agencies operating in the United States and found that nearly 90 percent of provider administrators (CEOs, CFOs) reported that they and their boards of directors felt that facility-based programs were indispensable for workers with disabilities and only 47 percent had a formal plan to expand integrated employment.[17] To make this point clear, roughly half the leaders from nonprofits receiving federal and state dollars to help people with disabilities get jobs reported having any type of formalized strategic planning to actually perform the tasks they are required to do by taking the funding from vocational rehabilitation and Medicaid. Imagine if these were CEOs of healthcare providers being surveyed, and they responded by stating that they had no definite plans to deliver primary-care services, to provide prevention services, or to pursue continuous quality improvement.

By 2010 I had left the machinations of the community rehabilitation provider system. I had worked inside the system for more than twenty years to try to make change, but now I felt that I could do more by training and providing assistance to states and nonprofits who wanted to truly help workers with disabilities leave subminimum wages. That would bring me to New Mexico, Rhode Island, Virginia, California, South Dakota, Maine, Utah, and other states. I took a job inside the DD network at the University of Georgia's Institute on Human Development and Disability, one of the nation's UCEDDs, and helped with training and implementing evidence-based employment practices mandated by Georgia's DOJ consent decree. During the decade of the 2010s, the nation had additional opportunities to overturn 14(c) and subminimum wages, and the battle intensified, resulting in the release of Wiki tapes to the public that highlighted the disability industrial complex and its scheming behind closed doors. NBC news coverage by Harry Smith investigated Goodwill's practice of relying on subminimum wages and the associated boycotts, but the most heart-wrenching stories of exploitation under 14(c) started in Texas and ended in a dilapidated bunkhouse in Iowa where law-abiding, legal citizens of the United States were treated as criminals and indentured servants because they had been born with intellectual disabilities and because it was legal to pay them differently from other men who worked in the processing plant doing the same work.

8

THE NIGHTMARE IN ATALISSA

Robert Canino knows how to tell a story. With his quick wit and command of language, it's easy to see that he also has a sharp legal mind, which he uses to simplify legalese—for writers and reporters, but also for juries, and most importantly for the people he represents. Listening to him talk reminds you of one of those guys in high school who didn't have to study and still managed to do well on pop quizzes. Canino can absorb new information and process it quickly so he can use his own experiences to arrive at similes and metaphors, a talent that the best attorneys seem to have been inherently gifted with. It would take these skills to understand his next big case, one that would propel him into the often strange and complicated disability systems that use phrases and terms that are either acronymic or simply incomprehensible (i.e., "enclave," "substantial gainful activity," "behaviorally challenged," and "borderline," to name just a few). What he didn't have to learn was compassion, a sense of justice, and a zeal for the underdog. He has spent his career trying to help others, if not to find it for themselves, then to prosecute those who have stolen it away. But before Robert Canino delved into the machinations of the disability industrial complex, he would first take on another case that came to light in 2001, one that later echoed and reverberated in his mind as he came to understand the plight of the men forced to work for subminimum wages at Henry's Turkey Farm.

Behind razor wire, fifty-two men of Indian origin were held against their will by the John Pickle Company, a silly name that belied the cruelty of its practices. All the men held captive were competent professionals, including high-tech welders, electricians, engineers, and other skilled tradesmen. The Pickle Company served the oil and gas industry, manufacturing pressure valves and steel pipeline couplings for oil transport. It was autumn in Oklahoma, a time of year in the state where temperatures can still climb to the eighties. Like most other rural places, though, the corn mazes and pumpkin patches were in full swing, some of them sponsored by churches. It was one of these churches that sounded the alarm. By this time in 2001, most of the men had been forced to stay in a cramped dormitory that Pickle had them build themselves shortly after they arrived two years earlier. Oklahoma red dirt can be hard, and digging it by hand and erecting a structure was backbreaking labor.

At first the men had been lured to leave India with the promise of excellent salaries, benefits, cell phones, apartments, and cars, all described to sound like the rags-to-riches movie tales of immigrants coming to America. An intermediary in India and a clandestine business associate of Pickle's, charged each man $2,500 to board the plane for America's heartland. Once aboard, they were told they would be receiving H1-B temporary work visas, which would allow Pickle to either renew the visas or return the men to India after six months. Once on the ground or perhaps better put, in the compound, which was dirty, unorganized, and greasy, Pickle and his staff began to immediately abuse the men. Because it was shortly after the 911 terrorist attacks in New York and at the Pentagon, Pickle often threatened the men with deportation or incarceration, and most of the time both. The men worked twelve- to sixteen-hour days, even after building their own shelter. Their IDs and visas were taken from them by Pickle's wife. Court records show that the men may have been paid as little as $1.20 an hour when the long days were figured in. They ate poorly, and Pickle liked to supervise them during grocery shopping, making sure they bought cheaply. Milk was only allowed once every three to four days. Food that was bought for the men was often expired, and many of the men, not used to American food, began to lose weight and suffer from lower energy. The Pickles now had control of the men's shelter, wages, diet, and movements.

The nights were hot and cramped and the days full of danger, with the facilities woefully unrepaired and a lack of caution and care from the overseers regarding safety. Some of the men tried to seek connections with the outside world. At the rear of the Pickle Company property, a fence was also in disrepair; apparently Pickle and his men believed threats and cruel treatment would keep the imprisoned workers from taking any significant initiative to improve their predicament.

At dusk one evening, once the guards who walked the property had settled into their routine of television and drinking, a few of the men crept to the fence and slid underneath, careful to remain quiet. Once under the fence and safely away from the perimeter of the Pickle compound, the men could talk more freely in their own language. Across the street sat a small church. Though only a few of the fifty-two men were Christian, they decided the Hale Pentecostal Church might be their only viable opportunity to find help. Time was short, and they knew Pickle and his men would notice they were missing when the meager dinner was provided later in the evening.

Fortunately for the men their first contact at the Pentecostal church was Mark Massey, a lay pastor. In Massey they found someone true to his Christian beliefs, a family man with a deep sense of morality about how to treat and care for his fellow human beings. Massey tried to make sense of what the men were describing to him about the Pickle working conditions, how their safety was being threatened, including insinuations by Pickle's Indian associate who had implied that the men's families back in India could be harmed if they did anything to disappoint the Pickle Company owners. Massey would eventually help nearly all the men escape, staging a late-night rendezvous with a van and offering his own home to house the men as he simultaneously began the search for an attorney. In the end Massey learned from the men that another group of Indian nationals was being held in a similar fashion in Louisiana, so he went on a mission to rescue them too. Massey's efforts, though, did not go unpunished. He was arrested in Baton Rouge and held for days while the men he had helped to flee the Pickle Company back in Oklahoma gathered money for his bail. A judge tossed out the case against Massey but not before he spent thousands on legal fees after it was alleged that it was the lay pastor who was the trafficker, rather than Pickle and the owners of the Louisiana company. Robert Canino took the Pickle case to the Equal Employment Opportunity Commission and won in court in 2006. The attorneys for the company argued that the practice used to pay foreign workers had some legal merit. "The pay was commensurate for a training program such as this." Canino recalled the details: "It was so egregious. Here we were in the twenty-first century with servitude, maltreatment, and human trafficking in the heartland. It was not difficult to see the same threads in the horrendous treatment of the men with intellectual disabilities at Henry's Turkey Farm."

The Pickle case prepared Robert Canino in other ways as well. As we saw in the congressional hearings on 14(c) dating back to the 1960s and 70s, the issue of what distinguishes an employee from a client, and from someone who is both of those and lives in a housing configuration where work is supposedly compensated in part by the exchange of labor for those living arrangements has been problematic for decades. In the Pickle case, the men were housed by their employer. The statute that allows for subminimum wages, the Fair Labor Standards Act, also grants some leeway to employers who house employees, known as 3(m) credits. Section 3(m) of the FLSA allows an employer under certain circumstances to count as wages "the reasonable cost . . . to the employer of furnishing such employee with board, lodging, or other facilities."[1] Of course, these 3(m) credits, like the 14(c) exemption, are often abused: they are not necessary exemptions for a worker who has stable housing, can communicate her needs and desires, and has equal power in the employer-employee relationship. This was the case with the Indian workers due to their reliance on Pickle for food and housing, communication barriers, their confusion regarding US labor laws, and the constant threat of deportation and incarceration.

At the time the Pickle situation was exposed, the owners of Henry's Turkey Farm (HTF) had been violating labor laws for more than thirty years. By 2003, though, the Wage and Hour Division at the US Department of Labor had finally become involved and begun an investigation into HTF's methods of paying men with intellectual disabilities. As early as the 1960s, the owners of HTF, also known as Hill Country Farms, Inc., had begun working with men with intellectual disabilities who had resided in institutions in Texas. In 1966 the Abilene State School agreed to allow the owners of HTF to run a pilot program that would send six men with disabilities to a Texas ranch where they would supposedly learn new skills working with sheep, poultry, and other livestock. This was just a few years after Burton Blatt had covertly exposed the conditions inside the country's "state schools" and "developmental centers." In stark contrast to Blatt's appalling findings, the idea that a for-profit company with "upstanding local owners" such as HTF would be willing to not only help the men but also teach them agricultural skills would have seemed cutting edge. The laws passed to ensure students with disabilities could receive an education that was free and appropriate would not be passed until 1975 and section 504 of the Rehabilitation Act as the cornerstone of disability civil rights became law only in 1973, more than a decade after the owners of HTF started picking up the men with disabilities from the institutional grounds for work on farms.

The idea for the initial pilot project of six men gained momentum, and by the early 1970s mental-health officials across the country were trying to find ways to deinstitutionalize people. In this arrangement not only did the men get to leave the institution, but they could learn and live in the community, all of it costing the state of Texas much less money. Oversight was steamrolled by the opportunities for good public relations.

Kenneth Henry and T. H. Johnson had jointly incorporated the business in Goldthwaite, Texas, a small town of fewer than two thousand residents in the center of the state. By 1978 Henry and Johnson had arranged to provide workers to a processing plant in West Liberty, Iowa, more than a thousand miles away. While the state officials in Texas who were associated with disability services greenlighted the practice, the Texas men with intellectual disabilities were essentially being trafficked from their home state to another for the purposes of cheap labor. The men with disabilities from Texas had been isolated and didn't have the same opportunities as others. The notion that someone wanted them, in another state no less, would be exciting for someone who hadn't had much freedom or respect in his life. As the situation in Iowa began in earnest, there was need for local housing. The owners of HTS found an enthusiastic partner just down the road from the turkey processing plant, in a place called Atalissa, whose population has hovered around 300 people for decades. An old schoolhouse was converted to provide shelter to dozens of men from Texas. It would become known as the bunkhouse, and the silhouette it cut atop a small incline on the outskirts of the tiny town of Atalissa seemed to perfectly coincide with its century-old frame. A single willow tree stood out front on one side, a maple on the other, and over the years the building had been painted different colors, including a strange sea-green shade with blue trim. A peeling flagpole and an elongated swing set with a single wooden seat had been erected along the sidewalk leading to the single-door entrance. The glass windows were painted over, some panes replaced with plywood. The owners of HTF rented the ill-kept and rundown building from the city of Atalissa for $600 a month, but of course, they charged the men much more. A few of the men with intellectual disabilities worked in the bunkhouse and not at the slaughterhouse, preparing meals, cleaning, and performing general chores, like shoveling snow and replacing rotted boards with slightly less rotted boards, but most of the men living in the bunkhouse were transported back and forth to the slaughtering house. It was a dawn-to-dusk enterprise. Tedious, dirty, cramped, and unlike what they had been promised.

After honing their model of exploitation in Texas, it seemed to Johnson and Henry that they could ramp up the demand side of their offerings using the legally permissive 14(c) subminimum-wage law, as well as the 3(m) housing credits. Like most people outside the disability industrial complex, it came as a surprise to ranchers and other agricultural reps that labor could come at such a low price. To make sure their business model had credibility in the eyes of the human-service agencies in Texas, it was given a name. For short, the program was called the "Magic of Simplicity," and it was outlined in a written document, essentially a piece of propaganda. The full title included the subtitle "Developing the Abilities of Developmentally Disabled Persons." If the owners of HTF were trying to emulate the state schools and human-service bureaucrats in Texas and elsewhere, they had accomplished the task. Johnson and Henry included an action phrase, "Developing the Abilities," meaning that their approach to training and employing men with disabilities had "habilitative" components. Since the scheme was all about billing state or federal funds, "intervention" is always needed.

As in any type of industry, word-of-mouth advertising is beneficial to sales. Hill Country Farms d/b/a Henry's Turkey Farm was getting its fair share of the spotlight, but by late 1978 cracks were emerging in the scheme. After nearly 600 men had been part of the project, there were allegations of poor record keeping, meager safety oversight, and a kind of macho, stoic approach to injury, working conditions, and the overall "ranch hand" lifestyle. The owners, Johnson and Henry, stated in the "Magic of Simplicity" manual that every man had annual physical and dental checkups and that the staff of HTF provided sick care to men in the bunkhouses, administering meds, including those aimed at reducing sei-zures and controlling diabetic symptoms. As in the copious congressional hearings over the years, the role of patient/client was at odds with that of trainee/employee, with a dose of resident/renter thrown in to confuse things even more. Imagine being sick in bed, and your job supervisor is your landlord, who also administers your medication. Taking a sick day is never more fraught with discrimination than under this type of predica-ment inside the disability industrial complex.

Initially, what Johnson and Henry were doing won them some praise. In 1968 the national Association of Retarded Citizens, as it was known then, gave Johnson an award for being an innovative employer. In 1972 Kenneth Henry, fifteen years younger, agreed to combine their two ag-ricultural companies to do business as Henry's Turkey Farm, under the umbrella of Hill Country Farms, Inc. Over the next decade men with in-tellectual disabilities from Texas institutions were sent to turkey insemi-nation farms in Missouri, Kansas, two sites in South Carolina, several in Iowa, and one in Illinois. Johnson's friend at the Texas Vocational Rehabilitation Commission referred hundreds of men to Henry's Turkey Farm. Johnson received $175 per month per person from Texas in the form of "training funds." Thousands of dollars a month went into John-son's coffers, and that was only the revenue from Texas. Labor contracts with Louis Rich and other processing plants also created a substantial revenue stream in addition to the human-service funds. Johnson was an enigma; he was critical of the red tape that government bureaucracies created, believing it a hindrance to business and entrepreneurs like him-self who just wanted to help. He reportedly believed that what he was doing was the best approach to remedy the problems that men with intel-lectual disabilities presented to state governments, especially those who didn't have family involvement. Johnson claimed he was training the men to do meaningful work, and housing them too, outside of institutions. He was even skeptical about sheltered workshops. Under investigation in 1979, he told reporter Margaret Engle about the common jobs done inside sheltered workshops, "Mickey Mouse things like packing little plastic forks and spoons in little plastic bags." In this way Johnson—and later Henry—was aligned with those advocates engaged in trying to close sheltered workshops but with a major distinction: Johnson was not critical of subminimum wages, just the type of work performed by workers with disabilities. Johnson referred to the men as "retardates" and viewed them as boys, rather than adults. At the time such derogatory terms were not uncommon with the general public or inside the disability industrial complex. Explaining why he wanted to help the men leave the institutions in Texas, Johnson told the *Des Moines Register*: "They resent being put in there with the vegetables," apparently referencing people still residing in the state schools who also had physical disabilities. Johnson spoke of the men's IQ scores, giving examples of men with IQs below forty now doing ranch work. If some of the men weren't as fast as the others, Johnson had them trained to bottle-feed calves. Farming is often rife with "survival of the fittest" mentality, and this worldview crept into Johnson's treatment of disability, productivity, and labor in general. The workers with disabilities were prodded to work through sickness like beasts of burden. They were housed similarly, and punishment was corporal and meted out with a focus on creating docile workers. The men were fed cheap food and expected to work extra hours if they wanted more to eat. The men labored in guts and blood, eviscerating poultry entrails and performing insemination, a physically challenging task, especially when it involves hundreds or thousands of turkey hens. Even in the cleanest poultry breeding compounds, where a table is used, workers still must bend and stoop over and over, picking up hens that can weigh thirty pounds. While more advanced farms have technology and additional insemination accoutrements, the men with disabilities were performing these tasks by hand, without the proper tools. Bending and picking up turkeys twelve hours a day can easily turn into the equivalent of tons of weight. There are also exposure issues related to insemination, and proper precautions are difficult to adhere to when the space is dirty, unorganized, cramped, and riddled with defecation, loose feathers, and the fine dust from corn and dried manure that is easily inhaled. At Henry's Turkey Farm all the equipment was rudimentary, and most of the process was done by hand. T. H. Johnson was nothing if not adamant about not having government, OSHA or otherwise, poking around his operations.

In 1979, thirty years before the men at HTF were finally rescued from these horrendous conditions, two reporters, spurred by an investigation by state officials, were reporting on the men's maltreatment and the strange business model that had been set up by T. H. Johnson and Kenneth Henry, in which they essentially rented out men with disabilities to meat processing plants, offering cheap labor. When the *Register* article was written, HTS was not only under investigation in Iowa but in South Carolina as well: human-service officials in that state believed a similar bunkhouse used for shelter for men with disabilities trafficked from Texas should be licensed as a group home. Johnson and Henry responded with characteristic antiregulatory rhetoric. "We're not an institution and don't want to be treated like one. Government red tape just costs lots of money and doesn't do any good." The official response from Henry's Turkey Farm in 1979 was reminiscent of the early workhouses from the late 1880s through the 1920s, where society's "less desirables" were expected to work for some philanthropic organization in exchange for housing and food, usually with religious ties, simply because they were poor, declared feeble-minded, or came from families deemed as having genetic problems. To Johnson and Henry the fact that they were happily providing training and employment to men with disabilities was enough, in their minds, to quell the concerns from officials. Johnson was difficult to work with, often relying on his own commonsense compass to guide and direct how workers with disabilities were punished, rewarded, and trained. He fired personnel who didn't agree with his tactics. A nurse who had worked for Johnson at Henry's Turkey Farm told the *Register*, "I won't say if he's a saint or the devil incarnate, but he does have a way with the MRs." If the use of the term "MRs" is any indication, the nurse and Johnson were like-minded, viewing the workers with disabilities not as human beings, but as a group, a herd with no individualization, requiring stern supervision. An official from the Social Security office in Dallas reported seeing an enormous paddle during a visit in 1972. When asked about the four-foot-wide paddle, Johnson commented that he used it on the "boys" to enforce the rules. At other times, Johnson denied using it, but because the workers with disabilities were all young men, they sometimes engaged in the typical boundary testing. Some ran away; others found ways to get alcohol. There were squabbles and personalities that didn't get along, and to these infractions the owners of Henry's Turkey Farm and their supervisors responded with more cruelty, eventually taking the extreme measures of tracking down runaways and capturing them for return to the bunkhouse, where they would be chained to the beds so as not to abscond again.

There was a great deal of window dressing, especially during any inquiry or investigation into the operations. During the heightened scrutiny in 1979, Johnson claimed that each of "his boys" would be receiving Christmas gifts valued at $100, and he often told people that he paid for medical care for the men who didn't have Medicaid. There is no proof that any of the men ever received the "extras" Johnson claimed to provide. It would not be an overstatement to say that Johnson believed he was bringing something new, maybe even innovative, to the debate related to disability, employment, and institutional settings, but he willfully ignored basic principles of humanistic supports.

It was with this backdrop that the two *Des Moines Register* reporters told the story of the burgeoning suspicions of some families and officials regarding Henry's Turkey Farm. Other inquiries and investigations into the use of 14(c) were going on simultaneously. The *Wall Street Journal* investigative reporters, Kwitny and Landauer, had covered the use and misuse of subminimum wages in their two-part series focusing on blind workers. "Blind people for years have entered the job market through so-called sheltered workshops, sheltered by law, that is, from having to pay the blind workers minimum wages." The reporters from Des Moines had published their pieces on Henry's Turkey Farm and the labor exemptions that resulted in horrible pay almost a full year before the stories in the *Wall Street Journal* appeared. By that time in 1979, Congress had held no fewer than a dozen hearings regarding the practice, specifically the unintended consequences and the abuse of the laws guiding it.

The story in the *Register* ran just two days before Christmas 1979, and it was a scathing piece of reporting with depictions that read like scenes from *The Grapes of Wrath*. There's good, evil, and plenty of scrutiny of the Henry's Turkey Farm owners' view of disability and common labor practices. The facts surrounding the case that were in clear view of the public, state officials, and advocates is what is most striking. The US

Department of Labor's Wage and Hour Division had begun an investigation in 1979 into how workers with disabilities were being paid, including how productivity was measured, the methods used to gather prevailing wages for similar jobs in the area, and the overall well-being of the men working on the turkey farms. There were other investigations too, some based on second- and third-hand gossip and others that stemmed from professional concerns regarding the "magic of simplicity" approach. It seemed to some that HTF and its owners were more interested in intrastate labor brokering than the training of workers with disabilities. After all, owners Johnson and Henry could make much more by leasing out cheap labor to poultry farms than simply by billing the state of Texas for their brand of rehabilitation—but they were doing both, and making lots of money from several streams of revenue. These private business owners exploiting a cheap labor force were taking direction from the way human-service agencies providing training and employment services operated. It was a shell game, and if there were some references to benevolence or ensuring that people were earning their keep, things were fine. Still, the success of their scheme in trafficking subminimum-wage labor had emboldened Johnson and Henry, and they began brokering even more labor contracts with bigger processing plants. It was a logical extension of Johnson's history with seeking out cheap, vulnerable workers.

Prior to getting workers from the state institutions in Texas, Johnson had made use of an infamous hiring plot called the Bracero program. Basically, this allowed a guest worker from Mexico to work in the United States for eleven months and returning to the United States after thirty days back home. The Bracero program was the result of a series of bilateral agreements between Mexico and the United States that permitted millions of Mexican men to come to the United States to work on primarily agricultural labor contracts. From 1942 to 1964, 4.6 million contracts were issued, with some workers returning several times on different contracts, making this the largest US contract-labor program in history.[2] It was cheap labor, from people with little to no power to dispute pay or working conditions or to organize in any fashion. If you were a troublemaker (e.g., asking questions about safety, pay, or working conditions), after your thirty days back in Mexico, you would not receive permission to return to the United States. The program was controversial, and the activists focused on farmworker justice.

According to Kenneth Henry, his business partner, T. H. Johnson, had wholeheartedly embraced the Bracero program, driving to the border to pick up workers. Now, since the Bracero program was being phased out, Johnson decided that he would need to replace the cheap, easily intimidated workforce. With his connection at the Abilene State School, he began discussions about using men with "mental retardation." Johnson had a bunkhouse in Texas where the Braceros had been housed that could just as easily be used by the workers with disabilities from the Abilene State School. The similarities between the Bracero program and section 14(c)were clear. Johnson's friend at the Abilene State School would have had knowledge of 14(c); by the early 1970s the practice had not only spread into communities throughout the United States, but institutional settings embraced 14(c) as well, particularly since state schools and other analogous institutions were under pressure to do more to provide training and life skills for those who had to live there. It was these factors, some the result of the policy's intended outcomes and others that were unintended, that created a suitable environment for Johnson and Henry to host and ultimately exploit and abuse the men with disabilities.

A labor arrangement was finalized with Henry's Turkey Farm, the Texas officials deeming it legitimate, and the processing plants in Iowa all too eager to participate; an entire system of labor trafficking had been put into place. At the West Liberty plant in Iowa, the men moved from insemination and cleaning up manure to taking spots on the meat processing lines, working alongside laborers doing the same work at the same speed, but the men with disabilities were paid only $65 a month, while the owners of HTF raked in hundreds of thousands of dollars under several contracts to provide labor. This configuration of "placing" disabled workers inside an existing factory, called an enclave, is a tactic that nonprofit agencies like sheltered workshops use. The word is defined as "a portion of territory within or surrounded by a larger territory whose inhabitants are culturally or ethnically distinct, or a place or group that is different in character from those surrounding it." The "enclave" model is embraced by human-service agencies responsible for training people with disabilities. They tout the workers as integrated because they are working near workers without disabilities. They use words like "inclusive" and phrases like "side by side with normal workers," meant to convey to funders that the agencies are engaged in community-based work that matches their flowery mission statements, but these arrangements do exactly what the definition implies. Workers with disabilities in enclaves are seen as different, set apart from the general workplace culture, and in the case of the men with intellectual disabilities doing the backbreaking work, paid much, much less.

The work of killing and processing turkeys for their meat is not pleasant. Loading and unloading crates of cramped birds with defecation from prior transports caked to the wire is repetitive. Lifting heavy bodies onto conveyors, turkeys' wings flapping and terrified guttural croaks as the soundtrack, is vile. An immersion scalder is used to kill bacteria as well as humidity cabinets where the bodies are sprayed with steam. A vacuum gun sucks out the bird's lungs. The lung removal gun is a gas pump handle and hose buoyed to the ceiling, while bird after bird, their body cavities open, continually pass on a rolling belt as if they are manufactured. The lung removal gun is shoved into and out of the opening. The operator repeats the motions three or four times on each bird before the next one is up, about twenty birds per minute. The motion to suck out the lungs reminds one of shoving a vacuum hose between car seats when detailing. All the lungs of thousands of turkeys are sucked up and deposited in large silver bins, and the thought of emptying the bins after a twelve-hour shift is nauseating. Blood, intestines, wet feathers with the associated smells, and the sheer quantity of all these elements makes for work that can seep into your soft tissues, leaving one constantly aware of the smells even when not working. In his seminal book *The Things They Carried*, Tim O'Brien writes about working in a meat processing factory; he uses those smells to remind the reader that the story is about death, for farm animals, of course, but also for the young people sent to Vietnam. The sense of smell can evoke visceral responses. I grew up on a farm, and one doesn't forget the reek of hundreds of confined animals. The men working against their will at the West Liberty plant had no say in their working conditions; they couldn't leave, couldn't decide that the stench and $65 per month was awful and warranted relocating and finding other work. They were expected to climb onto the vans every day at 4:30 a.m. in the dark and ride to the plant to work for long hours, and during winter, returning to the bunkhouse in darkness. The men were dependent on their overseers for shelter, food, and care.

Kenneth Henry recalled in a 2010 deposition that they had been supplying workers for the meat processing plant for over thirty-five years. He
testified that at times the dilapidated bunkhouse just down the road in
Atalissa held over sixty men. With such a long tenure of trafficking labor,
the inevitable happened—men aged, or their physical disabilities were ex-
acerbated by the backbreaking work in the slaughterhouse factory. When
a man was too old or couldn't keep up, he was simply shipped back to
Texas where state officials helped find cheap nursing home placements for
the men. For the most part, though, the owners of HTF kept the same men
for decades. In 2009, when the bunkhouse was raided, most of the men
ranged in ages from forty-two to sixty-three. The oldest man working was
eighty. Still, with age and the grueling work, some men got sick and died.

Alford Busby was a black man with intellectual disabilities who had
lived in Texas institutions and who was selected by both the Texas State
Rehabilitation Commission and Johnson and Henry to join the others in
Iowa. Alford was part of only 4 percent of black people living in Iowa
and the only black man in tiny Atalissa with a population of less than
300. He was a good worker who had been taught to do his best, but he
was also a person who needed positive feedback. Like most, he didn't like
to be teased, but at the West Liberty plant he was routinely badgered.
Mr. Busby often found the work and the treatment unbearable. At other
times he tried to make the best of the situation, to work harder, to try and
ignore the harassment; sometimes the men were allowed to go into town,
to buy a few things, go out to eat. Alford, like so many people habituated
to segregation, isolation, and institutional treatment, developed specific
reactions to the abuse. Erving Goffman first coined a phrase in his study
regarding the reactions of humans living inside "closed systems," meaning
those under institutional care who cannot exercise control over anything
in their daily lives. He called this the "mortification of self," whereby
a person loses any connection to his identify other than that permitted
by his controllers. In response, people will employ techniques to survive,
often craving the attention and approval of those upon whom they are
most dependent. Such reactions can be seen outside of psychiatric institutions, as in sheltered workshops, work activity centers, and in the operations at Henry's Turkey Farm.

Alford Busby had tried hard to make his captors like him, but the teasing and name-calling kept on. Insults about his race and ethnicity and his

label of "mental retardation" were the primary targets. While Alford had threatened to leave before, the supervisors would insist he couldn't make it on his own, that he had it good in the bunkhouse and on the slaughtering floor. To this, Alford would try once again to do his best work. He wanted to please the men who were tormenting him. The supervisors would remind him of life back in Texas in the institution. But when a supervisor made fun of him again, Alford Busby was ready to flee. It was a normal reaction, intellectual disability or not, but there was nowhere for Alford to go, and no one to go to for help. He had to do tasks he did not prefer, and while most of us have parts of our jobs that we do not like, we are not held captive. Alford was vocal and told the supervisors he was sick of working on the dock. He had a physical disability that impacted the right side of his body, likely a mild form of cerebral palsy, and it took him longer to lift, squat, and perform labor that required a lot of balance. The work of loading and unloading anything was difficult for Alford, but the dock in the poultry processing plant, even in the best conditions, was precarious, considering that a crate of live turkeys can weigh over a hundred pounds and a typical semitruck can hold 2,000 birds. Alford might be lifting up to twenty crates an hour from a truck, and the docks saw thousands of birds arrive daily, sometimes up to 21,000 turkeys in a day. Unfortunately for Alford, his complaints were either ignored, or he was egged on by supervisors, who relied on humiliation as motivation.

The tensions continued to build, and Alford Busby had endured about as much teasing and taunting as he could take. One late afternoon in the middle of an Iowa winter, Alford's feelings were hurt again when one of the supervisors began belittling him, and Alford stormed away. This was in January 1987, a year after the subminimum-wage floor had been done away with by USDOL, Congress, and the lobbyists for the nonprofit sheltered-workshop industry, effectively repealing the mandatory "50 percent of minimum-wage" rule. Whether or not these changes emboldened Henry's Turkey staff, Alford Busby and the other workers making subminimum wages were not a priority.

Reports also are contradictory about who reprimanded him, how old he was, how tall, and whether he'd "run away" before. Dan Barry, *New York Times* columnist and author of a book about Henry's Turkey Service, aptly called Alford Busby "the ever-present blur of the bunkhouse," because the details of his life and death remain shrouded in the kind of throwaway culture of becoming lost inside the human-service system. One fact is clear though—he was gone and not dressed for the winter cold, and the temperature was already eight below. The supervisors shrugged and joked some more, believing Alford would get his anger out of his system and return like before. Alford wasn't wearing a coat, or gloves. He had rushed off the docks and down a chute, heading for the frigid Iowa countryside. Dark comes early there in the winter, with grayness turning to black by 4:45 p.m. The cold and nighttime darkness on a farm can be disorienting; barn lights seem to hover and move off kilter; the wind can water your eyes and blot your vision. The awful smells trail away only to resurge as you round the next identical slaughterhouse. When we are upset, our bodies can sweat, our breathing increases, and our blood pressure rises. If we are emotionally upset, after people have been making fun of us, for example, we don't think as clearly either; if we have been devalued and our sense of self has been demolished from being in an institution, we might not be thinking about our own safety.

The railroad tracks in West Liberty, Iowa, have been upgraded over the years; what was once a single track is operational seven days a week and moves cargo to Omaha and Chicago, with access to the Mississippi River and Illinois River terminals. In the wintertime temperatures can fall to well below zero, as cold as minus twenty-eight degrees Fahrenheit. We know that there was a search, and that Alford had tried to leave before. We know that Mr. Busby was from Texas and that he'd tried to find his way back before. We know that if he was to survive, he would have had to have gotten more clothing, a ride, some money, and some kindness. It was winter in Iowa.

Alford didn't make it far—though accounts vary. He likely jogged some and ended up following the tracks and fence lines away from the slaughterhouse. Normal body temperature is 98.6 degrees, but if our core temperature drops to 95 degrees, hypothermia can begin, meaning that the body is losing heat faster than it can produce it. The human body moves from stage one, where shivering induces reduced blood circulation, to more advanced stages. The pulse weakens, with slower breathing, and the mind is also impacted, with significant loss of coordination, irritability, confusion, and sleepiness. The supervisors who gave him a hard time didn't bother to go after him, and Alford froze to death. Found several months later by a farmer in April once spring had arrived,

Mr. Alford Busby died of hypothermia. The death certificate reads, "Mentally retarded man wandered away from home in sub-zero temperatures."[3] The cause of death is listed as an accident. Alford Jerry Busby Jr. died alone, his head echoing with taunts, his hands and feet burning from frostbite, and his breaths painful from the cold. Reduced blood flow leads to shock and liver and kidney failure; ultimately the heart stops.

Alford Busby had been trafficked from Texas with the promise of something better, but he received only mistreatment and unkindness, all for the purpose of finding, keeping, and maintaining a cheap, pliant workforce. Our legal subminimum-wage policies put Alford there, but our refusal to take the multitude of congressional hearings seriously ensured that the consequences would not be acted upon. By the time of his death, no fewer than half a dozen hearings had been formally held and investigative reports at major news outlets had highlighted the concerns. Still, our taxpayer dollars went to sustain the abuse. Texas citizens underwrote the practices at the Vocational Rehabilitation Commission where officials selected the men to hand over to the owners of Henry's Turkey Farm. Since every state vocational rehabilitation agency is funded with a mixture of state and federal dollars, all of us helped fund it. Iowa taxpayers, including the city of Atalissa helped fund the death of Alford Busby. We all did, under legal provisions that purportedly are in place to protect workers with disabilities. It's a lie that spans decades.

One of the other men with disabilities in the bunkhouse reported that Mr. Busby "froze to death . . . made him run off . . . told him he wasn't doing his work right." Another man told social service workers, "We planted a tree. . . . They buried him under there and put a tombstone there in the front yard." The death of Busby also impacted the men in ways that kept them quiet, afraid to complain. "I had to stay. . . . I don't want to die."[4] It was later clear that what the men thought was a burial plot was some sort of service; the entire ordeal must have been terrifying. Fear is control, and the operators of HTS knew how to use it.

It's difficult not to see in the operations of the farm, and the treatment of the men with intellectual disabilities, as a kind of livestock analogy at play.[5] Social role valorization as developed by Wolf Wolfensberger provides a lens of critical analysis regarding the roles assigned to people with disabilities, who are often marginalized, warehoused in buildings and institutions.[6] In this way, the turkey processing plant, and the bunkhouse, can be seen as role influencers. The men are "bedded down" in an old barn-like structure; they are transported together; and they spend their days in toil, treated as less than human. They are fed. They are herded from one place to another; the group takes on one identity, and the individual disappears into the phrase most often used in Atalissa by the citizens, "the boys." They are placed into the roles of devalued workers, paid less, treated differently, and expected to withstand the conditions. If the men were sick, they were expected to work anyway—after surgery for throat cancer, during the active symptoms of the flu, with impacted teeth, and back injuries. Perhaps the livestock analogy related to social roles breaks down here, because most farmers and ranchers wouldn't force their animals to work in this way.

Robert Canino was ready to fight for the men in court after the raid in 2009. For expertise about the human-service systems that were supposed to support and safeguard the men of Henry's Turkey Farm, Canino sought out someone who could help him make sense of it all and who could be presented to a judge and jury as a seasoned expert. He was fortunate to find Sue Gant, PhD, who used her intellect to advocate on behalf of people locked away, segregated, and exploited by the very systems that were supposed to protect them. She had been a subject matter expert in a number of state class action lawsuits. From Georgia to Indiana, and Hawaii to Oregon, she had been instrumental in the closing of state institutions and a voice in ensuring that proper supports were in place for those leaving the walls and razor wire behind, including by focusing on opportunities for employment. Dr. Gant possessed all these skills, but her connection to the land and people made her a perfect fit for the work that lay ahead. Her family had lived and farmed the land in Iowa for generations. Their cattle were raised with care and attention to the details of expert husbandry. To this day, a yearly bull auction under the family name still occurs, almost a hundred years later. She had gone to college and graduate school to study special education, behavioral supports, and developmental psychology. As a young PhD she was recruited to serve in a consultancy role on the reformation of the infamous Willowbrook Institution in New York. She described her first view of the institution on Staten Island. "We flew in on a helicopter in the springtime, and they were doing some annual cleaning. From a distance, up in the air, I could see what looked like one of those big carousels that ponies trod around at fairs, only there were naked people tethered to it, and as they lumbered in a circle, attendants used hoses to spray the people down."

Willowbrook's abuses as a cauldron of hellish conditions are legendary. There are photos of children without clothes, cinder block walls covered in feces, rancid food being fed to people strapped into wheelchairs, unable to keep from ingesting it. Willowbrook was touted as a place where parents could trust that their children with disabilities would be cared for, but even now, some fifty years later, many of those same parents are finally finding out what happened to their loved ones, all under the cloak of the state's benevolent system.[7] The history of subminimum wages has always been tied to residential settings. From the beginning in 1938, housing and employment inside the disability industrial complex have been entangled with day rooms, like the ones in Willowbrook and other institutions, often purportedly serving the "vocational" needs of patients. Dr. Gant's introduction to the magnitude of abuses at Willowbrook formed her intellect and observational skills into a finely tuned set of tools she would use to help liberate thousands of people from so-called treatment, whether inside the walls of an institution or when those same practices were given new names, like "community care," which once again promised to be better for people with disabilities.

Gant can tell a story with the proper attention to details, and each one can break your heart. She's a tough human being, but even her voice quivers when she tells some of them. For decades she's done her work with care and an unflinching ability to stay the course. What she has seen and written about in reports, recommendations, and memorandas, reliving the stories over and over, would break most people; when asked how she does it, she's sincerely not sure. "I guess I pull on my mother's example. She was always friends with people others wouldn't speak to. She believed in dignity. I think I learned a lot from her."

Robert Canino knew he had to have Dr. Gant sign on to the Henry's Turkey Service case. A persistent litigator, he was convincing, telling Gant there was no one else on the planet as qualified as she to serve as an expert on the case. It would mean picking up where Canino had left off with interviewing the men at Henry's Turkey Farm. Thousands of words would need to be written, and her testimony would require the memorization of each man's story. That wouldn't be a problem for Dr. Gant, who's accustomed to processing and retaining massive amounts of details, most of which she can rattle off from years ago—full names, dates, and snippets of conversation.

I had the opportunity to meet Dr. Gant in New Mexico where she served as the court-appointed monitor for the state's complicated and intense class action lawsuit. It was an experience that Gant would leverage in the case in Iowa. I had been contracted by the University of New Mexico in 2012 to serve as an employment consultant on the state's long-running lawsuit known as the Jackson class action, filed in 1987 and named for lead plaintiff Walter Stephen Jackson. Mr. Jackson was labeled as "profoundly retarded" in court documents, a distraction from what New Mexico's state-run institutions allowed to happen, as if such a label somehow reduced the blame. It's a sickening trait of the disability industrial complex and its many systems: labels are used to deflect responsibility, secure additional funding, and essentially continue the narrative that deficit-based interventions are required, which don't resemble what most of us think of as work, housing, and relationships. It's a way to communicate to the public that they should just go on with their busy lives and let the professionals handle the "difficult behaviors of a special population," a phrase I recently heard during a state's legislative session, spoken by the CEO of a community rehabilitation provider organization. The debate concerned overhauling funding formulas, from a lump-sum payment method to an outcome-based system where milestones must be reached on behalf of the person being served. CEOs and CFOs of the nonprofit agencies receiving funding from vocational rehabilitation services and Medicaid HCBS funding loathe the idea of switching to an outcome-based configuration and will often resort to such outdated and disrespectful arguments. Labels like "profoundly retarded," as Walter Jackson was referred to in court documents, serve to create distance between who is and who is not considered an adult with inalienable rights; they function as a sidetracking tool that the disability industrial complex uses regularly.

Sometime in 1986 Walter was left unattended and ingested oven cleaner that had been left out and not secured. In addition, Walter was found to have broken bones, severe burns, and other injuries that had no feasible explanation. In short, Walter Stephen Jackson, through no fault of his own, was tormented, abused, and neglected under government care for twenty-two years at the Los Lunas Hospital and Training School, funded by taxpayers who believed the state of New Mexico was performing its legal fiduciary duties on behalf of citizens with and without disabilities. Unfortunately, Mr. Jackson was not alone, not in the country or in New Mexico. Another resident at Los Lunas was sexually assaulted and died two days later; others had unexplained abrasions, bruises, and injuries including knocked-out teeth, clumps of hair yanked out, and puncture wounds. In its 2010 review of the Jackson class action lawsuit, the *Santa Fe Reporter* revisited the history of the beginnings of the recorded abuse. "In May 1989, court observers saw the residents running around the room, screaming, and hitting each other. Thirty-nine residents were punished or restrained with ammonia, water mist, straitjackets and the papoose board, a flat board with arm and leg restraints. Others were seat-belted to toilets because only one staff member was available to assist six residents. One person had nine separate infirmary visits for human bites." Of course, there were "vocational programs" much like the sheltered workshops operating in the community, where residents of Los Lunas were ostensibly receiving some type of training, which usually meant they were cleaning up bodily fluid messes, working in groups at tables stuffing mailers, or doing work on the grounds. They didn't qualify for the 3(m) credits through USDOL as a way of paying for their room and board, but nonetheless that's how it was treated. These men and women, who had committed no crime, were paying for their lockup and its awful conditions. Burton Blatt died in 1985, and the Jackson lawsuit in New Mexico started in the late 1980s; one can only imagine his incredulity, believing the expose in *Christmas in Purgatory* would have made it impossible for any more of this state-run barbarism.

The Jackson lawsuit was one of the lengthiest attempts in the country to eradicate the neglect and abuse that citizens with disabilities had endured in New Mexico's institutional systems. In 1990 a judge found the state of New Mexico had violated the constitutional rights of thousands of people with intellectual and developmental disabilities—the same year that the landmark Americans with Disabilities Act was signed into law. New Mexico though, through its attorneys (and some elected politicians) wanted the Jackson lawsuit shut down or significantly altered for speedier resolution. Judge James Aubrey Parker, appointed by President Reagan to the US District Court for New Mexico, presided over the case from 1990 through several decades, trying to direct the litigation and an eventual settlement. In 1990 he ordered the state to improve institutional settings and move people with expediency into community-based alternatives; however, the path forward was fraught with competing interests. In states where the rural workforce often finds employment inside institutional settings, their closing means the loss of jobs, which can translate into a loss of votes. Judge Parker denied a motion to dismiss the case in 2000 and again in 2002, when lawyers for the state argued that Los Lunas and other institutions within New Mexico had been shuttered. Judge Parker agreed with the plaintiff's legal representation that there was much more to do in terms of ensuring community-based services, including vocational supports and primary-care access for the class members. In 2007 Judge Parker ruled that the state must reimburse the Jackson plaintiffs for 2006 attorney and court fees, which he said were "reasonable." It went on like this, and Dr. Gant fought hard for the rights of the Jackson class members. A formidable advocate, Dr. Gant researched best-practice models of providing community support, including employment; she visited people who had left the institutions in the community to see for herself that people were getting what they needed. It worked and, in the spring of 2019, the lawsuit in New Mexico was settled. Gant's signature advocacy and belief in the ability of people with intellectual and developmental disabilities to live, work, and participate in their communities was peppered throughout the agreement. There were ten broad areas of the improvement, such as unannounced visits to homes, quality primary care services, penalties for agencies that didn't provide excellent, evidence-based care. The state of New Mexico agreed to provide the Jackson plaintiffs with access to supported employment, so that the people with disabilities who had been held captive in the institution could forgo entering a sheltered workshop where they would earn subminimum wages.

The *Pickle* case for Robert Canino and the Jackson lawsuit for Sue Gant had prepared the two experts in their respective fields for perhaps the most important case in their lives. Both had gained insight into the mindset of those in power inside the disability industrial complex. Canino and Gant teamed up on the Henry's Turkey Farm litigation to deliver the largest settlement in EEOC history, but first they had to do more homework, starting with a journalist's story from back in 1979. In that *Des Moines Register* article on December 23, 1979, Margaret Engel and Mike McGraw, staff reporters, told the story of a businessman under investigation. The headline read, "Retarded Texas Labor in Iowa Turkey Plant."

It was subtitled, "They take home $65.71 a month." Stories matter, and it was providential for Canino and Gant, as well as the gentlemen from Henry's Turkey Service, that the record of abuse dated back thirty years.

As Gant began her investigation into the massive, heartbreaking failures at Henry's Turkey Farm, she had to face not only Alford's death but the deaths of others too. The men with disabilities told Dr. Gant about a coworker who had died during lung surgery. Another man died of a heart attack in his bed. There was testimony about another worker with terminal cancer who had been sent to a mental-health ward, where he succumbed to the illness. The bodies of some of these men were shoved into a van and driven back to Texas for burial in pauper graves, with Iowa funeral home officials providing the necessary paperwork to transport dead bodies across state lines.

Dru Neubauer, who was on the payroll as a supervisor and who took the men back and forth from the bunkhouse to the slaughterhouse, is quoted on February 7, 2009. "I've had some of them die in my arms. We had to take the bodies down to Texas, take them back to where they came from. We pulled the seats out of the van and loaded them up, you know, in the coffin, and drove their bodies back down to Texas." These were the same vans Neubauer used to haul the men to work at the turkey farm. As the men aged and contracted illnesses and aging conditions, some of them were also hauled in this way back to Texas, still alive but unable to work as they had. Texas officials once again helped Johnson and Henry "manage" their workforce and liability by placing the men in nursing facilities. The men didn't have a say about where or with whom they roomed with in these places, and to be clear, these facilities, while better than the bunkhouse, were still low-end nursing homes, where they became patients once again. Underfunded and understaffed, the nursing homes were little more than a stop before the end.

The men had been performing alongside others doing the same work and being paid gross wages of nearly $2,000 a month versus the $65 each worker with a disability was paid monthly. For the remaining thirty-two men, it would be a sister who ultimately saved the men from the chains of servitude and abuse. Thirty years after the *Des Moines Register* reports in December 1979, she called the EEOC in 2009 on behalf of her brother. By then, Johnson, the man who had first started working with Texas officials to take men from institutions and use them in turkey processing plants across the country, would be dead. Kenneth Henry, Randy and Dru Neubauer, and Danny Miles were the primary informants for the defense of their deeds. The surviving thirty-two men, Gant, and Canino would take up the work of attempting to expose the abuses at Henry's Turkey Service. As Gant interviewed the men, sometimes face to face and sometimes on Skype, her focus was on their well-being. "Some of the gentlemen needed lots of support to relive the horrors, and if they required it, I'd hold their hand. Others were eager to talk, and of course, a great deal of those conversations were also therapeutic."

In her final report to the court, she stated, "Defendants and their agents freely created a work and living environment of terror for the workers with disabilities. Incidents of assault and mistreatment were so pervasive at work and at the bunkhouse they did not know when the next act of abuse would occur."

Even their tormenters testified that the men were credible and able to distinguish fact from fiction. The men rose at 3:30 a.m. each morning to dress, quickly eat, climb onto the vans by 4:30 a.m., and arrive at the turkey slaughterhouse hours before sunrise. The entire enterprise reeked of killing and dismemberment, with terms like the "kill wall," "scorch vats," "blood troughs," and of course the "lung removal gun." The work environment served to reinforce brutality, and the effect was an overall atmosphere of death. Dr. Gant reported to the court on the atrocities:

> The abuse and negligence by the defendants allegedly occurred at the work site (plant) and the company bunkhouse. HCF/HTS and its agents engaged in disciplinary actions that violated the workers' right to be free from abuse as a consequence for what the supervisor claimed was unsatisfactory job performance. Consequences included physical, verbal and psychological abuse, harassment, denying workers access to their personal possessions, restricting freedom of movement and demanding labor without pay to benefit the employer. Conversely, there is no evidence of actions the employer took to improve job performance. According to testimony of the aggrieved men, and consistent with DHS reports and interviews, crew chiefs Randy Neubauer and Danny Miles, who supervised the workers at the plant and at the bunkhouse, engaged in a variety of abusive behaviors that included: hitting and kicking, yelling, name calling, withholding pay/wages, and ordering the handcuffing of at least one worker to a bed. Dru Neubauer, also a crew supervisor, but mostly a supervisor at the bunkhouse and Iowa manager of the

men's wages, actively engaged in abusive behaviors and neglected her responsibilities to oversee the worker's health.

Dr. Gant holds back no punches. Reading the report is to partially absorb the tragedies the men endured over the decades. To bolster the senselessness of their treatment, Dr. Gant invokes a similar argument I've tried to establish from the beginning of this book. That is, since the passage in 1938 of 14(c), there have always been better, more humane and science-based supports and interventions that could have been used for the benefit of the men at the slaughterhouse, and for all others as well. It's an erroneous conclusion to simply shrug our shoulders and say, Yes, this is not great, but what's to be done? The question being: If we know what works, if we know which interventions respect the dignity and honor the presence of everyone's talents, why then would we settle for anything less?

Punishment was high on the list for the owners and supervisors of Henry's Turkey Service. Once social workers and case managers from Iowa's human-service agencies descended on the bunkhouse in 2009, the stories started to be told almost immediately. One worker with a disability named Tommy told the officials that he sometimes only got $30 of his $65 a month. Tommy told stories about coworkers being denied breaks, and how the Neubauers favored withholding personal items like TVs and other electronics, cell phones, and VCRs and services to reprimand and control the men. Medical and dental care was also used as punishment. At deposition the HTS staff did not deny these forms of retribution, applied if a worker complained, didn't follow orders, or simply talked back. Keeping trafficked laborers quiet and afraid to talk is a common technique, as in Canino's Pickle case and the brutish approaches documented by Burton Blatt in the institutions he covertly visited.

One of the men told Gant a descriptive and corroborated story about Randy Neubauer's temper and management style. The incident occurred in the packing room at the plant, where the turkeys were prepared for shipment out to grocery stores. The worker with a disability was shoved by Randy up against the kill wall, where he proceeded to yell at the man and kick him in the shins. The same worker reported another supervisor, Danny Miles, had hit him in the left eye.

In fact, the HTS staff and supervisors were often the focus of the West Liberty Foods plant manager, Tom Alberti, who had taken the time to write a letter to Kenneth Henry relating his concerns over Randy Neubauer's abusive treatment of the men with disabilities. Alberti even asked that Neubauer not come to the plant. Still, Randy was reported to have used kicking the men as a primary tool for punishment. He kicked them in their crotches, in the shins, at the back of their legs. One worker reported to Sue Gant, "I learned to stay out of his way. Someone didn't do (the) job right, somebody paid for it. He'd yell and scream and cuss." There were reports from the men that they had seen other workers with disabilities with bloody mouths. One worker reported he was often kicked from behind, resulting in injuries to his testicles. When this worker was transported back to Texas because he could no longer work, it was reported that his testicles were "enormous" from swelling.[8]

The men were saved when the bunkhouse was raided in February 2009. The place was a death trap, with space heaters and tangled wires, cardboard boxes, and clothing spread out like a dump. There was asbestos in the ceilings. No light came in at the boarded-up windows. Rodents were a problem. The adjacent Quonset hut was packed with junk. It was never a secret about what was happening there and at the slaughterhouse, but somehow, with the light of national media on the place, town, and practices, it seemed like the horrors had been hidden in plain sight. Out front of the strange-colored bunkhouse, with its electric-teal paint and black, covered windows, there was a granite stone, a memorial for Alford Busby. Some of the men again reported that Busby had been buried there (perhaps they were told that), but he lies next to his mother in a Texas cemetery.

In the end, the human-service systems acted in 2009, not at glacial speed as they had from 1979 forward, but quickly, with coordinated care, and with direct action aimed at first helping the men find safe places to sleep and live. An order from the fire marshal carried the most weight; the bunkhouse was uninhabitable—and just like that, after decades of abuse and neglect, the best care and attention was provided. What came out, the deaths, the physical and verbal abuse, and the town's reaction, would shock most people but not those who had warned about the abuses in 1979. For them, it was an awful and sad example of what happens when people are devalued, segregated, and when an entire small town believes that "the boys" are being cared for by their overseers. Even now, there are those who don't believe the stories, the book, the documentary, and the sworn statements, admitting to the mistreatment, given by insiders at Henry's Turkey Service. What was noticeably absent from the media coverage was the issue of how little the men were paid. At most, it was a tertiary reference, but it was and is the central point of public policy. There are other issues—such as governmental oversight, and the myths and stigmas we as Americans hold of people labeled with intellectual and developmental disabilities—but the existence of the special rules under USDOL to allow special pay for these workers creates a rationale for regular community members to believe everything must be on the up and up.

Some of the men found places to live in Iowa, others found their families because of the media coverage. Several, like Willie Levi, also found jobs where they were paid fairly, more than minimum wage. So, what had changed? Did Willie suddenly develop skills he'd never had before? Did he lose his disability? Maybe he and others had somehow been miraculously cured. Of course not. Instead, they and their supporters found jobs and employers who saw their strengths and didn't highlight their weaknesses, like all of us do. Those employers bypassed the special 14(c) waiver and did the right thing. But we cannot rely on that to be the case; public policy is a guard against harmful practices, but it's useless when it embodies and emboldens the very unequal treatment under the law for which it was originally designed. Public policy must be updated continually in a capitalistic economy.

Four years after the bunkhouse was raided and HTS staff had given depositions, the case went to trial. Gant described the scene: "I was asked to expound on the final report I'd written and about the stories the men had told me. It was a brand-new courtroom with high-tech capabilities. We had a photo of each man projected from an LCD in the ceiling which made their photos enormous on the wall. They were getting their say, finally getting to tell, if not all their stories, at least the most salient parts. They weren't "boys" or "mentally retarded" or any of the other labels they'd been given. We used their names and gave them the respect their hard work deserved. We honored what they'd endured for so long."

The news regarding the litigation and the ultimate decision was powerful. The tales of the men traveled quickly, and emails circulated among people all over the country interested in justice for the men, but also in the larger picture regarding the future of disability wage policies. Curt Decker at the National Disability Rights Network believed the report that

NDRN had issued about HTS had helped usher along much-needed scrutiny. NDRN had been instrumental in 2011 and 2012 with a paper titled, "Segregated and Exploited: Call for Action," regarding the men in Iowa but Decker took the fight further. He wanted to get the attention of ordinary citizens, not just the professionals in the disability industrial complex. Some had claimed Decker wanted to put sheltered workshops out of business, but he insisted, "We are asking that they change their business model to focus on real jobs with real pay." It was working, with stories across the country in print and on television, focusing on Ohio, Rhode Island, Oregon, and Minnesota, and pieces airing on NPR and CBS. An article in the *Columbus Dispatch*, titled "Workshops Still Get Most Federal Funds for Disabled," examined the practice in Ohio as it was laid out in Decker's NDRN report. The sheltered workshops in Ohio received thirty-five times the amount of funding ($175 million) that the supported-employment programs did to help workers with disabilities find real jobs for minimum wage. "Seventy percent (70%) of the 21,000 Ohioans with disabilities who were employed and receiving services from county boards worked in sheltered workshops. About eighty (80%) percent were making less than $3.70 an hour."[9] Maybe, just maybe, there was a crack starting to widen in the walls of the disability industrial complex. With the story out in the open, exposing some of the best-hidden secrets of the practices that brought the Iowa men to their plight, there would be increased will on behalf of legislators and policy gurus to take a serious look at what had transpired and to change the public policies that allowed it.

The headlines related to the men with disabilities toiling away in Iowa were powerful. Robert Canino and Sue Gant had teamed up to deliver a result that was stunning:

On May 1, 2013, a jury in U.S. District Court for the Southern District of Iowa in Davenport rendered a verdict of $240 million in favor of the 32 workers. The jury found that for years the men went unpaid and were subjected to substandard living conditions, restrictions on personal freedoms, denial of medical care and harsh discipline as well as verbal and physical harassment.

This largest jury verdict ever obtained by EEOC was later reduced to $1.6 million, representing $50,000 in compensatory and punitive damages per man based on applicable statutory caps under the Civil Rights Act of 1991. An earlier award for unpaid market wages for a two-year period, together with the damages for the treatment, brought EEOC's total judgment to $3.74 million. Notwithstanding the elusiveness of the company's assets in the years surrounding the litigation, collection of the judgment through garnishments and liens had recently reached an accumulated amount of about $272,000 prior to this latest court order. The confidential agreement to change the beneficiaries of the Texas land deal to re-direct proceeds away from possible payment for discrimination was dated July 2013, only one month after the June 2013 final entry of judgment in favor of EEOC in the discrimination case.[10]

The city of Atalissa, Iowa, wanted to be known for more than the awful stories that had been exposed in the bunkhouse the town had rented to the owners of Henry's Turkey Service. Some residents felt they'd been portrayed as not caring about the men, while others had harbored some negative feelings about how the men were treated but had kept the thoughts to themselves. Sue Gant told me, "It's a sort of Midwestern notion. You work, and you don't often speak up. And you must understand that the church and the convenience store the men visited regularly, people in both places, tried to help even if they were not aware of their own biases."

The town had certainly been involved. In July of 2014, the bunkhouse was swept off the landscape, leaving smoothed-over dirt with tire tracks. Still, there were people who had not accepted the stories of abuse. Ryan Pace lived near the bunkhouse. "It's one of those things they say it happened, and I don't believe it," he told the *Quad City Times*. Carol O'Neill, also a resident of Atalissa, her home not far from what had been the site of the bunkhouse, said, "I'm sorry. I know they're men, but they were considered our boys."[11]

The rumors and heresy still exist in the town. Kevin O'Brien has a unique view of what happened in Atalissa. He was an employee of the Wage and Hour Division (WHD) of the US Department of Labor and had examined the practices of subminimum wages at HTS. His early investigations were included in court documents. A resident of Davenport, and a Catholic at the Holy Family Parish in the same town, O'Brien had spent decades at USDOL and worked inside the WHD, the same part of USDOL that has been tasked with oversight of section 14(c) for more than sixty years. Mr. O'Brien's faith played an integral role in his profession. "I've always been interested in fairness. I think this was one of the most significant cases of abuse I've been associated with," O'Brien told the *Catholic Messenger*, the newspaper of the diocese of Davenport, Iowa. He continued, "What each agency (involved in the case) needs to do—and maybe all of them together, and maybe Congress—is to ask: How did this happen?" O'Brien went on: "Someone taught me early on when I was a rookie: Follow the money—that's where the problems are." Of course, Congress had already held many hearings regarding the issue. In the congressional hearings as early as 1966, officials testified that WHD (the division O'Brien worked in) had extremely limited capability to oversee and ensure the correct and legal application of the special waiver allowing for subminimum wages.

The leveling of the Atalissa bunkhouse can be seen as a deeper sign of our own psychological views on human-service systems and the disability industrial complex at large. Our American reaction to abuse and neglect in relation to vulnerable citizens is often laced with the faux history of "pulling yourself up by the bootstraps." The foundations of independence, individualism, and the ideals of exceptional Americanism wind their tentacles into our reaction to something like the preventable tragedy in Iowa. Our collective values tell us that if we simply bulldoze the foundation of the bunkhouse, we have remedied the situation; we can build another structure, both physically and psychologically, and right the course of poor public policy. It is something that happens again and again in the disability industrial complex: old ideas that have no basis in proven interventions are recycled as new ideas, and somehow we believe if we just provide new buildings, with greater oversight, all will be made well. While that approach may feel good to our collective conscience, the disability industrial complex is an unresponsive conglomerate. O'Brien asked in the *Catholic Messenger*: "How did we not take action to eliminate this in 1979?" As Americans, we still carry those templates of deficit that were used to rationalize eugenics in the United States and then export it to Nazi Germany.

In the fall of 2012, I met Dr. Gant in person for the first time. I was in New Mexico working on the Jackson lawsuit for which Dr. Gant was the court-appointed expert. My role was to offer up expert advice and support so that class members could leave segregation and subminimum wages and find real work for real pay in their respective communities. By then, the stories of the men living in Atalissa and working at HTS had been exposed. I rode along with an official from New Mexico to a restaurant in Santa Fe. I was nervous to meet Dr. Gant because of her larger-than-life advocacy work. I'd heard Dr. Gant speak before, read lots of her reports, and admired her dedication and sharp mind, both put to serious use in advocating for systems change. We joined Dr. Gant and another colleague in a small booth, snacking on chips and salsa. The Southwest had been difficult for me to connect with; the mountains and desert unsettled me, since I was used to the flat farmlands of Indiana and the Georgia pine forests. All that open space with very few gas stations vexed me, and I told Dr. Gant about it. She smiled and asked me, "How's the work going in Gallup?" The Jackson class members lived all over the state, and I had been assigned to work with plaintiffs who lived in Gallup, who also worked in sheltered workshops. Dr. Gant really wanted to know how the work was progressing. She could read field reports, access data, and do her own investigating, but she wanted to hear from someone who had just been there.

One of the men for whom I was assigned to help find work outside the sheltered workshop was named Leo; he spoke using a mixture of Navajo, Spanish, and English, all mixed together into a musical pattern of speech that at times was difficult to follow. I told Dr. Gant about Leo, and I was smiling while telling the story because I'd connected deeply with him. I was eager to see him each month when I flew from Atlanta to Albuquerque and drove two hours west toward the Continental Divide. I was charged with organizing a team to assist Leo to find work. He was nearly seventy when I met him, and I told Gant how the staff at the sheltered workshop had labeled Leo as unproductive, off-task, and easily distracted. The staff at sheltered workshops evaluate workers with disabilities to determine the correct subminimum wages they should be paid, and it's a gamed approach, one that relies on very little science and even more guessing. Leo's chart stated that he should be paid seventy-eight cents an hour for work recycling cardboard. Dr. Gant shook her head; even after all she had seen and reported on, she was concerned about Leo. Still nervous, I told her Leo seldom showed interest in using the compactor to pack and bind stacks of cardboard but instead preferred music.

Our food was brought to the table, and we began eating. I kept talking too much. Dr. Gant placed her fork down beside her plate and held up a finger. "Leo spent decades in an awful institution," she reminded me. I nodded. "I know you're not working with the strongest of teams," she said, looking me in the eye, "but you're his last hope at having a life, remember that." She went back to eating, and I realized I needed to try harder for Leo. At the end of the meal, as we were preparing to go our separate ways, Dr. Gant gave me some parting words. "Leo is getting what the men in Iowa didn't get." She smiled, but I didn't understand. She said, "Leo's got you." I was stunned and humbled.

Leo began his first job outside the walls of a sheltered workshop in the fall of 2013. He was paid $8 an hour, about ten times more than what he had been paid on subminimum wages. We'd used a process called "Discovering Personal Genius" with Leo, a technique created and perfected by Cary Griffin and another strong advocate named Dave Hammis. Their work was built upon Blatt's angst and Gold's instructional values. "Discovering Personal Genius" (DPG) relies heavily on spending time with a person to learn about her strengths, interests, motivations, and—my favorite—her endearing traits. Instead of using tests, assessments, and rehabilitation remediation, DPG utilizes environments where the person is at his best, doing the kinds of tasks he likes and using a team to help figure out how best to support him in working a real job. DPG leads to Customized Employment, the approach demonstrated by the Office of Disability Employment Policy in its grants in the early 2000s.

As I spent time with Leo, it became clear that he loved music, especially stringed instruments. He stowed guitars under his bed, most of them handmade from cardboard. He had been labeled unproductive at recycling cardboard at the sheltered workshop, but he was a genius at using the same material to fashion guitars that actually played. One afternoon, while making toast with him in his kitchen, two women who worked in the group home told me how much Leo liked being called "abuelo" by their children. On his trips to the Dollar Store on Sundays, he made sure to buy Tootsie Rolls for the kids. With Leo's unique use of language, I needed to rely on getting to know him through other people as well, also a part of the DPG technique, so I interviewed as many people as I could find, those who had worked at the group home in the past, staff from the Los Lunas institution, case workers, coworkers he liked at the sheltered workshop. As with many people trapped inside the disability industrial complex, most if not all the people who knew Leo were paid to be with him. I heard about his love of being called a grandfather, his habit of making sure to offer guests whatever candy he kept in his jacket pocket, his unique way of talking that never failed to capture the imaginations of kids. An entry in his file identified a goal for him to "talk correctly" and to use English. His file also had other entries, all of them used to bill Medicaid and vocational rehabilitation for services. Still, at seventy years old he had not been deemed productive enough to work in a job in the community. Ever since he had left the institution some agency or another was making money off him by claiming to be working on whatever problems could be diagnosed. Just like the men in Iowa and in the work activity centers and sheltered workshops around the country, Leo was a commodity, a living, annual budget that could be tapped for billing. The nonprofits should be remunerated for their efforts, but those efforts should be focusing on the worker's strengths, talents, and skills. Funding should be driven by evidence-based practices that actually produce an employment outcome. Why had someone in the system that supported Leo not thought to use his best attributes and interests to make a job match in his community of Gallup, New Mexico? Just because a human being, regardless of disability label, is bad at one thing, or isn't interested in it, doesn't mean that they won't be good at other tasks they prefer. Why would those trained in human services assume that Leo would be unproductive in any job simply because they had observed him in a segregated setting? It's a recurring theme in this debate: if you don't believe someone can learn, and you are paid to focus on their deficits, then the system will perpetuate more problems to be fixed, making the cycle of rehabilitation an endless one that doesn't serve the person needing help. Arguing that we need subminimum wages for workers with disabilities and special places to work can be seen as the ultimate confirmation that those false assumptions are correct. Nothing supports low expectations better than investing in a system that promotes those same low expectations. Community rehabilitation providers need workers with disabilities who always need more training, more "fixing," because otherwise the business model doesn't work.

One of the approaches that DPG relies on is facilitating a team that can be enlisted to help a specific job-seeker find work that suits them best. Starting with music and guitars, the team searched the community and surrounding areas for others with the same interest. We stumbled upon a man named Robert Brochey in Blue Water, New Mexico, about thirty miles away. Leo and I met with Mr. Brochey to ask him for advice about ways that Leo could use his talents in his community of Gallup.

Mr. Brochey's business is named after the town he lives in. Blue Water
Guitars is an artisan enterprise run by a man who is talented beyond measure; Brochey has been playing guitar for over forty years and has worked
on acoustic instruments of all kinds during that period. He started re-
building older acoustic guitars first, learning how to repair and refinish
them, and has since been building different styles of instruments from
scratch, including archtop guitars and oud body–style guitars, a short-
necked lute-type, pear-shaped stringed instrument. Brochey specializes in
romantic period instruments and built a replica of an 1816 Jose Martinez
salon guitar. When Brochey saw pictures of Leo's handmade instruments,
he smiled. We met at Angela's café in the train station in Gallup. He didn't
ask about Leo's diagnosis or his productivity level, and he didn't suggest that Leo continue attending a sheltered workshop and day program.
He saw another person like himself—a guitar aficionado who liked building guitars. While Brochey used maple and purple-heart wood, Leo had
to rely on found items for his creations. They were kindred spirits, and
Mr. Brochey told me he could help. He wasn't a vocational rehabilitation
counselor or a remedial skills technician, but he would help create a job
for Leo. He put me in touch with the executive director of the Gallup Cultural Center, which was funded in part by a nonprofit called the Southwest
Indian Foundation, which serves the peoples of the Navajo, Hopi, and
Zuni nations.

Along the way there were a few human-service professionals who had
to be convinced that Leo could and should work. On one of my trips from
Gallup back to Albuquerque, I met with Leo's legally appointed guardian,
who was his advocate and who represented him to the judge since Leo was
part of the Jackson lawsuit. She didn't seem excited about the prospect of
Leo's getting his first real job, but she gave her blessing for me to continue.
On the next trip, a smart woman named Lupe, who was also working on
the New Mexico lawsuit, and I met with Colin McCarthy, the executive
director of the cultural center. We showed him pictures of Leo working on
his guitars and playing instruments. One of the goals of the cultural center
was to increase its relationships with the local elementary schools. Over
the course of several weeks, we continued to support Leo and promoted
his talents to McCarthy. We gave him Leo's visual resume (a customized-
employment tool that shows someone at their best, either using photos or
video). We learned that the cultural center had been thinking about ways

to support more field trips from the elementary schools to the cultural center. In the end, we created a pitch that McCarthy could take to the board of directors. Leo would host music exploration events on field trips to the cultural center for kids from third to sixth grade, and he would help them tour the Storytellers Museum upstairs. We assisted Leo in creating a presentation focused on his heritage, his time living at the institution, and his love for music, guitars, and life. He could play the presentation from a laptop and project it on a screen through an LCD. With funds from vocational rehabilitation, Leo purchased a kiosk from which he sold novelty musical instruments that the children could purchase. He wanted a sign on the kiosk that read: "Abuelo's Music!" The schoolkids loved Leo, and he relished his newfound role. The Southwest Indian Foundation approved funding to pay Leo above minimum wage. They created and advertised the new service that Leo oversaw at the Gallup Cultural Center, taking out a full-page ad in the newspaper to promote it. A vice principal helped to make sure that the teachers were aware of Leo's program and was delighted that the social-studies teachers could request a bus and driver to go on the field trips. The program was a success. Leo's talents were being put to great use in his own community. He had a socially valued role as an educator and as an entrepreneur, and he was helping to solve the needs of the cultural center.

Sadly though, Leo only worked outside the walls of the sheltered workshop for a year or so. He passed away and was buried in a cemetery in Gallup, where the pale desert sand is mounded to cover the body since the ground is so hard to dig. For just a little while, Leo was an abuelo to some kids who were fortunate to learn from him. Imagine what he would have been able to accomplish if the agencies with funding to help him for the last forty years had done better. How many children could he have taught? What would his impact on them have created in their own adult lives? Leo's community needed his talents not just for one year, but for decades. It's a story that has, and is, playing out all over the country. Policies like subminimum wages destroy a citizen's potential contributions. Segregating and separating people with intellectual and developmental disabilities from the broader community is bad public policy. The entire disability industrial complex has been conceived and operated within the strictures of prejudice and a paternalistic overlay that mimics the institutions of the nineteenth and twentieth centuries.

While it has become a tendency in the early years of the American twenty-first century to lobby for a specific voting bloc's public-policy desires (parents not wanting to vaccinate their children, earmarked tax dollars that can't be used for reproductive health, or bakers so offended by someone's love that they have special bills passed to exact their personal biases), things are not supposed to work that way. Public policy is an instrument that pervades our lives, from the mundane—like which days your recycling is picked up—to more significant issues—like labor conditions, access to healthcare, and disease prevention. The most important element in creating public policy is to value the common good enough that partisan balking cannot politicize its evolution. Section 14(c) of the Fair Labor Standards Act has not evolved because it benefits the prevailing forces inside the disability industrial complex to maintain it as is.

The powerful tools used to assist Leo were first developed by Marc Gold and carried on by Michael Callahan, Cary Griffin, and Dave Hammis. Those tools were codified by the USDOL at the Office of Disability Employment Policy, put into legislation, and defined in the Federal Register. The men in Iowa were never offered these services, nor were they afforded the opportunity to make minimum wages because it was more profitable to keep them defined as "disabled" and "retarded." Almost since its inception, there have been alternatives to 14(c) subminimum wages.

How did what seemed like a viable pilot project in Iowa and Texas (for the time back in the late 1960s) turn into such a corrupt and harmful scenario? Why did Johnson and Henry's labor trafficking not end until 2009, especially since the *Des Moines Register* reporters had not shied away from delving into the controversy in 1979?

To answer that question, I asked several people who have led the charge to end subminimum wages and support more employment for fair wages in real jobs. Nancy Brooks-Lane, who closed sheltered workshops near Atlanta, feels there's an insidious notion that keeps the current system in place.

When I first began in this field, there were people starting their careers with the utmost concern for how people were being treated, in the institutions, the sheltered workshops and day activity centers. They wanted to change the system, challenge the status quo, but as more and more layers of bureaucracy were created, their voices were muffled. Back then, it was common to hear all the time that disability rights are civil rights. So, the very best people who had started in this field began to drift away, taking jobs where they could effect change, in voting rights, in other social justice areas where they were needed. It left us with skeletal staffing and people who were just looking for a job. Talented, creative and dedicated people can change anything, and that scares the entirety of the Disability Industrial Complex. It took 30 years to put an end to the Iowa abuses for two reasons, one, we didn't have the best people working in the field and two, that leaves room for all kinds of motivations to take over, like money over dignity. The men in Iowa could've had good jobs and been healthy and contributing citizens but they didn't have access to the best people who were interested in their personal, civil rights.

Cary Griffin, who developed "Discovering Personal Genius" as an approach to get people jobs like Leo's in New Mexico, told me he thinks Henry's Turkey Service got away with their crimes for so long because of what Brooks-Lane mentioned plus a mindset of disability that hasn't changed much since Burton Blatt's time. "Chronic unemployment, and segregation isn't a flaw in the system, it is the system."

Curt Decker, the lawyer and activist who was one of the first to call for renewed action in 2011, using the backdrop of Henry's Turkey Service to put an end to subminimum wages, finds it extraordinary that 14(c) was not abolished as soon as the men had been rescued. Decker's paper, "Segregated and Exploited," which was distributed widely throughout state and federal systems, also found its way to investigative reporters. The paper had the backing of national advocacy groups, including the entity he leads, the National Disability Rights Network.

> I manned the phones for almost three days straight, talking with reporters, lawyers, families and people with disabilities who'd only been given the option of subminimum wages. It was somewhat overwhelming. Of course, at the time the *New York Times* hadn't covered Iowa so while we'd always had the goal of helping change the employment services for workers with disabilities, there seemed to be a real, tangible window for change. The fact that almost ten years later we've only seen marginal legislative changes doesn't surprise me, but it does make me wonder what it will take. If men being chained to beds because they ran away from abuse and wages of servitude doesn't make the abolishment of 14(c) a reality, I'm not sure what will.

Robert Canino, who led the way to a settlement for each of the men, wasn't through though. Not long after the HTS case was finalized, he received a tip about similar abuse in South Carolina.

The gruesome reality of hauling livestock to market is that death begins at the start of the trip. Chickens and turkeys are crammed into cages that are then layered onto semitrucks. Since death is imminent, no one spends much time worrying about losing some of the animals on the trip. Those that perish on the way are called DOAs, and the bodies must be removed and handled differently from live animals. That's the job that one of the men in South Carolina had. It is thought that social workers in Iowa who had helped the men of HTS find safe places to live had also uncovered a connection that led to South Carolina. The men in Newberry, South Carolina, had all originally worked for the turkey plant in West Liberty, Iowa. This time the nonprofit agency was called Work Services, Inc., an ironically named entity that supplied the men to the Kraft processing plant in Newberry. The story was remarkably like the one in Iowa. Robert Canino called it "one of the most uncomplicated" he'd seen related to violations of the Americans with Disabilities Act. "A clear-cut matter of an employer exploiting the trust of vulnerable workers."[12]

The South Carolina operation was smaller in scale, but the same tactics were being used. The men had been trafficked from Texas institutions to Iowa and then on to South Carolina. The living quarters in Newberry were also similar— decrepit mobile homes bunched together, the flimsy plywood and jerry-rigged heating devices operated from a tangle of extension cords. The five men in South Carolina were paid meager wages, and they were essentially held against their will by Work Services, Inc. The setup in Newberry, South Carolina, continued even after the extensive news regarding the men at Henry's Turkey Service had been prominently reported five years earlier. The trial that Canino pursued in Iowa, the depositions and newspaper headlines were all part of the public record, but Work Service, Inc., continued to abuse and neglect its workers with intellectual disabilities. Perhaps that was because no one was ever criminally charged in the Henry's Turkey Service case; or maybe Paul Byrd, the owner of Work Services, Inc., and a former HTS supervisor, knew that the safeguards inside the disability industrial complex were weak; or maybe, like the citizens of Atalissa, those in Newberry, South Carolina, believed that Byrd was doing the men a great service. In the *New York Times* piece on the Newberry story, Robert Canino tried to rally everyday citizens to take an interest. "And what we found here serves to remind us all to remain vigilant against such abuse of our neighbors and co-workers."

Canino and others, many of them the same advocates in favor of abolishing subminimum wages, began to ponder the unthinkable, that Henry's Turkey Service was not an isolated, decades-long anomaly. "Sadly, the discovery of this situation, answers, in part, the question that has arisen since the disturbing Henry's Turkey Service operation came to light in Iowa a few years ago," Canino said. "After seeing how workers with intellectual disabilities had fallen between the societal cracks, being virtually invisible for decades, many have asked, 'Could there be any other situations like this out there or right in our own backyards?'"[13] Unfortunately, the trail of congressional inquiries and testimony over the last six decades seems to run like a fuse from the policy of section 14(c) and the rise of the disability industrial complex to the powder keg of abuses Canino is alerting us to.

The aftermath of Henry's Turkey Service, spurred on by Curtis Decker's call to action in "Segregated and Exploited," set the stage for boycotts, state lawsuits, and a botched legislative solution whose implementation would depend on the Department of Justice's weakened Civil Rights Division enforcing the *Olmstead* Supreme Court decision. At the US Department of Labor, the Wage and Hour Division tried to ramp up its oversight of section 14(c). Workers with disabilities across the country hoped for a remedy. The disability industrial complex was increasingly exposed, but it wouldn't accept the scrutiny with dignity, opting to hunker down; instead of focusing on changes that could help workers with disabilities find parity in wages, it would use scare tactics and rationalizations to protect its billions of dollars a year from impact.

Part III

9

Boycotting Goodwill

Sometime during the middle of the 1990s, a notion began to spread throughout the system of nonprofit agencies that purported to be help- ing workers with disabilities. Midsize and small agencies, through their boards of directors and leadership personnel, believed they needed to act more like business. This idea was accompanied by yet another round of efforts to refocus on describing what had primarily been sheltered work- shops and work activity centers. More and more, the agencies used a host of alternative names: "community rehabilitation provider," "employment services organization," "disability nonprofit," and "supports provider." These two symptoms were part of a larger illness—the same one that had plagued these agencies in the past—What are we? Employer, trainer, or business?

To act like a business would be interpreted by most to mean that if only these organizations were viewed through the lens of business processes first, and human-service operations second, all would be well. This is a complaint I have heard since first starting work in the disability industrial complex thirty years ago, usually from a board member piping up at a meeting. Like other nonprofits, the agencies have volunteer board members, local business leaders, politicians, and others such as the area school superintendent, public-health director, and a few family members. In my experience it is those board members not in human services who are the most vocal. Eager to share their expertise, those folks would often say things like, "We've got to view this budget like I do at XYZ Inc." The premise is that human-service leadership and the accounting personnel do not have a clue about how to run a business. In my experience, however, it is these agencies that must figure out how to fund programs and services when the economy has a downturn and the tax coffers are depleted. Still, the notion that the community rehabilitation providers (CRP) would be just fine if they applied some fiscal discipline and listened to their business-minded board members took off rapidly. The discussion about vision, mission, and values happened after the board, and the CEO or executive director, had beat the drum loudly for a fervid calling to embrace some vague business practices. The idea trickled down to middle management, which pushed the idea to the staff doing the frontline work. "You're not in rehabilitation, you work for a business," is how one CEO started to put it. Of course, it's not unorthodox to approach nonprofit operations with the mindset of utilizing best-practice business tools, it's just that the concept, like many innovations in the disability industrial complex, didn't go much farther than slogans and jargon. "We've got to get serious about CQI," and "revenue maximization is the key," resounded throughout the late 1990s. As the 2000s began, more emphasis was put on looking to the field's top players for emulation. The belief began circulating that if the little sheltered workshops didn't respond, another, larger CRP would gobble them up, as in corporate mergers, buyouts, and cutthroat competition. Why and how these things were looming on the edges of the human-service system created to assist workers with disabilities was never clear, but at one point I was assigned business books to read and marketing conferences to attend, and I received what could only be called remedial Accounting and Budgeting 101. The boogeyman who would lay waste upon the little guys had a name: Goodwill.

Founded informally in 1895, Goodwill started from humble beginnings. Edgar James Helms, the man who began Goodwill, got his start through the ministry of the Morgan Chapel in Boston. The city had become a place where tenements and social vices were intricately linked together. Helms believed that instead of simply providing charity and public assistance, a man needed to find a way to contribute to his own betterment. Of course, that also included following specific religious principles, most of which had to do with resisting the temptation of known vices such as alcohol, prostitution, sloth, and gambling. Helms walked the streets, going door to door, carrying burlap bags from Thomas Wood and Company, seeking donations of anything of value. By 1902 Helms was asking the wealthy in Boston to fund his endeavors, but an economic downturn found those patrons with less money to contribute to his work with the poor. Instead, Helms began asking for on-hand donations, like clothing, used housewares, and furniture. To distribute the clothing to the poor, he would spread out the items on the church pews and invite people to take what they needed. The process proved burdensome, however, with some riots and arguing over prime pieces, so Helms came up with the idea of creating a small store at Morgan Chapel, where those same poor people could purchase clothing and other items of necessity for token prices. At the time the name of the organization was Morgan Memorial Goodwill Industries. Seven years later, in 1909, motorized trucks were first used in a more formalized fashion, replacing the burlap sacks as the mode of transporting donated items. In 1918 the Soldier's Rehabilitation Act was passed to assist veterans returning home from World War I; it created federal funds that could be used by nonprofits. Goodwill began the process of weaning its mission and practices away from religion, since the organization was now eager to receive federal tax funds to operate some of its programs. Perhaps a prescient Helms told the leadership and board at Goodwill, "We will be out of business if Goodwill does not take over work with the handicapped people."[1]

By 1938 a similar approach was being sponsored in Utah by the Church of Jesus Christ of Latter-Day Saints. Like Helm's approach with Goodwill, the Mormons created an informal program to address the same issues, identified not so much as social inequities but rather as weaknesses of the soul. They named the program Deseret Industries and claimed the approach would solve heathenistic tendencies. "The curse of idleness would be done away with, the evils of the dole abolished, and independence, industry, thrift, and self-respect be once more established among our people."[2] Like the poorhouses before them, these two religiously oriented organizations were rooted in viewing public assistance for the individual, whether from federal or state resources, as a type of sin. It could be said that Deseret Industries was one of the first human-service agencies that tried to emulate Goodwill. Today, Goodwill represents an operating budget of $42 million annually and has become one of the most recognized nonprofit organizations in the United States, with a worldwide network of 157 entities spanning twelve countries.[3] Goodwill was one of the first national organizations to obtain a 14(c) subminimum wage certificate from USDOL. It was these attributes, and the fact that most Americans know, at least topically, what Goodwill does, that instigated an expose.

The abuses and neglect in Iowa at Henry's Turkey Service, including the financial exploitation, brought closer scrutiny from disability advocates across the country. At the National Federation of the Blind, President Marc Maurer decided to follow in the footsteps of his predecessors at NFB and make subminimum wages once again an issue that must be addressed. He didn't need to look any further than the "Segregated and Exploited Call to Action" report from Curt Decker at NDRN. But if Maurer was going to get anyone's attention, the focus had to be laser sharp, attached to something that the average American had at least some familiarity with. Using human-service lingo like "14(c)" or even the phrase "subminimum wages" would only create more filters to understanding the issue. Maurer opted to use a household name to get the public's attention.

Maurer had been the president of the NFB for twenty-five years when he decided to arrange for the boycott of Goodwill over its use of subminimum wages. He was only the third president in the prestigious organization's history since its founding by Jacobus tenBroek. Dr. tenBroek was also a constitutional law scholar, a civil-rights activist, a leader in social-welfare reform, and a distinguished national and international humanitarian. He won the rights of blind people to apply for and be hired into federal civil-service jobs. He was a prolific and gifted writer, and Marc Maurer knew the presidency of NFB would always be measured against the impressive work of tenBroek. But Maurer was not a lightweight either. By the time he was a teenager, he ran a paper route, a lawn-care service, and had even created an enterprise producing and marketing maternity garter belts designed by his mother. This last venture was so successful that his younger brother took over the business when Maurer left home.[4] He had also taught himself to disassemble and reassemble an entire car engine, quite a feat for any young person, but Maurer, like all NFB's presidents, was blind, a condition caused by overexposure to oxygen after his premature birth. When he was just twenty, Maurer was elected vice president of the Indiana chapter of the National Federation of the Blind. He received his undergraduate degree from Notre Dame and went on to the University of Indiana School of Law, where he received his doctor of jurisprudence in 1977. By 1981 he was in private practice in Maryland, where he quickly became a subject-matter expert in legal cases where the plaintiffs' sole condition keeping them from fair treatment was their blindness. He took on cases of discrimination, using his keen mind and powers of articulation to win cases. In short, he was a force to be reckoned with, and he was keenly aware of the history the NFB had continued to play in the debate surrounding work, pay, and labor conditions for workers with disabilities.

In the summer of 2012, Maurer was ready to implement a tactic that he hoped would get the attention of average, busy Americans, most of whom would likely recognize the name of Goodwill but who would not know much about the NFB or its advocacy history. Maurer knew the approach, a concise and inciting flyer, would ruffle feathers, to say the least. He tapped Anil Lewis, the director of policy and research at the NFB, to ratchet up the salient points of the issue. To most Americans Goodwill's image centered on their store fronts, where one could donate, snag vintage clothing, procure used kitchen utensils, books, and even a couch for a dorm room. While some shoppers knew Goodwill also employed some people in the stores who had disabilities, however, they weren't aware of the 14(c) practices that supported some of the Goodwill employees. The NFB flyer read in part, "Did you know that some Goodwill workers with disabilities are being paid as little as **22 cents per hour**? *It may be legal, but it is not right.*"

The flyers went viral, at least inside the disability industrial complex. The NFB was bombarded with phone calls and emails; some were negative, from people who believed Maurer and NFB had ambushed Goodwill. Still, the boycott of the stores that fall of 2012 was not very successful. Only a handful of people showed up, passing out flyers, while some toted protest signs with "22 cents per hour" scrawled with exclamation points at the end. Only a few local news stations decided to make the effort to cover the boycott. Maurer was undeterred and set out to broaden the appeal. He sent a young woman named Rose Sloan, also blind, to attend the 99 percent rallies used during the 2011 Occupy movement in and around the DC area. Her technique was simple: she would ask the protesters in attendance whether they were aware that some workers with disabilities were legally paid pennies on the hour for their labors. Most were stunned to find out the truth. She passed out flyers. The approach was about raising awareness: Maurer and the NFB were focusing on Goodwill, but there were thousands of nonprofit rehabilitation providers around the country doing the same thing, embracing the law that allowed demeaning pay rates; they were not big names, though, and the goal, the reason to set out on the path in the first place, was to garner enough notice that news outlets might be interested in coverage.

It had been three years since the men had finally been rescued in Iowa, and just a year after Curt Decker at the NDRN had crafted the "Segregated and Exploited Call to Action." The window of opportunity was marginal, and the advocates and leaders working to abolish section 14(c) had seen at least some of this story before; that is, a news story of abuse is highlighted and after an initial round of outrage, not enough is done to use the exposés and coverage to effect real change (think Willowbrook, *Christmas in Purgatory,* the *Wall Street Journal* exposés, and the Jackson class-action lawsuit in New Mexico). The average citizen cares, but there's competition for attention; acting fast is good but acting so that the information is salient and accessible is better.

Curt Decker had been working behind the scenes with the large rehabilitation and disability trade agencies, some of them well funded and powerful, located in the heart of the capital's lobbying district. His decision to highlight the abuses of Henry's Turkey Service was purposefully crafted, with a focus on the unintended consequences of a lawful statute like section 14(c). He said, "I went to talk with the leaders of these trade groups, and of course it was already fraught with the intensity of disagreement." Decker had been a leader in civil rights and disability rights for decades, an attorney with a law degree from Cornell. He has been affiliated with the NDRN since its inception in 1982. As executive director of the nation's largest nongovernmental enforcer of disability rights, he has seen abuse and neglect that would shatter most people. "I'm a mix between an incrementalist and a staunch advocate. Change is a fight in any cause, but when it comes to something as misunderstood as disability and civil rights, one has to partner where they can, and trust that persistence and passion will be a catalyst for change." Before founding the NDRN with other like-minded activists, Curt served as director of Disability Rights of Maryland. Decker has been immersed in fighting the good fight in other human-service roles, serving as the director of an entity that served abused and neglected children. He was a VISTA worker prior to taking on the role of senior attorney for the Baltimore Legal Aid Bureau for five years. The meeting with the trade groups that were highly enmeshed in utilizing section 14(c) was intense. At first, in the blinding light of the story of the men in Iowa, there was an amendment on the table to reverse the removing of the "minimum, subminimum wage," that the trade organizations had lobbied Congress for back in the late 1980s. It could be seen as a paltry attempt by the trade organizations to appear to solve the most abhorrent issue under 14(c). Senator Harkin from Iowa and others suggested putting it back at half the current minimum wage, but the trade groups balked. More behind-the-scenes discussions occurred, and it was resolved to present the trade organizations with a floor for section 14(c) of one-third the minimum wage. "They kind of lost it," Decker told me. "I'd been on the record pushing for these organizations and their members to get busy with revamping their business models, but they were visibly upset at this meeting." The DD network, of which the protection and advocacy organizations in each state are a part and are funded by Health and Human Services, is in place precisely for policy issues like this. There's a natural push and pull between the trade organizations, which represent the desires of the providers agencies, including sheltered workshops and day activity centers, and the disability-rights organizations represented by the NDRN and Curt Decker. "They were vehemently opposed to changing the wage floor. They said they'd be out of business if they had to pay their workers a third of the minimum wage." That hourly wage would have been $2.39. It was inevitable that the issue of CEO pay at these organizations would be considered. Once leadership of the trade organizations raised claims of bankruptcy, this was the logical next step for many interested in pushing the issue of section 14(c) abolishment. Freedom of Information Act (FOIA) requests were made, furthering the animosity of some of the agencies that felt they were being targeted unfairly. There are many excellent nonprofit agencies operating within the disability industrial complex, some of which were started by families, but numerous organizations that were small five decades ago have grown into large enterprises, dependent on cheap labor and revenue from their sheltered-workshop contracts to fund operations, while also billing state and federal funders for training. Many of these organizations, some of which I've worked at or consulted with, will say the profits they make from paying subminimum wages are meager, but this is not true across the board; and while it may be true at some organizations, they are also deeply attached to a business model steeped in billing to "rehabilitate" or "habilitate" the people they are also employing. It's not surprising, then, that Decker and the NDRN encountered some conflict as the work to overhaul an outdated wage system was considered. Like a house of cards, once subminimum wages and its rationale are pulled from the foundation, all the other interventions that are billable are also at risk, and a system built upon erroneous beliefs instead of evidence-based practices is threatened.

Shortly after the exposure of Henry's Turkey Service, Iowa senator Harkin took another run at hosting congressional hearings related to section 14(c). The trade groups were on high alert, unable to acknowledge the abuses related to subminimum wages. For the most part, the trade groups tried to make out the horrific outcomes in Iowa as isolated incidents, perpetrated by bad actors. They called for each state to do more to provide oversight, but that wasn't exactly instructive: Wage and Hour personnel and Social Security investigators had been on site to do just that in 1979, to no avail.

ACCSES is the largest of these lobbyist trade groups, and its tagline is "the voice of disability service providers." On its website, it justifies its position regarding 14(c): "Successfully fought efforts to eliminate worker protections under Section 14(c)." Both state and national trade organizations inside the disability industrial complex use language to their advantage in this way. By stating that the efforts of ACCSES helped to fight the elimination of worker protections, the organization doesn't reveal that it fought to keep 14(c) exploitation legal and opposed any type of regulatory additions to provide safeguards.

ACCSES opposes the elimination or phasing out of the Section 14(c) program for all or a subset of the population of persons with the most significant disabilities. ACCSES also opposes the imposition of an arbitrary floor (e.g., 30% of minimum wage) with or without exceptions. People with disabilities must retain their right to make informed choices and exercise the right to self-determination. Individuals with the most significant disabilities must not be denied the opportunity to work in a center-based employment at a wage that reflects their productivity. Eliminating or repealing Section 14(c) or setting an arbitrary floor will simply have the effect of denying the opportunity to work for individuals with the most significant disabilities who cannot meet the productivity standards.[5]

This sounds like sincere advocacy efforts, and it is, but remember their tagline: The Voice of Disability Service Providers. To the public, most people don't differentiate between what Curt Decker and NRDN is doing versus ACCSES, and that's in part purposeful.

Senator Harkin's hearing before the Senate Committee on Health, Education, Labor and Pensions was set up to examine the systems, policies, and loopholes that had created the detrimental elements at play at Henry's Turkey Service, which had occurred unchecked for thirty years in his home state. Harkin was a powerful politician with connections to not only the landmark ADA legislation but to some of the leadership personnel at ACCSES, specifically Bobby Silverstein, a lawyer and behind-the-scenes player in the intergovernmental workings of creating the ADA and procuring political support for it in 1990. Bobby Silverstein was a lobbyist for organizations such as the Coalition to Preserve Rehabilitation, the American Congress of Community Supports, and the National Association of Rehabilitation Research and Training Centers. Silverstein, curiously, was against abolishing subminimum wages. In discussions off the record, several people said they believe Silverstein convinced Senator Harkin to wait, to include restrictions on subminimum wages in a larger bill, something that ACCSES had been public about in its legislative priorities. ACCSES was a staunch defender of keeping section 14(c) in place. In the end, these hearings did little more than those before. They informed the debate, brought out passions and set the groundwork for a flawed legislative solution.

The reaction of the trade groups vested in maintaining subminimum wages for workers with disabilities would also surface when the NFB pushed further on the Goodwill boycott. By the fall of 2013, there were over 220,000 petitioners signed onto an effort to get Goodwill to change its practices.[6] While the boycott had gotten a slow start, average Americans were beginning to understand a disturbing fact; as in corporate America, those at the top of the disability-employment programs were paid many times more than those at the bottom. After NBC aired a piece by Harry Smith, called "Wage Wars," regarding Goodwill and its pay practices, both the NFB and ASAN (Autistic Self-Advocacy Network) ramped up petitions at change.org. Word seemed to spread, and people responded. "A minimum wage is the absolute least a company can and should be able to pay their employees, regardless of disabilities. The minimum wage is already terribly low as it is, paying even less than that is horrible and should be criminal," said an observer.[7] Another put it bluntly: "The executives who are paid half a million per year or more enjoy their exaggerated wages through the underpaying of autistic workers who cannot defend themselves from being paid wages so minuscule that they should be outlawed. The millionaires are the parasites, not their victims of wage reduction by theft."

The country was just starting to recover from the economic downturn caused by the CEOs of corporate banks considered too big to fail, and sentiment was strong that something needed to be done. Hundreds of thousands of signatures demanding policy changes at Goodwill were delivered to the company's Rockville, Maryland, headquarters and to five regional offices in New York, California, Texas, Washington, and Rhode Island. On the main page of Bill Moyer's website, a photo depicted a Goodwill storefront replete with a sign asking for donations; the prominent caption read, "Thanks to a 75-year-old loophole, nonprofits like Goodwill can pay workers with disabilities as little as 22 cents an hour." The message the NFB set out to amplify was working, but Goodwill had lobbied behind the scenes to keep subminimum wages. Goodwill was not deterred by the coverage; Brad Turner-Little, a Goodwill spokesperson told *In These Times* that the NFB boycott had had no discernible impact on the company's retail outlets.[8] "We've actually experienced growth in retail sales." However, Goodwill had to realize a national news piece on prime-time television, and FOIA requests highlighting the extraordinary pay of its executives would certainly shine a light on disparate pay practices. The income of CEOs of Goodwill franchises across America totals more than $30 million annually. Goodwill understood its position and acted quickly.[9] Its corporate website page announced in all caps: "WE WELCOME THE CONCERN THAT MANY AMERICANS HAVE SHOWN FOR IMPROVING EMPLOYMENT OPPORTUNITIES AND QUALITY OF LIFE FOR OTHERS IN THEIR COMMUNITY, WHICH HAS BEEN A KEY ELEMENT OF GOODWILL'S MISSION FOR MORE THAN A CENTURY." Below, the justification continued: "As North America's leading nonprofit provider of employment training, job placement services and other local programs for people with severe barriers to employment, Goodwill takes these concerns seriously. Get the facts about Goodwill's employment of people with disabilities and learn firsthand from the people who have benefited from Goodwill services and work opportunities."

Perhaps it is understandable that Goodwill, its board of directors, and its leadership would feel they had been smeared; they have helped thousands of people find work, some with disabilities, others with barriers related to socioeconomic disadvantages through TANF (Temporary Assistance to Needy Families). Over the years I have met kindhearted, dedicated professionals who work at Goodwill. In the heat of the controversy, though, Goodwill could have stated for the record that it too believed that paying workers with disabilities so poorly, even if legal, was outdated. It could have said that the organization, its board, leadership, local agencies, and the corporate nonprofit in its entirety would work to design new practices, including changing their business model away from subminimum wages. Instead, like the smaller nonprofit sheltered workshops and work activity centers that looked up to Goodwill, it recruited families of the workers being paid subminimum wages to tell their story, an old practice in the disability industrial complex when a state legislature is cutting funds or asking provider agencies to show the outcome of the funds they receive. It doesn't take much searching to find references to "disability inspiration porn," a phrase meant to convey how we tend to place people with disabilities, and in this case, those with intellectual disabilities, at the center of our pity.[10] I'm always on the lookout for these stereotypes because the insidiousness of the pity mindset is likely one of our most significant challenges.

Goodwill used a variation on this mindset. It tapped its director of advocacy and legislative affairs to create a white paper on the use of section 14(c). The cover reads: "This paper provides an overview of Section 14(c), discusses why preserving the tool is important to individuals with disabilities and Goodwill, and provides recommendations to strengthen the use of special minimum wage certificates."

The white paper explains what the FLSA 14(c) special wage certificate is, and curiously cites the congressional hearings, which are both critical of and concerned with the way in which subminimum wages are determined and justified. The authors of the white paper tackle the history of Goodwill's use of section 14(c) and then lay out their perceptions of the issues, which again do not line up with congressional concerns Congress had with subminimum wages. There are solutions posed by Goodwill, and recommended actions, and then a portion that perpetuates the poster-child mindset, a story about a father and son. Goodwill's method of telling the story repeats something I've seen many times in many different states, usually during a legislative session proposing change or putting outcome restrictions on the use of the funds appropriated inside the disability industrial complex. In the Goodwill white paper the father and son are pictured, the grown son hugging his father—a sweet image, of course, but one that also propagates the notion of the "eternal child."

Even before we finish the short narrative (seven brief paragraphs) of the father and son, we know there will be multiple heroes, one of which is inevitably Goodwill itself. We are told that the man with the labels of trisomy chromosome imbalance and other disabilities was abused by another human-service provider, that he was assaulted at the age of ten. We can see the small child being hurt by those who are supposed to care for him, a heart-wrenching tale. We are let in on the child becoming an adult and how the father left no stone unturned but ended up again with a provider of services that his son didn't respond to. The father hears of Goodwill and decides to give them a chance. The son is transformed. We are to understand that subminimum wages are part of his miraculous recovery. A sentence reads in part, "Goodwill provides employment and vocational training to people with multiple and/or severe disabilities under a special minimum wage certificate." Here, we are to accept several things: One, these are workers with lots of problems! Two, though not referenced as "subminimum," the wage is described as "special." The authors realize that "subminimum wage" sounds bad, but "special minimum wage" invokes the Special Olympics and all that it has come to represent. Under the lens of disability studies, the story purposely summons the old stereotypes that citizens with intellectual disabilities in the United States are made subject to.

An internet search of the phrase "eternal child" produced an advertisement from Angel Sense, a company that markets a GPS device to be attached to the ankles of children and adults. A website with many photos of people with the label of Down syndrome, Angel Sense claims that it allows people to live independent lives, but it markets the GPS device to control "wandering or running off, oppositional behavior," and the vague and worrisome "changes in adulthood." It is uninformed and purposefully ignorant of concepts like self-determination, dignity of risk, and civil rights. The Goodwill white paper attempts to include self-determination in its solutions. In the disability industrial complex, the same one that Burton Blatt, Marc Gold, and others first identified as problematic enough that it might indeed be creating its own self-fulfilling prophecies, practitioners frequently take the strong, well-intended concepts of systemic change and transform them into their own interpretation. For instance, the Arc, the national organization at the forefront of attempting to ensure that citizens with intellectual and developmental disabilities have civil rights, defines self-determination in a way that is incongruent with the term as used by the Goodwill authors in their white paper that advocates to keep subminimum wages. The Arc interprets this concept as: "People with intellectual and/or developmental disabilities (I/DD) have the same right to, and responsibilities that accompany, self-determination as everyone else. They are entitled to opportunities, respectful support, and the authority to exert control in their lives, to direct their services, and to act on their own behalf." This is an important distinction. Since the early 1990s researchers, advocates, families, and people with disabilities have worked diligently to create a standard definition and set of principles by which to guide the application and implementation of self-determination inside the disability industrial complex by those who receive the bulk of the funding to support people with intellectual and developmental disabilities.

The Arc states, "People with I/DD have the same right to self-determination as all people and are entitled to the freedom, authority, and supports to exercise control over their lives. People with I/DD must understand that they can direct and influence circumstances that are important to them. This right to self-determination exists regardless of guardianship status."[11]

The principles of self-determination have been researched widely, and much of that work has been done by one man, Michael L. Wehmeyer, PhD, the Ross and Marianna Beach Distinguished Professor in Special Education and chairperson of the department of special education, as well as director and senior scientist at the Beach Center on Disability, all at the University of Kansas. Dr. Wehmeyer has received funding from multiple federal agencies to conduct research and model leadership preparation activities pertaining to the education and support of youth and adults with intellectual and developmental disabilities. He is the author or coauthor of more than 450 peer-reviewed journal articles or book chapters and has authored, coauthored, or edited 43 books on issues pertaining to self-determination, positive psychology and disability, the transition to adulthood, the education and inclusion of students with extensive support needs, and technology use by people with cognitive disabilities. Wehmeyer wrote a fascinating, but heartbreaking book on a family ravaged by the practice of eugenics, *Good Blood, Bad Blood: Science, Nature, and the Myth of the Kallikaks*. The book follows the true story of a woman who was given the pseudonym Deborah Kallikak and who became the poster child for the cultural fear generated by American eugenicists. Those same eugenicists provided the Nazi regime with the excuse to take the eugenic horror to its ultimate conclusion.[12] Wehmeyer is coauthor of the widely used textbook *Exceptional Lives: Special Education in Today's Schools* (2020), published by Merrill/Prentice Hall and now in its ninth edition. Wehmeyer's text *Development of Self-Determination through the Life Course* (2017) is a seminal look at the impact of embedding self-determination at early ages on the adult lives of people with intellectual and developmental disabilities; it has been used in creating life paths for neurodiverse youth. Not surprisingly his dedication to reform resonates, and he was awarded a Burton Blatt Humanitarian Award for his work. I asked him whether self-determination can ever include subminimum wages, segregation, and poverty. Are people with intellectual and developmental disabilities truly choosing anything if the principles of self-determination are hijacked by the very agencies that benefit from making those choices align with their funding? He responded, "It's a misapplication of a very powerful set of principles designed to liberate youth and adults with disabilities from the systems that tend to focus on programs rather than people. The real question for these types of misnomers of best practices lies in the creation of a set of choices that reflect those that we all make. In other words, it's not about self-determination in relation to systemic choices, but having the power to choose how to get what we all want, which includes work, family, community, connection and safe places to live."

Like most large, bureaucratic multilayered systems, the disability industrial complex tends toward mirroring what a funder is asking for; since that requires taking strong, fidelity-based approaches like self-determination to scale, the organizations believe they must water down the original value-based concepts into easily tracked check-off lists. This tendency can be seen in special education, vocational rehabilitation, and the Medicaid waiver programs designed to support people in community settings rather than day programs, sheltered workshops, and congregate living schemes.

The fuller fleshing out of these concepts and the implementation of them in relation to personal and community lives is reflected by the national Arc, on which Wehmeyer has had a significant influence. "Family members, friends, and other allies play a critical role in promoting self-determination by providing supports and working collaboratively to achieve the individual's goals. Families, friends, and other allies should understand, recognize, and promote the rights and responsibilities of self-determination and respect the limitations on their own authority. Service providers, educators, and substitute decision-makers must recognize and respect the individual's right to self-determination and the limitations on their authority."

To this end, people with I/DD must be able:

- In their personal lives to:

  o lead in decision-making and problem-solving about all aspects of their lives and have the supports they want to make decisions;
  o advocate for themselves with the assurance that their desires, interests, and preferences will be respected and honored;
  o choose their own supporters, friends, and allies;
  o direct their own supports and services and allocate available resources;
  o hire, train, manage, and fire their own staff;

o acquire additional skills to assist in determining the course of their lives;

o use adaptive communications devices and other assistive technology; and

o take risks to achieve the lives they desire.

• In their community lives to:

o participate fully and meaningfully in the community;

o receive the necessary supports and assistance to vote and exercise other rights as citizens;

o become valued members and leaders of the community;

o serve as active members and leaders of community boards, advisory councils, and other organizations;

o take leadership roles in setting the policy direction for the self-determination movement; and

o have representation and meaningful involvement in policy-making at the federal, state, and local levels.[13]

This is important because the concept of self-determination reflected above is about the person, not the system, or the nonprofit agency receiving taxpayer funding. Nowhere in this specific definition or in the set of guiding principles does it state, imply, or enumerate the right or responsibility to be subjected to unequal pay, subminimum wages, or other exploitive vocational configurations unlike those of average American citizens. Goodwill's white paper uses the concept of self-determination to rationalize keeping an unfair, outdated, and specious set of practices. That's precisely why the example of the father and son is deployed, to give the reader a sense that adults with intellectual and developmental disabilities and their families have the right to choose to be exploited. Goodwill is not the only organization insinuating that it is acting on the choices of the people it is funded to rehabilitate, but it is the largest, most recognizable nonprofit agency to do so. Similar language exists in most of the country's network of provider agencies. Goodwill's white paper includes recommendations for increasing the investigations the USDOL performs on section 14(c) subminimum-wage certificate holders, the same division investigating Henry's Turkey Service in 1979. That investigation proved useless, and it took the sister of one of the men thirty years to get both state and federal government to act. As with the congressional hearings over the decades, USDOL itself has testified that it is not equipped to do much more than a fraction of the oversight investigations of the 14(c) program. The question is not one of increased oversight; the legality of paying subminimum wages should be the issue that's thoroughly investigated, not an unfair and exploitive loophole that should be better monitored.

I spoke with Ari Ne'eman about his role in 2013 in forcing the issue to the surface by supporting and leading the second boycott of Goodwill. Through Change.org he and the organization he cofounded, ASAN, obtained more than 200,000 petition signatures, and a piece about Goodwill and subminimum wages aired on primetime television. He told me he believed it was the right step, and that without the exposure, the general public would still be in the dark regarding subminimum wages. "It was strategic. After so many decades of nothing being done, with one congressional hearing after another, it seemed the timing was right to up the ante. People on social media responded and we're furious with Goodwill." Ne'eman had been a standout in the NBC piece when he asked Harry Smith whether he could stand up to the practice used in section 14(c) wage payments of using a stopwatch to rate his productivity. There with Ne'eman was a married couple, both vision impaired, who had worked at a Montana Goodwill facility hanging clothes. Harold and Sheila Leigland are the epitome of a hardworking American family. Writing for the NFB blog, Sheila provides a testimony of the harm that 14(c) created for her family. It's reprinted here with permission.

Hello, my name is Sheila Leigland and my husband's name is Harold. We live in Great Falls, Montana and have been married for thirty years. We both have attended college and have bachelor's degrees. My degree is in music education, and Harold's degree is in social science with an extended minor in psychology. We have raised one child, and my husband worked as a massage therapist for over thirty-five years. We are active in our church and are members of the National Federation of the Blind. Two years ago, we had the privilege of participating in the Rock Center piece and speaking at the National Convention of the National Federation of the Blind on the issue of subminimum wages.

We wanted to make extra money to help make ends meet, so we both tried to find work and were eventually placed in a sheltered workshop. We both started working in 2009. I was told that eventually we would make minimum wage, which turned out not to be even close to the truth. Disabled workers are forced to take timed productivity tests every six months so that wages can be reevaluated. Because of the timed-test method, wages fluctuate wildly. It is pretty hard to set up any sort of budget when you never know how much you will be making from month to month.

In February of this year, Harold was up for another timed-test evaluation. We were very concerned because a committee met to discuss changes in the format of the timed test. It turned out that Harold's test was extremely long. In the past, the tests took thirty minutes to an hour, but this one took four hours on the first day and fifty minutes on the day of his next shift. Harold was to place five toys in a bag and divide them as objects that were alike in some way. Sounds easy, right? No, it wasn't easy at all! Many of the items weren't identifiable by touch, and many of the features that would help with their correct placement were exclusively visual. Harold and I are both blind. Even some people with perfect vision had difficulty with the task, so they resorted to sorting the items by color, which of course Harold could not do.

As I said, both Harold and I are college-educated adults. There are many jobs that Harold can do, but he was deliberately assigned a task that would be difficult or impossible for him and then timed on how quickly he could do it. Rather than placing Harold in a job that matched his skills and interests, the sheltered workshop appears to have set him up to fail so that he could be paid a lower wage.

When my husband came home from work, I knew that the test had not gone well because he told me that he didn't want to talk about it. I told him that we would work through this together. When we finally talked about it, I found myself talking with a person who was demoralized and felt that he was letting me down. It wasn't true, but it is hard to accept that you are a capable adult when you are still being treated like a child. It broke my heart to see the man I love in such pain.

I knew that the test had not gone well, but I wasn't prepared for Harold to be set back to a wage of $2.75 per hour. His previous wage was $7.61 per hour. He is angry and humiliated. I am so angry that it is legal to discriminate against people just because of blindness, or for that matter any disability. It makes me sick that so little is expected of us, and we are treated like children. In fact, I know children that get more money as an allowance than my husband receives in his paycheck.

It is a tragedy that there are people who claim to be advocates for people with disabilities but believe that this is okay. There are people with disabilities who believe that they can do no better because the agencies

who exploit them have repeatedly told them and their families that subminimum wages are all they can or should expect. In truth, they are victims not of their disabilities, but of the low expectations held by their
employers and society.

I want to see Section 14(c) of the Fair Labor Standards Act abolished.
I strongly encourage our members of Congress in the House of Representatives to support H.R. 188, which would phase out this law over a three-
year period. I also want to see a similar bill introduced in the United States
Senate.

We can't do this alone.

We need your help to get this accomplished. I thank you in advance for
your help in this important matter. Section 14(c) is immoral and discriminatory. All that we are asking for is fair treatment. We need and want to be
awarded first class citizenship in our own country and this includes making
a fair wage. Please, help us live the lives that we want to live.

When I spoke with Sheila Leigland five years after her eloquent and
impassionate blog was published online, her feelings had only intensified.
From their home in Great Falls, Montana, she told me how she was keeping the fight up. "We tried to get a bill to ban subminimum wages here in
Montana, but it was shot down. We knew that would be the case, but you
must try. When I worked at Goodwill some of the younger workers with
disabilities believed if they took a day off to go to a sporting event they'd
be fired. Yes, the legality of 14(c) is still there, but I just don't know how
anyone could think it's a good practice."

The NFB remains in the fight. From his Washington, DC, office, the
new president, Mark Riccobonno is as creative and energized by advocacy
efforts as his predecessor Dr. Maurer. "We've never taken a federal dollar
because that compromises your advocacy efforts. I see it all the time. No
one wants to lose their funding, even a little bit, so a threat to a budget
if an organization joins a boycott can be significant." Riccobonno understands the way the disability systems work, especially their perspective of
low expectations.

The Goodwill boycotts would provide an avenue for other organizations to join the fight. The awareness that the boycotts had stirred,
along with the NBC piece, created a unified protest to keep intact the
legality of subminimum wages. On the twenty-first anniversary of the
Americans with Disabilities Act, the groups conducted protests in opposition to the legislation. The focus was on the members of the Senate

Committee on Health, Education, Labor and Pensions, where the reauthorization was to occur.

Dr. Marc Maurer, president of the National Federation of the Blind, said, "We are extremely pleased that these organizations are joining us to advocate for equal pay for equal work and an end to the outrageous practice of paying subminimum wages to workers with disabilities. We hope that other members of the disability rights community will join us in speaking out against this unfair, discriminatory, and immoral practice and opposing any legislation that authorizes and perpetuates it."[14]

Serena Lowe, who was at the time the executive director of Collaboration to Promote Self-Determination, said, "We are pleased and proud to join the National Federation of the Blind to stop the exploitation of workers with disabilities. It is time for our political leaders to take a stand against exploitation and to fight for true equality for American workers with disabilities."[15]

Something critical had been exposed, certainly not for the first time or even the hundredth, but there was a conscious and strategic vision behind the boycotts that had moved from the household name of Goodwill to the more abstruse congressional committee and the recondite underpinnings of sheltered workshops. The NFB had been instrumental in the fight. Anil Lewis, the director of policy and research at the NFB, who doesn't shy away from the truth, enlightened me in an interview. "I'm a black, blind man from the South. I know racism, but the kind of insidious benevolence that these nonprofits engage in is deeply rooted in the use of segregation and subminimum wages and it's hard to fight against. And, as I started trying to advocate for the law to be overturned, I had to convince myself that they truly believe they are doing what they think is best for people with disabilities." Lewis is a man for whom self-reflection is a personal necessity, and he uses that mindset to make sure his actions don't inadvertently hurt people. He's reached out to parents of workers with disabilities being paid subminimum wages, and he's tried not to demonize the people and organizations in the disability industrial complex who fight to keep section 14(c) legal. "When Dr. Maurer came to me and asked me to find a way to introduce a bill to ban subminimum wages, we decided to double down when I was the Director of Strategic Communications." What Maurer and Lewis in their roles at the NFB were doing was expanding their opposition to paying blind workers with disabilities subminimum wages so that their efforts encompassed all people with disabilities, including those with intellectual and developmental disabilities. It was a powerful and inclusive decision, one that would reverberate throughout the many lobbyists, trade groups, and billions of dollars of funding. It was a statement, but for Lewis, it fit with his views of how human beings should be treated. "I told Dr. Maurer, well that's simple, a no-brainer, it's a law that's still on the books because no one has gone at it directly." But Anil Lewis was surprised at the reaction to his efforts. "Man, I could not have been more wrong. The whole other side was revealed to me. I realized there was going to be a great deal of political theatre involved." Lewis was instrumental in pulling in the CPSD Coalition, which has in its membership the National Down Syndrome Congress, The National Rehabilitation Association, and several others. On a call with CPSD, Lewis was confounded when he heard the lead members tell him that they preferred to slow down. "These were organizations that represented, at least in part, those most adversely impacted by subminimum wages, but still they were opposed. It was the beginning of my evolution of understanding what we were up against."

This battle was different from the congressional hearings over the decades. Sites like Change.org, and the capability to film the protests and upload to social media were ubiquitous. Regular citizens saw, heard, and in some ways, albeit vicariously, participated in the protest. A quick internet search shows people holding protest signs that read, "CEO Salary $500,000, worker pay 20 cents," or "We need good jobs, not goodwill."

The message had finally reached the public. By the fall of 2012 and into 2013, it had also resonated with the Department of Justice, which would institute class-action lawsuits on behalf of workers with disabilities in sheltered workshops, in one state on the East coast and another on the West coast. Once again, those battle-weary advocates, Anil Lewis, Lois Curtis, the men from Atalissa, Iowa, and reformers across the country were hopeful that the crack in the facade was widening. The end result was a mixed bag. The other side had money, lobbyists, and their insidious benevolence to fall back upon.

10

OREGON, RHODE ISLAND, AND THE
PROMISE OF A WAY FORWARD

If you're Vanita Gupta, it would be difficult to ignore or rationalize what had transpired in relation to disability and employment over the four years from 2009 to 2013. As a litigator and a person deeply steeped in a sense of civil rights for all, Gupta was appalled at what the men endured at Henry's Turkey Service, but she also knew, as Anil Lewis did, that violations of a human being's basic rights can come shrouded in benevolence, cloaked in a facade of care, protection, and paternalism. She started her career at the NAACP where she was a staff attorney. Her career was meteoric, but Gupta is a brilliant thinker, possessing a legal mind that misses nothing. At the NAACP she used her talents and sense of justice to save thirty-eight people in Texas who had been wrongly convicted, pardoned by Governor Rick Perry. By 2006 she had moved from the NAACP to the ACLU where she continued her focus on helping those with few options for representation, including forcing a privately run prison to stop its unlawful and immoral practice of detaining immigrant children. Appointed by President Barack Obama as the chief civil-rights prosecutor for the United States, Gupta oversaw a wide range of criminal and civil-enforcement efforts to ensure equal justice and protect equal opportunity for all, including LGBTQ rights, criminal-justice reform, human-trafficking cases, voter ID violations, and investigations into the police forces in Ferguson, Missouri; Chicago; and Baltimore. Serving as acting assistant attorney general and head of the US Department of Justice's Civil Rights Division, Gupta didn't shy away from cases involving disability rights, even ones like the case in Oregon, which on its surface could be explained away with faux pity, the misapplication of the concept of self-determination, and involvement from lobbyists for the disability industrial complex and parents of workers with disabilities being paid pennies per hour in sheltered workshops in Beaverton, Oregon, and elsewhere in the state.

Before Gupta had left the ACLU and was appointed by President Obama a year later, the attorneys at the Department of Justice had already provided a statement of interest in an initial complaint coming from workers and families in Oregon. The basis of the initial investigations focused on violations of the Supreme Court *Olmstead* decision, along with wanton disregard for the ADA and the amended Rehabilitation Acts of 1973. The DOJ attorneys signaled their mounting pressure for the state of Oregon to adhere to those landmark pieces of legislation. The DOJ released a statement: "The unwarranted placement of persons with disabilities in sheltered workshops similarly perpetuates 'unwarranted assumptions' that such persons are 'incapable or unworthy' of working in competitive employment or interacting with non-disabled co-workers or customers."

While the Henry's Turkey Service case had been explosive inside the disability industrial complex, with violations of 3(m) housing credit and the obvious pay exploitation, the Oregon case highlighted a new and intimidating development for the nonprofits running employment programs that relied on paying workers subminimum wages. HTS had been something that lobbyists and trade organizations tried to label as an exception to the rule. They believed more oversight by USDOL's Wage and Hour Division and closer auditing, both financially and programmatically, by state officials was the answer. But Oregon was different in that the attorneys for the DOJ were not solely arguing against the use of subminimum wages, but in addition and with more emphasis, the placement of people with intellectual and developmental disabilities into the sheltered-workshop system on a wholesale basis. Students in special education and those people applying for services in Oregon were routinely shuttled into a pipeline to programs that offered very little employment in real jobs, but rather almost entirely focused their use of taxpayer dollars on underwriting the operations of the 14(c) sheltered workshops, denying workers with disabilities access to "the least restrictive setting" and instead relying on outdated modes of intervention and support. It was as if nothing had changed in terms of the state's funding, provider expectations, and the application of civil rights from the 1970s until 2013. The four decades of progress with the courts, public policy, and the advent of supported employment and customized-employment methodologies had been largely ignored, and the operations of the sheltered workshops had gone on robustly, with cheap labor for the secured in-house contracts, while state and federal funds were used for the purported outcome of "rehabilitation," and "habilitation." Now the gig was up, and someone other than Congress, lobbied by the state and national trade groups, had taken an interest in how the sheltered workshops using 14(c) were continuing to operate. The bill from Rep. Stearns of Florida and others two years earlier had failed to pass, yet here was the country's premier law enforcement agency seriously scrutinizing the setting (segregated disability programs) and the options presented by those programs as a possible violation of laws already on the books, most specifically, *Olmstead* and the ADA. It was not just Oregon though; more than forty-four states were using subminimum wages, and sheltered workshops were still widely in use—but the state was quickly becoming a bellwether for the country.

Almost immediately the lobbyists and trade groups kicked into high gear once again, aiming to put a halt to the DOJ's interest in Oregon's sheltered workshops. If that linchpin was allowed to be pulled, not only would other states' subminimum-wages practices become embroiled in the scrutiny but so would the low expectations and lack of concrete outcomes that the disability industrial complex relied upon. This wasn't some businessman from Texas trafficking men from state institutions to a tiny town in Iowa to slaughter and process turkeys; this was the federal government looking closely at a little-known and obscure system that had thrived and largely been untouched by congressional attempts for six decades.

Shortly after the case in Oregon became of interest to the DOJ, I was scheduled to provide training at the offices of NISH, the National Industries for the Severely Handicapped—now known as SourceAmerica. In 2015 the name change became important after an insider handed over audio recordings of backroom dealings where special considerations were being given to some of its network of nonprofit agencies for kickbacks. Wiki tapes were released, and the story made the investigatory arm of CNN.[1] SourceAmerica officials denied any wrongdoing, and the case against it was partly found to be lacking merit. "We continue to stand fully behind our prior statements that the allegations being made against SourceAmerica in recent media stories are simply without merit. These allegations are the same that were made against SourceAmerica last year and are being made by the same disgruntled nonprofits and individuals. A recent court decision rejected similar accusations in a separate lawsuit, and SourceAmerica is continuing to vigorously defend itself against these unfounded allegations."[2]

I had worked with programs across the country that were affiliates of SourceAmerica. Most were hard working and dedicated, but they often found it difficult to bypass their reliance on the government contracts that employed workers with disabilities. I had been asked to provide training on the use of the powerful tools of customized employment: taking time to understand someone's ideal conditions of employment, looking at interests and strengths, rather than trusting the vocational assessments used inside the disability industrial complex that rely on outdated and spurious assumptions. The training I was to give would focus instead on working with local, smaller businesses to customize a position that meets the needs of both the employer and the worker with a disability.[3] I use a framework from the pioneer of adult learning, Malcolm Knowles, who was at the forefront of arguing that adults cannot be taught as if they're in elementary or high school. Knowles challenged the methodology of training adult workers. Rather than relying on the way universities and human resource departments used the framework of "pedagogy," which means "leading children," Knowles and others presented the notion of "andragogy," literally meaning "leading man." For example, adults must collaborate to learn; they need to understand how a new concept is different from their typical way of working; they cannot be coerced into learning (as in withholding rewards); and most importantly adults crave understanding why it is important to use the new methods they are being taught. So I began with a list of developments that had occurred and what that meant for learning a new set of skills to rise to the occasion.

I suppose I should have known better than to have referenced the Goodwill boycotts and the various DOJ inquiries into sheltered work, but these were professionals from all over the country who had paid money to receive the training I was delivering. I believed, and still do, that using Knowles's adult learning principles to capture the interest of trainees is both effective and respectful, but almost immediately I noticed a woman in the back of the room with a sour look on her face. Now, that's not uncommon, any trainer can tell you that; sometimes people are made to attend trainings, and there's little you can do to assuage their bitterness at having to sit through something they don't believe they need. Still, this person seemed to become more displeased as I went on. I covered changes in employment services for people with disabilities; I reviewed the Henry's Turkey Service story (even today I am amazed that most people in the field do not know the story), how the men suffered, and mentioned that it was one of the few times that the USDOL had actually revoked a 14(c) subminimum-wage certificate—which should not be interpreted as the first time it had found serious abuses.

Later, I learned that the woman was an employee of NISH/Source America: one of the country's largest players in the disability industrial complex was bothered that I was taking time to provide an analysis of current changes in a field rife with stagnant thought. Once I returned home, I was summoned to be on a call with the person I had offended. The call was brief, but I was told and asked to repeat that if I ever had the opportunity to train for NISH/SourceAmerica again, I would stick to the training and not offer my input on the legislative or advocacy efforts involved in overhauling or changing the way 14(c) subminimum wages are applied. That one instance is indicative of the way in which systems change is viewed inside the disability industrial complex and could be translated as: "Never amplify the problems, always rely on pity, and keep those who seek to make changes in line."

For an organization that had vehemently objected to the Wiki tapes and the CNN story, it nonetheless wanted to control the narrative around a pivotal issue that it and its affiliate nonprofits found objectionable.

Of course, it has also tried in recent years to reconsider how it applies its taxpayer-funded budget, but the customized-employment project that SourceAmerica operates is a tiny fraction of the annual budget of some $2.6 billion dollars. Window dressing? I don't know for sure, but I can say without a doubt that in my experience in the corporate offices, they didn't want me talking about the phase-out of 14(c) or the Goodwill boycotts.

It would be inaccurate, though, to paint SourceAmerica as the only part of the disability industrial complex that had concerns over changes to section 14(c). Beginning in 2011 I started traveling to Rhode Island to train provider agencies in the principles and implementation of customized-employment tools. For almost twelve years, the Centers for Medicare and Medicaid had funded Medicaid infrastructure grants, or MIGs. Authorized by the Ticket to Work and Work Incentives Improvement Act (the "Ticket Act") of 1999 and administered by the Centers for Medicare and Medicaid Services (CMS), the Medicaid infrastructure grant (MIG) program afforded states the opportunity to develop infrastructures and initiatives that promoted, supported, and facilitated the competitive employment of people with disabilities. Specifically, the MIG program aimed to increase the number of people with disabilities participating in competitive employment by (1) developing Medicaid infrastructure by facilitating targeted improvements to a state's Medicaid program and/or developing a comprehensive employment infrastructure that coordinates disparate state service delivery systems; (2) removing barriers to the employment of persons with disabilities by creating systemic change throughout the Medicaid program and coordinating with other programs to further remove barriers; and (3) developing infrastructure that offers sustainable and significant improvement in the ability of the system to provide adequate health coverage, personal assistance, and other supports for people with disabilities who are competitively employed.[4] For the most part CMS mandated that MIG funding was not to be used for the direct provision of services, but rather to change the systems surrounding and supporting the employment of individuals with disabilities. States had to have the support and approval of their Medicaid agency, which meant some states had the funding for more than a decade, while others, like Georgia, only had the funding for eighteen months. There was a wide range of reasons why a state didn't compete for funding, but much like expanding Medicaid coverage for citizens without insurance, the MIGs were sometimes seen as part of that expansion. From 2001 through 2011, over $450 million in MIG funding was awarded to forty-nine states plus the District of Columbia and the US Virgin Islands.[5]

This was an important initiative, one that—like so much inside the disability industrial complex—came with some successes and some failures to sustain the changes in the long term. Some states tried to impact their use of 14(c) subminimum wages but most focused on cross-agency collaboration, expanding their Medicaid buy-in program, which allows workers with disabilities to maintain their healthcare coverage when income and assets would otherwise make them ineligible for traditional Medicaid coverage. Many of the states used the MIG funds to offer more training and systematic change in the use of evidence-based employment services, which is how I found myself working in Rhode Island. Before the DOJ filed a lawsuit against the state of Rhode Island and the city of Providence, I was providing training to the agencies that still either operated sheltered workshops or had work activity centers. One participant in the training was a distinguished man with an expensive shirt and tie, sleeves rolled up. I liked him; he was attentive and thoughtful, but when I started going into the Goodwill boycotts and the Oregon lawsuit that seemed to be taking off, aimed directly at violations of the civil rights of workers with disabilities in the sheltered workshops, he became negative. He listened but moved in his seat. He had been a board member of a large agency and had recently taken on the role of an interim CEO as the remainder of the board did a national search for a replacement. He could no longer remain quiet and spoke up as I laid out the specifics of the potential changes to the system in Oregon. "That would never happen here, Doug," he said, with a kind, knowing smile, as if I hadn't yet grasped the politics in Rhode Island. "We've always had the ear of our elected officials in DC. They back what we do." I nodded; I wasn't there to debate or even spend a great deal of time on a lawsuit on the other side of the country. Still, he continued talking about their state trade organization, families of workers with disabilities whose adult children worked in a sheltered program earning subminimum wages for contract work performed for the prestigious jeweler Tiffany's. Finally, I held up my hands and told him that perhaps he was right, I only meant to share with the group what was happening with the lawsuit in Oregon. Less than six months later, Rhode

Island found itself agreeing to a consent decree with the Department of Justice. It found that the state and the city of Providence had essentially created a pipeline from its special-education programs and linked it with the adult provider agencies operating the sheltered workshops as a matter of course. Students' civil rights were being violated. The expectation was a lifetime of pennies per hour. The consent decree with the DOJ in Rhode Island called for a ten-year agreement to fundamentally change the practices of subminimum wages.

Back in Oregon, a progressive provider affiliated with United Cerebral Palsy signed onto the lawsuit and aligned its focus and advocacy with that of the DOJ. Oregon was the perfect laboratory to bring a lawsuit questioning the state's reliance on sheltered workshops and subminimum wages. It wasn't that Oregon's practices were more egregious than those of other states; in fact, Oregon was an early adopter of the use of supported employment and had formed one of the earliest initiatives, "Employment First," a set of values, principles, and techniques aimed at shifting the focus of a state's funding agencies away from sheltered work and day activity programs and toward spending those dollars on helping people find suitable, customized and supported employment scenarios for at least minimum wage. As in several states the DOJ has pursued in relation to civil-rights violations for citizens with disabilities, in Oregon there was a cadre of people, mostly professional bureaucrats with a bent toward advocacy, who welcomed the lawsuit, seeing it as a way to force the changes they were trying to bring about inside their own version of the national disability industrial complex. Molly Holsapple is one of those freedom fighters, working for almost half a century to assist people in leaving institutional settings for real homes, focusing on making sure that workers with disabilities had a choice in leaving a sheltered workshop for a real job with fair pay. She was instrumental in restructuring the funding streams to ensure that provider agencies were being paid based on outcomes. In other words, she was attempting to fundamentally change her little corner of the disability industrial complex. Holsapple worked to make sure that there were independent case manager professionals whose sole job was to assist people with disabilities in making informed choices regarding how, where, and when they spent their time, wresting the power away from the agencies, and putting the control in the hands of the person most reliant on the services. Personal budgets, where a person could see how much their provider agency was receiving to support them, were a cornerstone of Holsapple's efforts. She had been designing the supported-employment system in Oregon long before the DOJ lawsuit began. In many ways she was a one-woman dynamo, trying to make change where there was resistance, but she relied on others too. "We kind of all grew up together. Folks at the state agencies, the trade organizations, all of them. We didn't always agree and still don't, but we could trust one another, and that's so important in any wholesale systems change."

The first amended complaint in the Oregon class-action lawsuit was filed in May 2012, brought by eight plaintiffs ranging in age from twenty-seven to fifty-one, with an average time spent in sheltered-workshop settings of nearly fifteen years: Paula Lane, Andres Paniagua, Elizabeth Harrah, Angela Kehler, Lori Roberston, Gretchen Cason, Zavier Kinville, and a young woman named Sparkle Green. United Cerebral Palsy of Oregon was also a plaintiff, and most importantly, all workers in the state's sheltered workshops, referred to legally as "and all others similarly situated." Governor Kitzhaber, and several Department of Human Services officials along with the administrator of the state's vocational rehabilitation services, were named as defendants. In this way, the lawsuit was directly attached to two of the most significant funding sources, both configured with a blend of federal and state dollars: 1) long-term Home- and Community-Based Medicaid waivers; and 2) services delivered under the 1973 Rehabilitation Act, section 504, the basis of the DOJ action against Oregon related to violations and shortcomings related to Title II of the ADA. Title II applies to state and local government entities and protects qualified individuals with disabilities from discrimination on the basis of disability in services, programs, and activities delivered within their home state and community.[6]

The argument of the amended complaint is that informed choice and self-determination are for individuals to invoke, not providers, associations, PR staff, trade groups or lobbyists. The pertinent terms were defined:

> A sheltered workshop is a segregated employment setting that employs people with disabilities or where people with disabilities work separately from others. Sheltered workshops are usually located in a large, institutional facility. Workers with disabilities in these settings have virtually no contact with their non-disabled peers, other than agency staff, and are typically paid

sub-minimum wage. By contrast, integrated employment is a real job in a community-based business setting, where employees have an opportunity to work alongside non-disabled co-workers and earn at least minimum wage. Supported employment services are vocational training services that prepare and allow people with intellectual and developmental disabilities to participate in integrated employment.

The plaintiffs were represented by lawyers with the organization Disability Rights of Oregon, who argued that there is no reason for the incessant reliance on subminimum wages in sheltered workshops. Workers with disabilities are capable of work, each qualifies for access to Supported Employment services, and they have a desire to work in real jobs in the community. So, the question is, why haven't they and others been afforded their rights under the ADA and the Rehabilitation Act of 1973? Oregon, through the DHS's Medicaid waiver program and its state vocational rehabilitation program funds the Supported Employment service necessary for these workers to find and keep real jobs in the community. As the amended complaint noted:

> DHS currently funds *some* supported employment services that permit *some* persons with intellectual and developmental disabilities to work in integrated employment settings. But thousands of other similarly situated individuals are unable to obtain such supports because DHS administers, manages, and funds an outdated employment service system that primarily relies upon segregated sheltered workshops. DHS and the other defendants have failed to timely develop and adequately fund supported employment services, despite their demonstrated knowledge of how to provide these services to support people in integrated employment, their acknowledgment of the benefits of integrated employment, and their repeated public commitment to policies designed to expand integrated employment.

As in most states in the country, the leaders, often appointed by governors, have other constituents with more access, more money, more at stake than workers earning subminimum wages.

Perhaps another lens from which to view a state's obligations to use its tax dollars to fund evidence-based practices is the fiduciary relationship in which a beneficiary puts her faith in a body to perform its duties as a trustee. The issue arises from the significant confusion inside the disability industrial complex, the muddled relationship between the operators of the sheltered workshops and the workers with disabilities. If the latter are indeed workers, they can organize, negotiate, and enter into contracts, but if those same people are also viewed as clients, as in receiving some sort of treatment to ameliorate specific conditions, then that relationship is restricted by another, different set of values, more in line with the doctor/patient relationship. That consideration constitutes the framework of the argument in the Oregon case. It's likely that the state is trying to balance these relationships. A simple way to determine who is at the front of the queue is to follow the money. If the state relies on the use of section 14(c) and sheltered workshops, and if it places supported-employment services lower on the list of priorities (with lesser funding for those services), it is knowingly denying workers with disabilities the ability to leave segregation.

The complaint argues: "The named plaintiffs and the class they seek to represent are harmed by their placement in segregated sheltered workshops. Without meaningful supported employment services, the named plaintiffs and the plaintiff class are stuck in long-term, dead-end, facility-based sheltered workshops that offer virtually no interaction with non-disabled peers, that do not provide any real pathway to integrated employment, and that provide compensation that is well below minimum wage."

The plaintiffs' injury was made clear: "Although each of these eight citizens is qualified and would prefer to work in an integrated setting, the plaintiffs remain unnecessarily segregated in sheltered workshops, as a result of Oregon's Department of Human Services' administration, management, and funding of its employment service system."

The litigation sent ripples throughout the disability industrial complex. By 2011, New Jersey staff inside the same state agencies being sued in Oregon began tightening their expectations with providers, and the trade organizations and lobbyists in New Jersey responded. After administrators in the state pursued an "Employment First" approach, as lawyers were arguing for in Oregon, Governor Chris Christie reversed their actions, even though his administration had endorsed the concept of spending taxpayers' funds on real jobs first. Administrators in the New Jersey Department of Human Services' Division of Developmental Disabilities had tried to push provider agencies to wean their services away from a reliance on subminimum wages, but Christie became volatile and reversed their actions, moving the $7 million dollars from DHS to the state's vocational rehabilitation program, whose state counterpart in the Oregon case was listed as a defendant.[7]

There's a playbook that trade associations for provider agencies use, much like the one in the national press release from Goodwill. First, find families and their adult children with disabilities to showcase as being harmed by asking provider agencies to deliver on their taxpayer funding. The narrative is often steeped in stereotypes and revolves around the individual's deficits rather than strengths. Second, get these families in front of their elected officials to stop whatever change is being proposed. It worked in New Jersey. Governor Christie could then claim that he had saved the sheltered workshops. Joseph Bender, the executive director of a sheltered workshop in New Jersey, the Occupational Training Center, stated, "They are grateful the Legislature saved their work. . . . It's their choice to work, and that's what we wanted to preserve, not have someone else dictate to them what was in their best interest."[8]

Still, the ACCSES affiliate in New Jersey was concerned about the precendents from the cases in Oregon and Rhode Island. They had been able to control the congressional oversight commissions and hearings, but two DOJ lawsuits seemed to signal something new.

11

A Legislative Fix Was In

"Training through Placement" was a sheltered-workshop program in Rhode Island with several subminimum-wage contracts with businesses in the community. One of those contracts involved recycling outdated and obsolete remote controls. The remotes sat on skids in cardboard frames, two and three feet deep, some of the remotes so old they were as big as footballs, with batteries that needed to be pried out and plastic casings and multicolored buttons that needed to be separated from the jasmine-green circuit boards. Some of the old remotes had acid leaks, and if they'd come from hotels, they had been handled by hundreds if not thousands of people. The task was boring and dirty. The tan building said "TTP" on the upper facade, and in passing one might think the place was just another structure in an otherwise unimpressive light-industrial park, but over the years it had become the end point of a pipeline that began with a program called Birch Academy inside Mount Pleasant High School. By 2013, when the interim settlement agreement was reached between Rhode

Island and the DOJ, almost 130 workers with disabilities had been sent to TTP, which considered special education at Birch Academy a feeder program. Students at Birch and other special-education programs were rarely offered supported-employment services and instead headed straight to subminimum wages.

After I had been working in Rhode Island for several months, I met Steven Porcelli. Steven has a strong accent and an easy smile. He's matter-of-fact when talking about making less than $2 an hour at a sheltered workshop. "It was a pretty bad place, and I didn't get to focus on the things I'm good at." Steven had been one of the people sent to TTP. He didn't have many options but tried to make the best of it. The DOJ lawsuit in Rhode Island would impact him directly.

With an interim plan in place, by 2014 Rhode Island had agreed to a permanent, more detailed, ten-year consent decree that would revamp and update the disability and employment systems, with a focus on younger adults still in special education as well as those workers in sheltered work-shops, like Steven, who had been telling staff they wanted to work in the community. Instead of 130 people, the newly reached agreement would cover more than 3,000. In part, the settlement was reached after the DOJ performed a deeper investigation. The Rhode Island case rested squarely on the ADA, and the Supreme Court *Olmstead* decision in 1999. It was hoped, since the state was small and the officials and provider agencies knew one another well, that it, like Oregon, could be used as a laboratory to show the way forward in fundamentally improving a series of systems that were broken. Rhode Island was not somehow more neglectful than other states; bringing lawsuits rooted in civil rights has always been about timing, place, and the possibility of creating precedent. The road ahead for Rhode Island would be a winding one; at least five state administrators tasked with overseeing the human-service agencies' adherence to the settlement were leaving in short order.

When the permanent consent decree was signed, a young student named Michael Coyne was receiving special-education services in Rhode Island. His mother and father had always had high expectations for him, but while they loved him dearly, they also set obtainable goals, from Michael's doing his fair share of chores to learning new skills at school. The DOJ case in Rhode Island would coincide closely with Michael's transition from high school to adulthood, but it wasn't clear whether the systems charged with changing and overhauling their funding, purpose, and outcomes would be able to do so quickly enough to address Michael's needs.

By the start of 2016, Oregon too had negotiated and agreed with the DOJ lawyers regarding the primary claims of the lawsuit. That case would be influenced by the Rhode Island case, including a focus on young students with disabilities who would most likely have been entered into the sheltered-workshop and subminimum-wage systems. Oregon would assist just over 1,100 people in sheltered workshops find jobs by 2023 and would focus on almost 5,000 students, helping them to bypass the old systems and assumptions of productivity and receive supported-employment services to obtain real jobs in the community, jobs of their choosing, that did not focus on their weaknesses, but rather the tasks they were good at, could be taught, and had an interest in learning, as students without disabilities were treated.

The budget figures varied from what Oregon believed were the funds sent along to the sheltered-workshop systems in the state, but on the long-term care side of the equation, meaning Medicaid waiver funds and the much smaller amount of state funds, the DOJ determined that Oregon spent roughly $30 million dollars annually segregating approximately 2,300 people, workers with intellectual or developmental disabilities, estimated in the amended class-action complaint to mean that Oregon was funding sheltered workshops with close to $2.5 million dollars a month.

One of the most puzzling parts of the disability industrial complex is accounting and outcomes. For the eight named plaintiffs the average time spent in a sheltered workshop amounted to fifteen years. During that time Oregon officials were funding both rehabilitative interventions as well as habilitative interventions. "Rehabilitative" means returning a person to their previous skills and functioning, and "habilitative" means the recipients of the service intervention are being taught new daily living skills, things that will help them live more functionally. But inside the disability industrial complex, it can mean simply plopping people down in front of an ancient VHS player to watch the same videos over and over. There should be an outcome associated with the billions of dollars being spent, and only recently did CMS begin guiding states to more fully steward the funds they bill for. There is a debate about the length of time that someone can be in prevocational services. For years provider agencies kept people in these prevocational services (which can mean anything from soft-skill development to resume writing) without even thinking about when, where, and how the vocational outcome occurs. Imagine if you were going to a physical therapist after a torn ligament, and that professional never indicated when you'd reach your rehabilitated state but instead informed you that the average rehabilitation took fifteen years. That was the plight of the plaintiffs—a lack of response to their desire to leave subminimum wages for a community job even though the provider agency had billed a decade and a half of rehabilitative and habilitative services.

In 1988 in Oregon, 50 percent of the 2,300 people served in the Medicaid waiver program were receiving supported-employment services, but by 2010 only 7 percent of those 2,300 were receiving individualized supported-employment services.[1] Oregon had once had robust employment numbers, which had declined. It returned to sheltered workshops and subminimum wages beginning in the 2000s, even as the state wrote its own white paper about the regression in 2005, adopted an "Employment First" policy in 2008, and received funding under the Medicaid infrastructure grant in 2009 to systematically remove barriers to real employment for beneficiaries. Oregon officials, like others in the country, were trying but losing to stagnant services, uninspired leadership, and a congregated and segregated approach to employment and work activity services.[2]

While the state was equivocating a young woman named Sparkle Green found herself in a sheltered workshop in Beaverton, Oregon. Though she remained connected to her mother, she tried to find some independence and lived in an adult foster-care home in the same town. Sparkle had attended special-education classes where she did some work at a food bank, and without many alternatives, she entered the sheltered workshop in 2009. As the DOJ investigators reviewed the billing documents and Sparkle's performance, they found details that are repeated thousands of times across the country. She was eligible to receive supports to work for at least minimum wage in the community but was still unnecessarily segregated in the sheltered workshop. Of the many times I've taken a business owner to visit a sheltered workshop, one stands out. This owner was interested in hiring people with disabilities. As we walked around and I introduced him to people I knew, he grew increasingly irritated, his facial expression a mixture of confusion and concern. As we watched people packaging surgical gown kits, he was exasperated, "All of these workers could be employed at my place or others I know of. Why are they here?"

Sparkle's records showed that she was engaged in similar bagging and packaging tasks. The sheltered workshops have traditionally gravitated toward contracts of this type because it is easy to quote rates, find prevailing wage data, and, they contend, the tasks can be used to accurately determine one's productivity level. Sparkle's attendance records were nearly spotless for over a year, no small feat even for adults her age without disabilities, working for the first time. In August 2011 Sparkle earned only $26.59 for almost sixty hours of work— about fifty cents an hour. Her rate went down further in September, to thirty-nine cents per hour; in October it went down another ten cents, to twenty-nine cents per hour. The trade groups and CEOs of the sheltered-workshop programs and the defenders of maintaining the legality of section 14(c) would argue that Sparkle could work more and increase her productivity, but she chooses not to. They are being funded by taxpayers to support Sparkle in rehabilitating or habilitating her skills, but it appears that the more the intervention, the worse Sparkle's performance becomes, a phenomenon I have observed many times. When workers inside a sheltered workshop were referred to the employment services I ran to help secure and support those workers in real jobs in the community, the referral almost always arrived on my desk with a chart. Inside, I would see the same kind of reports that the DOJ reviewed on Sparkle. Time and time again, the individual seemed to start out productively, then their work worsened, and their supposed productivity was impacted. Qualitatively, the charts often included statements of "easily distracted" or "won't stay on task." This is a standard that applies largely to workers with disabilities inside the sheltered workshops and not in other places of work. There are dozens of situations where a person's chart contained diminishing productivity assumptions while he was performing boring, repetitive work with little to show for it in a paycheck, but that same person earning minimum wage or above performed satisfactorily in jobs in the community, where fair wages gave him more interest and where having coworkers for social contact provided a more stimulating work environment. If the job match was a very good one, those same workers who had been labeled either "unemployable" or who had labels of poor attention span and distractedness could excel. Inside the disability industrial complex boring tasks that anyone would dislike after more than an hour are often used to predict a person's future employment success. Add to that the strange "readiness" precursors that workers with disabilities must demonstrate to prove they can work outside the constraints of subminimum wages, and the disability industrial complex can keep its hooks in one for virtually a lifetime, as we saw with Leo in Gallup, New Mexico.

The Oregon lawsuit was aimed at transforming the entire state system and the tens of millions of dollars spent on employment and disability so that Sparkle, her seven coplaintiffs, and others similarly situated could find work outside the sheltered workshops. It took the DOJ presence, more than half a dozen lawyers, and years of litigation against the governor and his administration to make that happen. If it could not get the eight plaintiffs jobs, could the action truly change the entire disability industrial complex in Oregon for the thousands of others similarly situated?[3]

Michael Coyne was in ninth grade when the Rhode Island lawsuit began. For most parents, the state and its political and budgetary inner workings are not at the top of their list of concerns, but those who have children with disabilities do not have that luxury. What a state does and does not do—such as expand Medicaid waiver access so kids can get services in the home rather than a facility, or increase teacher pay and provide more aides—has a direct impact on their children. Sheila Coyne and her husband have military backgrounds, and Sheila worked as a correctional guard in one of Rhode Island's prisons. They are smart, tough, hardworking people, even homesteading on a small farm outside South Providence. They take work and community contribution seriously, and they made sure that Michael received not only the necessary special-education supports, but they also advocated that Michael work for part of his school days. Michael is tall and thoughtful. When he goes some place, he always makes sure he brings along a gift. At a meeting I attended, Michael brought the entire group barbecue sandwiches from one of the many famous eateries in Rhode Island. Still, as the lawsuit began to take hold in the state, even with an emphasis on improving special-education services, Michael was left with very few options.

Sheila Coyne reflected on her son's experience: "We were really proud of Michael working in the community during his high school years. Since it was part of his educational plan, the students didn't get paid, but he was learning skills, building confidence, and learning what he could do, what he liked and what he needed help with."

For the last thirty years or so, after the Individuals with Disabilities Education Act (IDEA) was reauthorized and improved, there has been a debate on how best to help youth make the transition from the school setting to employment and adult life. IDEA makes available a free appropriate public education to eligible children with disabilities throughout the nation and ensures special education and related services to those children. Prior to IDEA local school systems could simply say, "We don't educate children with disabilities," a refrain you will hear if you talk to parents of an adult child over forty. IDEA and the corresponding Office for Civil Rights at the US Department of Education have afforded and reaffirmed the rights of children with disabilities and their families, but special education is also part of a bureaucratic system that often struggles to innovate. The answer is not more private or religiously based charter schools.[4]

As Employment First initiatives and the class-action lawsuits in Oregon and Rhode Island began to influence policy making, many started looking at the special-education practices provided to Michael and hundreds of thousands of students with disabilities. Low expectations drive the values framework of the disability industrial complex, and that can be seen in the way that students with disabilities are afforded employment experience during their high school years. Essentially, there are two very different paths that American youth travel when it comes to making the transition from a school setting to work and adulthood. Youth without disabilities are expected to work and to pursue vocational or college degrees. From a very early age those expectations can be seen in everything a child engages in, from daycare experiences to chores, first jobs, summer work, and classroom learning. For youth with disabilities, those same expectations are watered down and often nonexistent in educational settings. Many special-education programs have significantly altered their curricula to include employment-related activities, but those are often rife with the same failings of the disability industrial complex. As an example, the National Technical Assistance Center on Transition, funded by the US Department of Education's Office of Special Education Programs (OSEP) and the Rehabilitation Services Administration highlights as an evidence-based practice (EBP) cleaning a toilet. The EBP is referenced as: "**Response Prompts to teach cleaning a bathroom**: Student is taught how to clean a bathroom mirror, sink, and toilet using a cassette player to provide an auditory prompt system with a fading component to teach the task analysis for each skill."[5] I can't think of any example in my own child's educational path, or any friend or family member whose child without a disability was taught in a school setting how to clean a toilet, and yet here it is referenced as an EBP.

Many special education programs rely on the school setting as the primary location for learning job skills, so students with disabilities are often tapped to do cafeteria cleaning, locker room duty, and other janitorial services. Administrators and teachers who believe such tasks are appropriate to teach job skills to students with disabilities argue that most youth in America have first jobs in fast food and that is what they are doing with students with disabilities. But having all students with disabilities doing such tasks reinforces stereotypes, forgoes the individualization of the student's IEP, and furthers the insidious assumption of low expectations. One student in California found it appalling that her classmates with disabilities were picking up trash and wearing vests while students without disabilities did not perform the same work.[6] In Arizona in 2018, a mother reported that her daughter was spending four of her six school periods in "job training" in the cafeteria.[7] All over the country this is a problem. "They call it food, flowers and filth. Those are the programs for people with intellectual disabilities," says Ron Hager, senior staff attorney for the National Disability Rights Network. "They (special education administrators in Arizona) should be embarrassed that they're doing this. It's supposed to be based on the individual student's needs, preferences and interests."[8] And that's exactly why the DOJ focused so much on how the city of Providence and the state of Rhode Island operated their "pipeline from special education to sheltered workshops."

Michael Coyne was luckier than most; though unpaid, he worked at several community jobs in and around Providence during his last years in high school. He performed the typical cleaning and food service work, but at least it wasn't on the school grounds, and he received support and feedback that helped him mature and gain new interpersonal skills. "He really blossomed on the job sites," said his mother. "I think it helped him understand teamwork and getting things done." She and her husband were happy that his IEP included a focus on work, and they felt supported by the teachers and the para-pros who helped Michael on the job. The Coynes appreciated the employers and businesses that had cared enough to participate in the school work program. However, they were soon disappointed. "We just thought it would be a matter of filling out an application and helping Michael apply for a permanent job." But it didn't work out that way; since employers can obtain free labor from special-education programs, they essentially have a new crop of free help each semester. The employers that Michael worked for during school hours wouldn't hire him. "We were just kind of stunned," said Sheila. The Coynes were just starting to learn how difficult navigating the space between special-education services and the transition into the adult-services arena could be. The disability industrial complex looms large, often blocks out individualization, and can even create more supposed problems which then need to be remedied. The Coynes, like so many other families, were in for a tough lesson and an eye-opening revelation.

As the cases in Oregon and Rhode Island moved forward, each with appointed court monitors who were required to regularly provide DOJ with updates related to progress with systems overhaul and the conditions of the plaintiffs' working lives, Congress was trying to once again address the issue of subminimum wages. Senator Harkin's efforts, after the appalling conditions of Henry's Turkey Service were brought to light, to reinstitute a "minimum, subminimum wage floor" had been effectively curtailed by lobbyists. In 2011, when a bipartisan bill was introduced called Fair Wages for Workers with Disabilities, the large provider agencies, along with more trade groups like ACCSES, shot down that effort too. Most legal advocates believed that the class-action lawsuits in Oregon and Rhode Island would make the difference this time, however, and along with groups like the National Federation of the Blind, they upped their political pressure in 2013 and 2014. A special committee was formed to advise on phasing out the use of section 14(c) exploitive wages. The reauthorization of the Workforce Investment Act of 1998 was to be the conduit, but its replacement had already been passed. The first meeting of the special committee, the Advisory Committee on Increasing Competitive Integrated Employment for Individuals with Disabilities (ACICIEID), was held on January 22–23, 2015, but as Serena Lowe, the woman who had led the Collaboration to Promote Self-Determination, told me, "The timelines weren't in sync. By the time the advisory committee started meeting, the legislation was nearing implementation." That legislation was the Workforce Innovation and Opportunity Act (WIOA), which was signed into law by President Obama in July 2014, with Title IV of WIOA amending the Rehabilitation Act of 1973, which authorizes funding for vocational rehabilitation services for individuals with disabilities. The Advisory Committee included some familiar names, some of whom had fought for decades to eliminate subminimum wages, but some of the most powerful subminimum-wage proponent agencies were on the committee too, notably Goodwill. In all, the secretary of labor appointed eighteen members, some with disabilities, but the committee lacked a significant membership of workers with labels of intellectual disability, the group of workers that section 14(c) impacts the most. Essentially the ACICIEID deliberations centered around intent and implementation of WIOA, since it had already been signed into law and would be implemented in 2016. Some excellent recommendations were made in the final report, but WIOA hadn't abolished section 14(c). Section 511 of WIOA went as far as it could politically, according to two anonymous sources. "The trade groups used all their power and the advocates pushed back hard too. In the end, all we could get into WIOA was restrictions on the use of subminimum wages. It was heartbreaking."

The Obama administration and Congress were seeing changes in their ability to get bills passed as the political cycles tightened and the focus was on keeping the economy in rebound mode from the housing and banking crises. Both parties had highly contested primaries in 2016, and some advocates saw the issue of subminimum wages as having been sufficiently addressed. If they were disappointed in the outcome of section 511, they hoped it was a start. In the end, the restrictions on subminimum wages that followed were reiterated by USDOL's Wage and Hour Division as late as 2019 in "Fact Sheet #39H," a fitting bureaucratic nomenclature for exploitation. In the following text, SMW stands for "subminimum wages."

Workers Age 24 or Younger Hired After July 22, 2016: Section 511 prohibits section 14(c) certificate-holders from hiring and paying SMWs to any individual with a disability who is 24 years of age or younger, unless the employer has reviewed, verified, and maintained documentation that the youth has completed three requirements:

1) Transition services under the Individuals with Disabilities Act (IDEA) and/or pre-employment transition services under section 113 of the Rehab Act;
2) Vocational rehabilitation (VR), as follows: a) The youth applied for VR services and was found ineligible OR b) The youth applied for VR services and was found eligible AND i.) had an individualized plan for employment (IPE) AND ii.) worked toward an IPE employment outcome for a reasonable period without success AND iii.) the VR case was closed; and
3) Career counseling, including information and referrals to Federal and State programs and other resources in the employer's geographic area.

The Designated State Unit (DSU), typically the vocational rehabilitation (VR) agency in the state, is required to provide individuals with documentation of services provided. The fact sheet explains:

All Workers, Regardless of Age, Who Are Employed at a Subminimum Wage

Section 511 also prohibits section 14(c) certificate-holders from continuing to pay SMWs to any individual with a disability, regardless of age, unless the DSU provides him or her with career counseling, information, and referrals ("career counseling") every six months during the first year of employment, and annually thereafter. An employer may refer employees to the DSU for this mandatory counseling, or the employer may choose to contact the DSU and inform that agency of the need for counseling. The employer must verify completion of this requirement and review any relevant documents that an employee may provide as a condition of paying SMWs to that employee. In addition, the employer must provide information about self-advocacy, self-determination, and peer mentoring training opportunities ("training opportunities") available in its local area to each employee every six months during the first year of employment, and annually thereafter. The training opportunities may be provided under applicable Federal or State programs or other sources but must not be provided by an entity that has any financial interest in the individual's employment outcome, including any entity that holds a section 14(c) certificate.[9]

By 2017 workers with disabilities had had two DOJ class-action lawsuits underway for almost four years, together with the restrictions that WIOA had put on the use of subminimum wages. Like most major systemic overhauls, however, there was a significant gap between the intent of the law and the way states and their agencies would implement the changes. There still remained the unresolved issue of nonprofit agencies being both employer and service provider to workers with disabilities. In the restrictions on section 14(c), the term "employer" is used exclusively, but that doesn't resolve the issue. Let's consider one of the most significant requirements: "In addition, the employer must provide information about self-advocacy, self-determination, and peer mentoring training opportunities ('training opportunities') available in its local area to each employee every six months during the first year of employment, and annually thereafter."

Here is where the labor union is once again an operable overlay to examine the statement above. Imagine if your employer, who is paying you much less than other employers in your area, were given the role of referring you to, say, the local labor union, or simply to workers being paid much better than you. What priority would your employer give that expectation? Would they be the most logical entity to take on that role? What if in your local area there was no such entity to refer you to? It's also important here to once again visit the lingo and strangeness associated with the phrasing. Do you think of yourself as having self-advocates in your life, or spend time pondering if you're being self-determined? What about feeling like you are peer mentored? Terms like "self-advocacy," "self-determination," and "peer mentoring" are powerful concepts and values; they can be operationalized, but few outside the field of disability services would be able to decipher their meaning. Even with the best intentions, the requirements are cloaked in human-service language, and the roles are clouded by loosely defined expectations. There now exist some constraints on the use of subminimum wages, but they can still legally be paid by jumping through some hoops. Some states have taken the counseling more seriously than others, using third-party advisors to help workers with disabilities understand their rights as related to section 511, but others are doing the bare minimum. Professionals in some states roll their eyes at the restrictions; one agency leader told me the feds are always dreaming up new ways of trying to interfere. One mother was simply told her son needed to go to a sheltered workshop. Reminiscent of the congressional hearings of forty years ago when workers with disabilities earning subminimum wages could appeal their case to the secretary of labor, these remedies seem to be unrealistic.

Steve Porcelli told me in an interview about his memories regarding the sheltered workshop he had been attending in Rhode Island for thirty years. One day while playing cards with his friends, agents in FBI windbreakers entered the facility and locked it down. "I guess I knew it would happen someday." Steven had been working on the contract work that paid subminimum wages, mostly putting earrings on cardboard backing and refurbishing remote controls. "It was boring, and the pay wasn't very good. I had friends there and we're all working jobs on the outside now."

Steve was assisted in finding a job in the community that fit his skill sets. Advanced Business Solutions hired him part-time. "The pay is much, much better. I stay in touch with friends and have made some new ones." Steve had been asking for help in finding a job "on the outside," a phrase that lots of workers with disabilities who've been segregated and exploited inside sheltered workshops use to define the difference. Steve Porcelli is an example. Did the decades on subminimum wages prepare him for a real job with real wages, and did that process culminate just at the time the FBI and state officials shut the place down? Or could the powerful tools of job coaching, customized-job development, and the underlying Blatt principle that all human beings can learn and be trained have been used at any time during Steven's work history? The tools and evidence-based practices have been available for decades, but those inside the disability industrial complex built their core functions of budgeting, programmatic design, and lobbying efforts around congregated settings, where a mass of people could be "trained" or "employed." When both, the administrators and CEOs of these programs can continue to muddy the waters, to call for more oversight from USDOL as a remedy, to insist that their practices are based in self-determination and the peculiar labor right they have invoked as "protecting a continuum of employment options."

By 2016, the year the restrictions under WIOA were to be implemented, the DOJ lawsuits had taken a toll on the number of section 14(c) certificates held by nonprofit agencies. There was evidence of a downward trend in the overall number of workers being paid subminimum wages, but those figures continued to be a point of contention. A USDOL Wage and Hour spreadsheet listed 2,413 special subminimum-wage certificates active in the United States. The list included some of the names that continue to propagate the notion that Anil Lewis calls "insidious benevolence." The phrase "opportunity" in the names of these organizations appears hundreds of times, as in the Work Opportunity Center in Agawam, Massachusetts. Some of the names confuse the role of employer with that of rehabilitation, as in Westlake Enterprises in Weyerhaeuser, Wisconsin, and the Wheeling Area Training Center for the Handicapped in Wheeling, West Virginia. Many of the programs try to sound as if they are a business and use "industries" in their names. Easter Seals and Goodwill pop up regularly in their local forms. The historical connection to religious charity houses is prevalent too, with sheltered workshop names that include phrases like Golden Rule, Good Shepherd, Genesis, and Gentle Brook. Some are inexplicable, as in Ragtime Industries, Rainbow of Challenges and Rhea of Sunshine. Others are clearly not only employers and rehabilitation providers, but they also control an individual's living situation, as in Res-Care, Resident Home Association, and Reliant Living Centers. Some are small, local agencies while others are multistate operations and have budgets in the millions of dollars. Alexandria Opportunities Center in Minnesota has almost 14,000 workers earning subminimum wages while hundreds of organizations have just fifteen to twenty workers. The average in 2016 was around 100 workers with disabilities being paid under the 14(c) subminimum-wage certificate holders. The total number of workers being paid subminimum wages was 241, 265 according to the spreadsheet. And we know from the Oregon, Rhode Island, and Iowa cases that many of these workers had been toiling away for paltry wages for decades. I have met a mother whose son was paid subminimum wages for over forty years. He had passed away, and she told me how he had always wanted to work outside the walls of the sheltered workshop, but she feared he would not be able to hold down a regular job with equal pay. She wondered this aloud, and I could feel her pain for the loss of her son and the anxiety about the decisions she had helped him make. He could have certainly worked in a job in the community, and it was the organization's responsibility to help her and her son take the risk; they were the ones receiving the funding for his supports, rehabilitation, and skill development. The organization had done them a grave disservice.

One of the sheltered workshops holding 14(c) certificates in 2016 was a bland sounding nonprofit named UCO Industries, in Marysville, Ohio. UCO listed seventy-seven workers with disabilities being paid subminimum wages. One of the contracts UCO held was with an automotive company named Honda. One of the seventy-seven workers was a man named Mr. Denoewer who had been labeled as an adult individual with intellectual and developmental disabilities who was autistic, nonverbal, and epileptic. From July 2008 to December 2015, Mr. Denoewer held the job at UCO of production associate. He was paid a subminimum wage by UCO—as little as $1.38 per hour after taxes—for the entire time that he worked there.[10]

More than ever before, the Wage and Hour Division at the USDOL was increasing its oversight of the section 14(c) subminimum-wage program, even listing some applications as pending, which had been a rarity in the past. A flood of stories made their way into the mainstream media, as more and more journalists became aware of the practices of subminimum wages. The boycotts of Goodwill had helped, but now real data seemed to be making its way around the internet. For many people it was shocking that as we moved nearer the beginning of the second decade of the twenty-first century so many people with disabilities were impacted by the practice. At the DOJ, Regina Kline, a young attorney with a sharp sense of fairness, learned in 2011 that workers with disabilities could be legally paid far below the norm, and she was incensed. She had been hired at Vanita Gupta's DOJ, who was appointed by President Obama. The Department of Justice then was led by strong, determined women, with backgrounds in civil rights and a penchant for fighting the good fight. Kline was under the tutelage of Eve Hill, who had joined the DOJ after serving at the Burton Blatt Institute at Syracuse University, where she had learned in 2008 that it was legal to pay workers with disabilities pennies per hour. All the threads from the past, including Blatt's legacy, the *Olmstead* decision, the hard work to get disability rights recognized as civil rights, and the historical failings of the section 14(c) program seemed to be aligned. However, by the fall of 2016 the country had chosen a reality TV star as its new leader, and everything, including the issue of subminimum wages, was an unknown. Trump advocated for bringing back mental hospitals and spent airtime talking about his and his family's great genetics, two points of view that frightened advocates and harkened back to the days of eugenics.[11]

Regina Kline understood that even the DOJ had a shortened memory, and if she were not around to keep up the momentum that she, Vanita Gupta, and Eve Hill had begun, at least there should be a guiding report on the status of the cases in Oregon and Rhode Island and their impact on state agencies of Medicaid and vocational rehabilitation. She wrote a "Statement of the Department of Justice on the Application of the Integration Mandate of Title II of the Americans with Disabilities Act and *Olmstead v. L.C.* to State and Local Governments' Employment Service Systems for Individuals with Disabilities." Like Robert Canino and Sue Gant in the Iowa Henry's Turkey Service case; Sue Jamieson, Lois Curtis, and Elaine Wilson in *Olmstead*, and Anil Lewis, Rose Sloan, Marc Maurer, and Mark Riccobonno at the National Federation of the Blind, the DOJ women understood that change within massive systems is fragile and reliant upon precedent, both legal and communal. An entire page of Kline's report was dedicated to the issue of section 14(c) and employment services for workers with disabilities. For the first time, there was a resource that advocates, workers, family members, administrators, and state agency personnel could utilize to make better decisions. The document was disseminated widely, and it was extremely helpful in my own work with state and local provider agencies. There is a strange force within the disability industrial complex when one speaks about forthcoming changes. It is common to hear naysayers comment, "The feds have been saying that for years and nothing's happened yet." The sentiment also shows up with leaders of provider agencies but directed at their respective state systems. That makes it more difficult to get leaders, whether legislative, appointed, or leading local disability employment programs, to take change seriously. The guidance Kline had written for the DOJ website had weight, and behind her words stood the lawsuits that were still playing out.

Thus it was disappointing when Attorney General Jeff Sessions removed the guidance that Regina Kline had written, along with many other disability- and employment-related resources, from the federal website. It was as if President Trump had not only mocked people with disabilities by disrespectfully imitating a reporter with cerebral palsy, but the administration was signaling that it didn't care enough about the strides that had been made in the fight against subminimum wages to keep a resource active on the nation's top law enforcement agency's website. The date was December 10, 2017. Defiant, and already at a private law firm in Washington, DC, Regina Kline and Eve Hill posted the guidance on the website of their new employer, Brown, Goldstein & Levy. Even in the spring of 2017, they had been devising a plan to keep the momentum up, after leaving the DOJ for private practice. In October of 2017, Kline and Hill kept their promises to workers with disabilities without a voice, launching Inclusivity Strategic Consulting, with the tagline: "Inclusivity is the first of its kind to offer supply chain analysis to help companies divest from suppliers that exploit workers with disabilities."

Focusing on the supply chains that have kept sheltered workshops and subminimum wages alive and thriving, Kline and Hill were taking on something only they could do. Many advocates over the years had talked about the economic inequalities in the practices of section 14(c), such as the Goodwill boycotts highlighting the pay of its staff compared to that of workers with disabilities, but few had dared to think about going after the companies that benefited from subcontracts with sheltered workshops. Kline and Hill were clear. "Many companies have taken steps to ensure their supply chains are free of child labor, unfair wages, or human trafficking, but most have yet to find a way to identify whether their suppliers are exploiting people with disabilities," said Kline, who had previously served as senior counsel in the Office of the Assistant Attorney General for Civil Rights. "Our experience at DOJ gives us a unique insight into the opportunities and challenges organizations face when it comes to building a workplace that works for everyone."[12]

One of the most frustrating parts of the saga of the exploitation of workers with disabilities is how difficult it can be for people outside the disability industrial complex to determine whether an entity is a friend or foe. Names alone cannot provide the clues regarding allies. Over the last decade, I have encountered advocates I believed felt the same way I did about the need to abolish subminimum wages, only to find out they had reservations, usually articulated in phrases of caution. "I believe in incrementalism. We've got to make change slowly." Of course, the glacial speed of this approach has already taken more than eighty years.

A common comment is, "If we shame the companies that contract with sheltered workshops, they won't want to really hire people with disabilities." Another defies logic: "I don't think we should be focused on the salaries of the leaders in nonprofit agencies, it's distasteful." To those who hold these points of view, apparently the notion of paying workers with disabilities pennies an hour isn't distasteful.

With their mission clearly defined, Regina Kline and Eve Hill would take on the case of Mr. Denoewer and help him challenge the nonprofit that had paid him subminimum wages, as well as Honda, a massive international company that has spent almost a quarter of a century on the global Fortune 500 list.

12

OHIO AND THE FUTURE OF
SUBMINIMUM WAGES

By 1998 Nike's manufacture of sports clothing and equipment was fully global. Founder Phil Knight had always intended to outsource the work to areas of the world where labor was cheaper, but he didn't intend to act unethically. However, as information became available much faster through the internet, stories about working conditions in some of the factories that sewed Nike products came to light. In 1996 *Life Magazine* ran a story about the iconic brand that forced Knight to act. The image of a child stitching footballs with the Nike logo emblazoned on the side produced an instant outcry, with reporters using phrases like "sweatshop" and "child labor" in their coverage of the story. At first, the company denied any wrongdoing, then stated that the photo was staged, and after more pressure from the public, insisted the contractor had not followed protocols. Images of the Nike logo were circulated, with the "swoosh" used as the "v" in the word slavery.

Knight decided to act boldly and take responsibility. During a press conference he said, "The Nike product has become synonymous with slave wages, forced overtime and arbitrary abuse."[1] The company released the locations of the factories they had used, vowed to provide detailed audits and release their progress on improving safety, and immediately eliminate any contractor found using child labor. New watchdog groups popped up, like NikeWatch and an initiative called the Clean Clothes Campaign. But by 2006 a contractor in Pakistan had broken Nike's rules and sent out soccer balls to be worked on at home. Soon the image was everywhere: an adolescent boy in a squat, surrounded by Nike soccer balls, his head bowed, as he concentrated on hand sewing a section of a ball, a concrete wall with graffiti behind him. Nike pulled the business at the cost of $100 million dollars and led the world in demanding ethical practices. The company was admired for its commitment to fair employment practices, safety, and sustainability. Other companies with similar manufacturing agreements in the Middle East and elsewhere were forced to follow Nike's lead. The combination of social media and a new generation of shoppers with a sincere interest in the way the products they used were made created an awareness that permeated companies around the world. It was clear that consumers did not want to be associated with brands that acted irresponsibly, at least when it concerned child labor.

Over the years of operating sheltered workshops, the disability industrial complex grew ever more eager to land contracts associated with high-profile companies, believing that if they could put a prominent brand on their marketing brochures, they could interest other companies to also outsource some of their packaging and assembly tasks. At conferences there were sessions that claimed to help sheltered-workshop leaders learn how to engage with businesses; marketing and sales techniques became part of the new lingo. Board members were recruited to help "get a foot in the door" at companies in the community who had not yet participated in supplying work. Before long the strategy worked, and recognizable companies, large and small, began sending their work to the local sheltered workshops, even as other parts of the system were trying to get those same companies to hire workers with disabilities on their payroll, to do jobs on site for real pay rather than inside the sheltered workshop for subminimum wages. While trying to find employment for workers, I would often be told by someone in human resources that they preferred to send their work to the sheltered-workshop programs. Most of the time, that HR person had no idea that the tasks were being performed for subminimum wages; when I told them so, they had various reactions, from wanting to understand more fully to simply stating that they left those pay details to the sheltered workshop. One part of the system was advocating for businesses to hire workers with disabilities directly, while the other was telling them that they needn't worry, that all would be fine if only more companies provided work to the sheltered workshops. Rarely did the nonprofits inform businesses that they had a choice in the matter. In that way, those nonprofits inside the massive disability industrial complex failed their responsibility as sound stewards of taxpayer funding.

UCO Industries sounds like a small company in a modern light-industrial park. In 2017, UCO in Marysville, Ohio, had seventy-seven workers working for subminimum wages. UCO was not much different from the thousands of other sheltered workshops in the United States; in fact, it was about a third smaller than the average nonprofit using a section 14(c) certificate. On its website, UCO states, "An employer of over 130 associates, UCO Industries, Inc. has been an active member of the Union County business community for over 40 years. We exist and love to share our mission because of our wonderful and amazing employees. They are why we're in business. It is because of their dedication and spirit that we love coming to work each day."[2] Not a bad mission statement—with its history, concern, and passion for its employees. UCO doesn't use the word "client," or "patient," or any other of the terms the disability industrial complex likes to switch up, including the vague "individual," the food-chain-sounding "consumer," and the strange buddy-ism, "our guys." UCO says it's an employer, that it has over a hundred employees. Nowhere does UCO state that it pays subminimum wages. You might think it was just a local business specializing in document handling and shredding, but above the large photo of the expansive building is a tab that reads, "Employment and Support for Individuals with Developmental Disabilities." That link has photos that appear to highlight UCO as a healthcare provider, pictures of people using walkers and wheelchairs against a backdrop that looks like the hallway of an urgent-care facility. The duality of these programs causes confusion, not just with respect to outsiders but also with the leadership, board, and staff. Are we getting people jobs, training workers, rehabilitating patients, or billing different sources to do a little bit of each? Adding to the confusion, UCO decided to perform "reverse integration" of the sheltered-workshop operations.

The faulty thinking is that if nondisabled workers labored alongside workers with disabilities, the mandates around inclusion, pay, and opportunity for advancement would simply be overlooked. This is what Henry's Turkey Service did as well. In the regulatory change called for by the Centers for Medicare and Medicaid (CMS) for people with disabilities under the Home- and Community-Based services waiver regarding settings, CMS requires states to ensure that the funds are used in integrated, regular environments instead of segregated "disability-specific" settings. In this case, UCO was attempting to fulfill its obligations to one of its newest and most prestigious customers, Honda, while still operating as a "community rehabilitation provider."

On December 14, 2017, Mr. Denoewer through his attorneys, Regina Kline and Dr. Marc Maurer, who had been executive director at the National Federation of the Blind and who supported the Goodwill boycotts, filed a complaint in the United States District Court for the Southeastern District of Ohio. Tamara Basil was denoted his "next friend," a legal term for someone who acts on behalf of another, since Denoewer was considered nonverbal. The complaint pleaded Denoewer's subminimum wages (as low as $1.38 per hour after taxes) and his disability labels: autism, nonverbal, and epileptic. The attorneys explained that UCO had gone from being only a sheltered workshop to having employees with and without disabilities so that the employees of UCO were both subminimum-wage earners and above-minimum-wage earners. Some of the areas inside the building had nicknames, not uncommon, but unlike other businesses those nicknames also delineated workers with and without disabilities. There were the "tables" where Mr. Denoewer worked, unpacking the separate components of what would be assembled as the complete Honda owner's manual; the separate items consisted of plastic sleeves, covers, and bound paper documents. It was boring work, at piece rate, which according to court documents ranged from $1.38 an hour but never up to minimum wage. Like Sparkle Green and many others in sheltered workshops, Denoewer's initial productivity was higher but fell off as the years went by. Why? Most of us paid piece rate for repetitive tasks not of our choosing would steadily decline in output. If our pay were set not as an hourly wage at or above the minimum, our income would suffer. However, inside the disability industrial complex, this common human tendency to resist performing tedious tasks is not viewed the same way;

rather, it's taken as a sign of the worker's deficits. Since the nonprofit can also bill federal and state programs for "interventions to fix these problems," they make money off the worker either way.

Denoewer was not provided the opportunity to move from the "tables" to other areas of UCO operations that were more profitable to the worker. UCO ran a shredding operation called "File 13" and other Honda-focused work that was referred to as the "line. These jobs were not offered to Denoewer even though Tamara Basil, as his advocate, had filled out surveys from UCO in 2014 asking that Denoewer's tasks be varied so that he might have an opportunity to learn and grow. That's what taxpayers in Ohio are funding UCO to do—to support and assist with advancement; the funds aren't earmarked for maintaining the productivity level of a worker with a disability but rather to "train, teach, and rehabilitate" the worker. The funds from Medicaid and vocational rehabilitation are supposed to be used to support someone in attaining new skills and abilities. But UCO represents the worst of the confusions inside the disability industrial complex when it comes to mixing purposes, pay, and profit: a nonprofit that receives taxpayer funds to pursue a mission, supporting people with disabilities; that same organization has a mixture of subminimum-wage earners and minimum-wage earners, competing with similar for-profit private companies that would also like a subcontract with Honda but can't get it because the lowest wage in any shop lowers the wages of all. This type of amalgamation is what the advocates for abolishing subminimum wages warned Congress about decade after decade. Add to this identity maelstrom the fact that UCO as a community rehabilitation provider is mandated to carry out the ADA, *Olmstead*, and the Rehabilitation Act as amended. Instead, the board, leadership, and local funders are apparently unaware of the laws meant to guide their fundamental existence. The fact that the nondisabled workers brought into a rehabilitation facility are then given preferential treatment in terms of jobs and training violates the fundamental trust that taxpayers put in the nonprofits that receive local, state, and federal funding.

Such a configuration is not new. From my entrance into the disability industrial complex, organizations have tried to muddy the waters when the challenges they are presented with are deemed too difficult. Our funding systems and laws require adherence to the basic belief that Burton Blatt articulated nearly sixty years earlier; that is, people with the labels of intellectual and developmental disabilities can learn, can be productive. The organizations that receive the financial benefits of that belief refuse to embrace it, or only slightly, opting instead to focus on people with "mild disabilities" as in the SourceAmerica operations, where the billions they receive in funding are not used to support those workers connected to their original name: the National Industries for the Severely Handicapped.

Citing precedent from the United States Court of Appeals for the Sixth Circuit, Denoewer's lawyers contended, "The thesis of the ADA is simply this: That people with disabilities ought to be judged on the basis of their abilities; they should not be judged nor discriminated against based on unfounded fear, prejudice, ignorance, or mythologies; people ought to be judged on relevant evidence and the abilities they have."[3]

As a culture we have reinforced outdated, ignorant views of people with disabilities. While some of that is changing, biases remain within the disability industrial complex. Court documents reveal that some UCO workers with disabilities reportedly made as little as fourteen cents an hour.[4]

Paragraph 33 in the First Amended Complaint in *Denoewer v. UCO Industries and Honda of America* alleges that the two entities "relegated Plaintiff to lower-paid, less fulfilling, and dull work, and Defendants acted in conscious disregard of his statutory rights in a way that was highly probable to cause substantial harm." That's what's so wrong with the disability industrial complex in America: it knows it causes harm; it is fully aware of its responsibilities to workers with disabilities and taxpayers, but it chooses to act on interventions that are unproven and nonbeneficial to their primary stakeholders and to hide behind that insidious benevolence that Anil Lewis talked about at the beginning of this book.

To read the *Denoewer* complaint is akin to diving into a primer on the disability industrial complex, revealing the inherent issues that persist. One might conclude that UCO advised Honda with faulty information, without a proper knowledge of evidence-based supports, that UCO created the configuration Denoewer was subjected to, and that Honda therefore is the recipient of bad advice from an entity that is supposed to be aware of laws, interventions, and practices at the intersection of disability, employment, and training. UCO did not assess Mr. Denoewer's individual skill and abilities to determine whether he could advance in pay, be assigned new tasks, or needed reasonable accommodations to do so. In some instances workers without disabilities were placed in positions instead of workers with disabilities in order to meet the demands of Honda's contract. Although state and federal funding is not for the benefit of Fortune 500 companies, but rather workers with disabilities, even as late as 2017 several states proposed in their state plans to CMS that they would use "reverse integration" to address the settings rule aimed at ensuring that people receiving home- and community-based services under a Medicaid waiver have full access to integrated employment in the community. In February of 2018, Honda moved the court to be dismissed from the case, arguing that it had no connection to the plaintiff other than contracting with UCO. The motion was granted, the judge ruling that "Honda has no connection to Plaintiff. Honda simply contracted with UCO as a supplier." Nevertheless the internationally recognized Honda name had helped shed light on the issue of subminimum wages and provided an opportunity to get the attention of policy makers who had been slow to react.

A year later, in December 2018, Kline and Maurer took the next step in the fight to highlight how corporate supply chains were the beneficiaries of the cheap labor derived from section 14(c) subminimum wages. They found other examples of abuses in Ohio. Roppe Corporation, a manufacturer of rubber and vinyl-flooring products, based in Fostoria, Ohio, had been working with its local sheltered workshop since the middle 1980s. Roppe's annual sales in 2017 were almost $73 million. The provider agency, Seneca RE-AD Industries, located in Tiffin, Ohio, had 178 people working for subminimum wages in 2018. It had held a section 14(c) USDOL certificate for decades. Seneca RE-AD chose to leverage its subminimum-wages capabilities and partner closely with Roppe, essentially running its sampling division. Seneca invested its time and efforts as a community rehabilitation provider in focusing on the operation of Roppe's samples division, the first examples of new flooring products their worldwide customers saw. The complaint alleged: "Seneca does not perform work for any other business beside Roppe." Thus, Seneca didn't have an array of tasks that workers could try; if one didn't like manufacturing, he was out of luck. Who is the primary customer here? Roppe? People with disabilities? It seems clear that the mission of Seneca wasn't about providing services to support workers in vocational rehabilitation, but rather the one corporate entity.

The three plaintiffs were all employed in the sampling division at Roppe and alleged that they were segregated from other employees without disabilities; they were paid less; and they were denied the same benefits and privileges of their nondisabled peers. The legal basis of the litigation was Title I of the ADA and several Ohio state statutes. Besides Roppe and Seneca, plaintiffs' lawyers named the funder, the Seneca County Board of Developmental Disabilities, as a defendant. Ohio's system for delivering services and supports to people with intellectual and developmental disabilities is centered in county boards, which essentially coordinate, oversee, and distribute funding to the community rehabilitation providers, among others, in the county. As late as 2016, the Seneca County Board was still using the phrase "mental retardation" in its name on the USDOL 14(c) spreadsheet. Over the last decade advocates have worked diligently to rid systems of this demeaning term, and its use is a barometer of an entity's awareness of current practices. The Seneca County Board essentially helped to recruit workers who would end up at Roppe.

The two cases in Ohio will impact not only the plaintiffs but workers with disabilities in general. The violation of the ADA and *Olmstead* in the context of corporate supply chains will echo across the country. Although both cases are still pending and the final outcome unknown, the practices of low pay and discriminatory practices initiated and funded by the very agencies that are supposed to put workers with disabilities first are no longer cloaked in mystery. They further demonstrate the lack of a consistent set of national policies.

The Rhode Island consent decree expires in 2024. To date, the state has worked to promote employment for people who have not had an opportunity to work outside the segregated, sheltered system. Using state dollars, BHDDH has seeded agencies to use best-practice supports. The special education-to-sheltered-workshop pipeline could be said to have been inactivated. Signed in 2014, the consent decree stipulations were essentially stalled for two years, prompting a federal judge to threaten to hold the state in contempt if it didn't act swiftly and with increased focus on making sure the benchmarks were accomplished. By the end of 2019, roughly 860 people had been supported in real jobs in the community earning minimum wage or above, but nearly 1400 additional workers with disabilities were still waiting for services. The state monitors employment data by three categories: youth exit from special education, prior sheltered-workshop worker, and day program attendee. The total number of people with disabilities covered under the DOJ consent decree is 2,225, with 857 employed, or 38 percent. The state's last official sheltered workshop closed in 2018. The state has invested in a process known as Person Centered Supported Employment Performance Program in order to continue to support a transformation of the state's employment services. In March of 2020, the Rhode Island House of Representatives introduced a bill to repeal subminimum wages. House Majority Leader K. Joseph Shekarchi stated, "Disabled individuals are entitled to the same rights, protections and dignity as all Rhode Islanders. Of course, they should be protected by our minimum wage laws. While I'm relieved that state day programs for the disabled stopped engaging in this practice a few years ago, there's no excuse for any law that allows anyone to take advantage of disabled people and pay them less than other workers. We must repeal this law to ensure that no one abuses disabled Rhode Islanders in this way ever again."[5]

Oregon's DOJ consent decree expires in December 2022. In October of 2020, the last sheltered workshop in the state closed, and subminimum wages will be phased out by 2023. Of the eight named plaintiffs, most have had opportunities to work in jobs outside the subminimum-wage setting, but their experiences, which include the typical grocery store and fast-food jobs, make clear that more needs to be done to support workers with disabilities in accessing career pathways, with opportunities for advancement, pay raises, and on-the-job-learning.

At the US Department of Labor, audits of 14(c) certificate holders were increased, with the Wage and Hour Division (WHD) ramping up its oversight. The agency completed 193 subminimum-wage investigations in fiscal year 2017–2018 and ordered the payment of nearly $2 million in back wages to employees. Reports of the number of workers with disabilities still being paid subminimum wages are conflicting. The National Disability Rights Network stated in 2017 that there were half a million people on 14(c) certificates; APSE often gives a figure of approximately 100,000. In the National Council on Disability's report to the Trump administration in October of 2018, the number of workers under 14(c) was also not clear, with a range of 141,081 workers to 321,131.[6] While there has surely been a decrease in the WHD figures, there is no clear evidence that the workers who have left sheltered workshops are working in real jobs in the community. According to data submitted by the states, the number of people in facility-based work (subminimum wage) has decreased but the number of people in facility-based nonwork has increased.[7] This means that those workers who had been earning subminimum wages have not left for jobs in their communities but rather have simply been moved into a day program setting where they may continue to work on prevocational tasks or spend time on supposed daily living skill building or other "habilitation" activities. This is the shell game played inside the disability industrial complex. Held to account, community rehabilitation providers did not shift their focus to supporting workers with disabilities in community jobs, but simply moved people to services inside a building, where more billing can be done under different codes. Anecdotally, I have seen this in action: agencies talk openly about shifting services to more facility-based nonwork activities in light of changes in their state to prioritize employment in the community. Participation in facility-based nonwork has grown steadily for states that report it as a service, from 18.7 percent in fiscal year 1999 to more than 40 percent in fiscal year 2017.[8] Instead of work, people are spending time in day rooms participating in "activities." From the National Disability Employment Policy report comes a staggering statement: "There is a limited amount of data on the structure, activities, and outcomes of facility-based non-work services, and states have not established clear service expectations or quality assurance strategies." One hears the echoes from the congressional hearings on subminimum wages over the decades: data is lacking, there is no proof that the interventions produce outcomes, and the quality of the services are in question, but the disability industrial complex represents billions of dollars each year in taxpayer funding. If the trend continues, those community rehabilitation providers who were reluctant to give up subminimum wages will be able to adjust their business models not to reflect real work for real pay, but with the primary focus on continuing to bill with no clear outcome in sight.

From 2017 onward, the focus on section 14(c) produced more USDOL-WHD audits, and the Rhode Island case, especially the focus on the "special education to sheltered workshop" issue, brought more attention to the use of subminimum wages outside the community rehabilitation provider system. Known innocuously as the school work experience program (SWEP) at the federal level, USDOL-WHD issues 14(c) certificates to school systems so that students can legally be paid subminimum wages. These certificates and the use of subminimum wages in special education have declined but remain legal in contradiction to the *Olmstead* decision and WIOA regulations. In Sonoma, California, for instance, there were nearly 1,750 students with disabilities being paid subminimum wages in 2018, the highest number in the country.

Perhaps one of the strangest circumstances of section 14(c) subminimum-wage certificates is a USDOL category termed the business establishment list (BEL). These are private employers in local communities who are legally permitted to pay workers with disabilities subminimum wages, sometimes for the same jobs performed by workers without disabilities who earn minimum wage or above. When FLSA was passed in 1938, this category envisioned veterans returning from war who had worked in manufacturing and because of a service-related disability, needed a modified job to return to. According to the report of the National Council on Disability sent to the Trump administration in October 2018, the USDOL had very little information about this category: "WHD could not identify or report its enforcements efforts of the BEL, and so the public currently has no way of knowing whether WHD has conducted oversight audits with the private businesses participating in the program." This is an astonishing admission, given that the workers would most certainly qualify for reasonable accommodations under the ADA, which could include the use of customized employment supports codified in the law via the Workforce Innovation and Opportunity Act of 2014. One business on the BEL list, Riverview Productions in Wellston, Ohio, submitted documentation to the USDOL stating that they paid workers with disabilities as little as twenty-five cents per hour for work that involved assembly tasks that were being done by workers without disabilities for $8.15 an hour.[9]

As long as the use of subminimum wages remains legal pursuant to section 14(c), exploitation and abuse will follow, and the possibility remains that we will find out much later about abuse, as in the case of Henry's Turkey Service. One bright spot from the last five years is the fact that the Goodwill boycotts, the DOJ cases, and private litigation have increased the general public's awareness of and interest in what happens inside the disability industrial complex. It doesn't take much research to find examples of 14(c) being at best misapplied, and at worst used as a mechanism for unscrupulous behavior.

Maine had been at the forefront of forgoing subminimum wages, with early adopters like Gail Fanjoy choosing to lead her organization, KFI, in the direction of community employment; the state's other nonprofit agencies had followed. Over two decades Maine was pushing its funding systems toward Employment First. By 2017 there was only one organization left with an active 14(c) certificate—Skills Inc., a nonprofit based in St. Albans. A sawmill for all practical purposes, like many of the organizations that pay subminimum wages, the entity also housed people with disabilities, billing Medicaid and the state of Maine for both vocational and residential services, with total revenue in 2015 of almost $14 million dollars. Reminiscent of the big-name nonprofits in the stark difference between the pay of workers with disabilities and the CEO's, Skills seemed to have embraced the practice. Some of the workers with disabilities made $2.14 an hour, lifting heavy wood planks, sorting, sawing, and moving thousands of pounds of lumber each day, while two administrators were paid nearly $3.5 million over seven years, with bonuses. In one year alone, the organization paid one manager $570,000, all approved by a board of directors. As far back as 2001, Skills had nearly seventy-five violations related to the Fair Labor Standards Act. Based on a Wage and Hour report from the USDOL, there were 77,855 subminimum-wage violations across the country from 1997 through 2016, requiring employers to pay their workers with disabilities about $16.5 million in back wages.[10] Sixty-one of those violations occurred at Goodwill facilities. However, the abuses are widespread, and in many of the cases, the nonprofits that purport to support workers to "achieve their greatest potential" remain in business.

In the Randolph County Sheltered Workshop in West Virginia, workers with disabilities spent their days assembling and packing fishing lures for Leland's Lures in Arkansas. While Randolph County Sheltered Workshop had previously obtained a legal section 14(c) certificate authorizing the provider agency to pay subminimum wages, it had lapsed, and in late 2017 and early 2018, the agency was audited. In the past this had not been much of an issue; over the last three decades there has been an informal approach to making sure the paperwork is in line, resulting in laxity in performing correct time studies, making certain productivity is measured per each worker rather than as a team, and permitting an overall laissez-faire approach on the part of USDOL-WHD and the community rehabilitation providers paying subminimum wages. This attitude was evident not just in the Congressional Hearings, but in relation to viewing these issues with the same sense of urgency we see elsewhere in labor, law, pay, and worker's rights. It seemed, since this financial configuration had to do with workers with disabilities—and more specifically "clients" with intellectual disabilities—it just wasn't necessary in the eyes of policy makers, enforcement personnel, and leaders at provider agencies to get too concerned about the details.

The Wage and Hour Division at the USDOL, however, was trying to ramp up oversight considering the effective efforts from the NFB and other advocacy organizations in getting section 14(c) on the journalists' radar. Tips started to arrive, and concerned citizens and family members began to inquire about the practices of the sheltered workshops in their communities. Randolph County Sheltered Workshop in West Virginia was ordered by the US district court to pay $119,040 in back wages to thirty-four employees. Through an analysis of payroll data, the investigation found that the organization had violated the minimum-wage provisions of the Fair Labor Standards Act (FLSA) and failed to post and make available in alternative formats the rights that workers with disabilities have under the law, especially the procedures for filing a complaint if the worker feels her pay is not correct.

In Lowndes County, Georgia, USDOL investigators found that the sheltered workshop run by Lowndes Advocacy Resource Center (LARC), a nonprofit, had underpaid 130 workers with disabilities by $160,000 in 2018 and 2019. Most ordinary citizens would think the organization's name would imply it did the opposite of exploiting people and that's precisely how the assistant director responded to the media. "It was a 1,600-page document. We missed one sentence. Yes, we take responsibility for missing that sentence," said Steve Jaramillo, the assistant director, trying to make it sound as if all would be fine if it not for the cumbersome feds and their bureaucratic red tape.[11]

In the spring of 2018, USDOL-WHD found violations serious enough to revoke the section 14(c) certificates from Rock River Valley Self Help Enterprises, Inc., a community rehabilitation provider in Chicago. According to the press release on the USDOL's website, the violations were significant, persistent, and even involved obstruction. "The WHD investigation revealed a failure to timely perform appropriate wage surveys and failure to conduct proper time studies on all jobs performed by workers with disabilities. The investigation also revealed that the employer attempted to mislead and obstruct WHD's investigation by concealing relevant information from WHD during the investigation, hiding work that the employer had not time studied but had the workers perform. On some weekends, Self Help unlawfully paid workers with gift cards instead of wages."[12] This is painful to read even in brief. Perhaps it's the ridiculous name, or the fact that leaders in a nonprofit believed it was fine to provide trivial payment through gift cards, or the fact that USDOL states clearly that NONE of the time studies were conducted properly on ALL the jobs performed by workers with disabilities, but it is disheartening that this type of brazenness inside the disability industrial complex persists despite all the warnings, hearings, news stories, and legislative committees that have occurred. These cases highlight the fallacy of one of the claims that trade groups and large provider agencies make regarding section14(c), that more oversight will correct the inherent problems. After eighty-two years the field still cannot perform its rudimentary tasks of properly documenting wage and hour studies, proving that the practice of using subminimum wages in supposed vocational rehabilitation is rotten at the roots, is fundamentally bad public policy that will only continue to permit more exploitation under the guise of self-help, as in the widespread violations in Chicago. Rock River Valley Self Help Enterprises was ordered to pay back wages up to at least $7.25 an hour for all workers dating back two years, totaling $575,000.

In October 2018 USDOL's investigators found that ninety-two workers at a sheltered workshop in Selma, North Carolina, had not only been paid incorrectly ($52,000 in back pay), but youth with disabilities under the age of twenty-four had also not been provided services under the Workforce Innovation and Opportunity Act. Under WIOA, the youth should have had opportunities for regular training and employment supports rather than simply being put into work for subminimum wages. Johnson County Industries violated both the FLSA of 1938 and the WIOA of 2014.

In 2019 USDOL investigations in Montgomery, Alabama, found that the local Arc had violated workers' rights by deducting thirty minutes each day for breaks whether the worker took the break or not. The larger portion of the case, though, found that workers at two of the Arc's ancillary sites, the Hanan Center and the McInnis Recycling Center, were not provided the mandated services under WIOA regarding learning about options other than subminimum wages. The press release from USDOL states in part, "Individuals with disabilities receive career counseling, information and referral services from the state vocational rehabilitation agency and information about local opportunities for self-advocacy, self-determination and peer-mentoring training from the employer each year while working at subminimum wages under the FLSA's Section 14(c). WHD found Hanan Center and McInnis Recycling Center failed to ensure workers were provided these services during subminimum wage employment. Investigators also determined the employers failed to conduct a prevailing wage survey and to adjust wage rates annually, as required." The subminimum-wage worker with disabilities is entitled to counseling about jobs outside the sheltered workshop by the very entity (the employer) who benefits the most by not providing the worker with employment options for minimum wages and above, a significant flaw in the regulations. These are the most recent stories reported by USDOL and reflect only a fraction of the oversight audits performed under section 14(c).

Even when not pressured by USDOL Wage and Hour investigations, the disability industrial complex reacts to oversight in some predictable ways. In July of 2019, in response to the state's increase in minimum wages, Sharon Durbin, CEO of the Land of Lincoln Goodwill told dozens of employees with disabilities that they would no longer receive paychecks due to the Illinois legislation on livable wages. Durbin made an annual salary in 2018 of $164,000 plus a bonus of $6,000.[13] The wage law in Illinois was set to increase the state minimum wage gradually through 2025. Durbin and Goodwill tried an old trick of the disability industrial complex, claiming that the state vocational rehabilitation program only pays for part of their thrift-store employees. Most of the successful human-service nonprofits don't rely on only one or two funding sources; they find foundations, donors, and grants to make up the mix of the operating budget. Every year, in every state capital, budgets are passed related to workers with disabilities and employment supports; and the standard approach for trade groups and community rehabilitation providers is to plead that they are not sufficiently funded by the state.

By the fall of 2019, advocates for the abolishment of section 14(c) had managed to get hearings before the US Commission on Civil Rights (USCCR) in Washington. Those hearings focused on the same issues that have been addressed in countless other settings, from Congress to national and state self-advocacy groups. There were references to the Oregon and Rhode Island lawsuits and what had been learned about transforming state systems away from segregated and exploitative sheltered workshops and toward jobs in the community for at least minimum wages. The USCCR hearings created another step forward, however, one that would live on, presided over and documented by one of the country's most focused federal entities concerned with fair and equal opportunities for all Americans. The commissioners at the USCCR spent the next ten months engaged in research, site visits, and a review of stakeholder public comments with the hope of issuing a report on 14(c) by the fall of 2020.

Sometimes, the financial abuse of subminimum wages and segregated settings is linked to other types of mistreatment. In September 2020, during the same week that the USCCR issued its full report with recommendations, a sheltered-workshop director in Bartow County, Georgia, was arrested on forty counts of felony theft by taking, plus two counts of exploitation and intimidation of adults with disabilities. Misty Dawn Baynard directed the program at Good Shepherd Foundation that also paid workers subminimum wages. Just a year earlier, the organization had received $750,000 to renovate its buildings from the county's community development block grant administration.

In 2018 NPR launched a multiday exposé on the rampant rate of sexual assault on people with intellectual disabilities, calling it "the sexual assault epidemic no one talks about."[14] Several brave men and women came forward to tell their stories. James Meadours, a self-advocate who exudes dignity and unwavering commitment to honesty, shared his story, including sexual abuse and mistreatment while living in a group home. Meadours also spoke about being paid fifty cents an hour in a sheltered workshop. People with intellectual disabilities, who represent the largest number of workers being paid subminimum wages, are sexually abused at seven times the rate of people without disabilities.[15] Being segregated in a sheltered workshop or work activity center puts people with disabilities at risk for exploitive wages, as well as other forms of abuse, verbal, sexual, and physical.[16]

On September 17, 2020, just a few days before the director of the Good Shepherd Foundation was arrested, the US Commission on Civil Rights released its report "Subminimum Wages: Impacts on the Civil Rights of People with Disabilities." It called for the repeal of section 14(c), albeit once again "a planned phase-out." Harkening back to the work of Dr. Paul Wehman at Virginia Commonwealth University, the commission also suggested ramping up funding to supported-employment programs. There were the familiar nods to "more oversight" during the phaseout and more stringent reporting, very much as had been heard during the numerous congressional hearings over the decades. But there was also a recommendation to "increase enforcement of the Olmstead integration mandate to determine whether state systems are inappropriately relying on providers using 14(c) certificates to provide non-integrated employment in violation of Olmstead."[17] Overall, the commission stated, the practice of subminimum wages is inconsistent with the civil-rights protections to which people with disabilities are entitled. "The Commission today calls for the end of the Section 14(c) program, because it continues to limit people with disabilities from realizing their full potential," said commission chair Catherine E. Lhamon. "In addition, the program suffers from wildly insufficient federal oversight and civil rights review, and apparently routine noncompliance, begging the question why we as a nation continue its operation."[18]

The USCCR report made national, mainstream news, with pieces on NPR and elsewhere. In January 2019 a bill was passed in the House to address the issue. The Transformation to Competitive Employment Act (H.R. 873) mandates that states, service providers, and subminimum-wage certificate holders transform their business models to help workers with disabilities transition into competitive, integrated employment. Another bill, known as the Raise the Wage Act (H.R. 582), also addressed subminimum wages.

A handful of states have already banned subminimum wages for workers with disabilities; these include Vermont, New Hampshire, Maine, Alaska, Oregon, and others (by 2023). Other states have tried to address the issue by ceasing the entry of new workers with disabilities into sheltered workshops or have passed state legislation with a focus on employment in the local economies at minimum wage or above. In the United States in 2022, however, it will still be legal to pay workers with disabilities pennies on the hour and enshrine the practice in shades of goodwill, altruism, charity, and best practices, all while billing state and federal funding sources for billions of dollars a year.

If the phaseout occurs through 2027 following the recommendations of the US Commission on Civil Rights, or if either of the two House resolutions reaches the Senate for a vote, subminimum wages for people with disabilities pursuant to section 14(c) will have been the law of the land for ninety years. It will have taken us nearly half a century from the exposure of the abuses at Henry's Turkey Service in 1979 to abolish the law that encouraged the abuse. More insidious, we have allowed large trade groups to lobby Congress; we have permitted multinational community rehabilitation providers to design the funding they receive; and we have turned away when these entities have repeatedly abused the very constituents they claim to fight for. It has been difficult for me to admit to myself that I'm part of the American disability industrial complex. We are all part of the disability industrial complex. Our tax dollars go to its machinations and prop up the false assumptions and discriminatory practices invoked in our names.

It is entirely likely, though not a foregone conclusion, that subminimum wages will be wholly abolished by at least 2030, an important, long overdue step in reconciling what we tell ourselves about how we care for people with disabilities and the kind of public policy we make. But industrial complexes do not just go away; they find other ways to make sure the funding keeps flowing. In addition to the recommendations from the US Commission on Civil Rights, let's add a caveat. If you represent or work for an organization that has spent time and money advocating to keep workers with disabilities earning pennies per hour, you have forfeited your right to help fix the issue. You and your organization, board members, staffers, lobbyists, and highly paid CEOs don't deserve a seat at the table. Fill those spots with people with lived experience, with those who have had to endure ridicule, mistreatment, and abuse. Unfortunately, there are hundreds of thousands of American citizens who can fulfill those descriptions. Self-determination and informed choice belong to people, not organizations. The story of subminimum wages for Americans with disabilities is one whose painful consequences must not be forgotten. The disability industrial complex has shown us who they are; we should believe them.[19]

NOTES

Preface

1. US Equal Employment Opportunity Commission, "EEOC Sues Comfort Suites for Disability Discrimination" (Washington, DC, 2010), https://www.eeoc.gov/newsroom/eeoc-sues-comfort-suites-disability-discrimination.

2. Parke Rouse, "Workhouses in Virginia: Certainly a Poor State to Be In," *Daily Press*, February 19, 1989, https://www.dailypress.com/news/dp-xpm-19890219-1989-02-19-8902190007-story.html.

3. National Federation of the Blind, "Anil Lewis," https://www.nfb.org/about-us/national-headquarters/executive-directors/anil-lewis.

1. The Stage Is Set for Broken Promises

1. Cheryl Bates-Harris. "Segregated and Exploited: The Failure of the Disability Service System to Provide Quality Work," *Journal of Vocational Rehabilitation* 36, no. 1 (2012): 39–64, https://doi.org/10.3233/JVR-2012-0581.

2. US Equal Employment Opportunity Commission, "Jury Awards $240 Million for Long-Term Abuse of Workers with Intellectual Disabilities" (Washington, DC, 2013), https://www.eeoc.gov/newsroom/jury-awards-240-million-long-term-abuse-workers-intellectual-disabilities.

3. Ibid.

4. Ibid.

5. National Federation of the Blind, "National Federation of the Blind Urges Boycott of Goodwill Industries," June 7, 2012, https://www.nfb.org/about-us/press-room/national-federation-blind-urges-boycott-goodwill-industries.

6. National Federation of the Blind, "A Source of America's Discrimination against Workers with Disabilities," video, September 23, 2014, https://www.youtube.com/watch?v=IyLLzM5Bmkc.

7. There are numerous names for the organizations that are funded to provide employment services for people with disabilities. I use "agency," "sheltered workshop," "nonprofit," "work activity center," and "community rehabilitation provider" interchangeably because those terms are used interchangeably inside the disability industrial complex. Each of these descriptors can hold a 14(c) subminimum-wage certificate and can legally pay subminimum wages.

8. Alice Minium, "The Dark Reality Behind America's Greatest Thrift Store Empire: How a Saturday Night Internet Wormhole Effectively Ruined My Favorite Store," Medium, April 22, 2018, https://medium.com/@aliceminium/the-dark-reality-behind-americas-greatest-thrift-store-empire-183967087a1e.

9. Fair Wages for Workers with Disabilities Act of 2013, H.R. 831, 113th Cong. (2013).

10. Next Steps New Hampshire, "Work Early, Work Often: Parents/Caregivers of Young Adults with Disabilities," video, March 2016, https://nextsteps-nh.org/video/work-early-work-often-parents/.

11. Tom Cotton, "Cotton Statement on Sheltered Workshops That Serve Arkansans with Developmental Disabilities," April 6, 2018, https://www.cotton.senate.gov/?p=press_release&id=920.

12. Wikileaks, "Wikileaks—The Sourceamerica Tapes," November 16, 2015, https://wikileaks.org/sourceamerica-tapes/.

13. Karin Allison, "Time Study Information" (National Institute on Severe Handicaps, 2016), https://silo.tips/download/time-study-information-introduction.

14. US Government Accountability Office, "Employing People with Blindness or Severe Disabilities: Enhanced Oversight of the AbilityOne Program Needed," GAO-13-457 (Washington, DC, 2013), https://www.gao.gov/assets/660/654946.pdf.

2. From Evil Intentions to Unintended Consequences

1. United States Holocaust Memorial Museum, "The Murder of the Handicapped," https://encyclopedia.ushmm.org/content/en/article/the-murder-of-the-handicapped.

2. Nathan Nelson, *Workshops for the Handicapped in The United States: An Historical and Developmental Perspective* (New York, NY: Thomas Publishing, 1971).

3. Steven J. Taylor and Steven D. Blatt, eds., *In Search of the Promised Land: The Collected Papers of Burton Blatt* (Washington, DC: American Association of Mental Retardation, 1999).

4. Wolf Wolfensberger, "Normalization," https://www.wolfwolfensberger.com/life-s-work/normalization.

3. Subminimum Wages and Disability Rights

1. SRVS, "History," https://www.srvs.org/history.

2. William G. Whitaker, *Treatment of Workers with Disabilities Under Section 14(c) of the Fair Labor Standards Act*, RL30674 (US Library of Congress, Congressional Research Service, February 2005).

3. Ibid.

4. Ibid.

5. *Wyatt v. Stickney*, 325 F.Supp. 781 (M.D. Ala. 1971).

6. Global Macro Monitor, "Manufacturing Employment in the U.S.," April 30, 2012, https://global-macro-monitor.com/2012/04/30/manufacturing-employment-in-the-u-s/.

7. American Presidency Project, "Department of Labor Nomination of Xavier M. Vela to Be Administrator of the Wage and Hour Division," May 23, 1977, https://www.presidency.ucsb.edu/documents/department-labor-nomination-xavier-m-vela-be-administrator-the-wage-and-hour-division.

8. Whitaker.

4. The Floor Is Gone and Modern Lobbying Arrives

1. MODAPTS: The Language of Work, "Welcome to International MODAPTS Association," https://modapts.org/.

2. *Southeastern Community College v. Davis*, 442 U.S. 397 (1979), https://supreme.justia.com/cases/federal/us/442/397/.

3. Whitaker.

4. Ibid.

5. Ibid.

6. National Federation of the Blind, "History," https://www.nfb.org/about-us/history-and-governance.

7. *Cleburne v. Cleburne Living Ctr.*, 473 U.S. 432 (1985), https://supreme.justia.com/cases/federal/us/473/432/.

8. College of Workers' Compensation Lawyers, "Donald Elisburg," http://www.cwclawyers.org/html/donald_elisburg.html.

9. Whitaker.

10. Ibid.

11. Ibid.

12. Ibid.

5. The *Olmstead* Supreme Court Decision and Freedom Fighters

1. Joanne Finnegan, "Survey Finds More Than 9 in 10 People Say Doctors Are the Most Trusted Professionals," Fierce Healthcare, 2019, https://www.fiercehealthcare.com/practices/survey-finds-over-9-10-people-say-doctors-are-most-trusted-professionals.

2. *Bayh v. Sonnenburg*, 573 N.E.2d 398 (1991).

3. *Bayh v. Sonnenburg*, Case Brief Summary, May 3, 2013, http://www.casebriefsummary.com/bayh-v-sonnenburg/.

4. Robin Nelson, "Unlocked: The Lois Curtis Story," Robin Rayne: A Southern Photojournalist's Notebook, November 27, 2010, https://assignmentatlanta.wordpress.com/2010/11/27/unlocked-the-lois-curtis-story/2010.

5. Robert Evert Cimera, Lauren Avellone, and Carol Feldman-Sparber, "An Investigation of the Outcomes Achieved by Individuals with Intellectual Disabilities and Mental Illnesses," *Journal of Vocational Rehabilitation* 43, no. 2 (2015): 129–135, https://doi.org/10.3233/jvr-150762.

6. Sue Burrell, "Trauma and the Environment of Care in Juvenile Institutions," National Center for Child Traumatic Stress, 2013, https://www.nctsn.org/resources/trauma-and-environment-care-juvenile-institutions#:~:text=This%20brief%2C%20written%20by%20Sue,best%20practices%20and%20support%20for.

7. Derrick Henry, "Elaine Wilson," *Atlanta Journal Constitution*, 2004, https://www.legacy.com/obituaries/atlanta/obituary.aspx?n=elaine-wilson&pid=2907375.

8. John Elflein, "Mental Health Treatment Facilities by Setting of Services in the U.S. 2019," Statista, August 2020, https://www.statista.com/statistics/450277/mental-health-facilities-in-the-us-by-service-type/.

9. Ibid.

10. K. Charlie Lakin et al., "Factors Associated with Expenditures for Medicaid Home and Community Based Services (HCBS) and Intermediate Care Facilities for Persons with Mental Retardation (ICF/MR) Services for Persons with Intellectual and Developmental Disabilities," *Intellectual and Developmental Disabilities* 46, no. 3 (2008): 200–214, https://doi.org/10.1352/2008.46:200-214.

11. US Department of Justice, "Special Litigation Section," 2020, https://www.justice.gov/crt/special-litigation-section.

12. Olmstead Rights, "Sue Jamieson's Story Continued," https://www.olmsteadrights.org/iamolmstead/history/item.5402-Sue_Jamiesons_Story_Continued.

13. *Olmstead v. L. C.*, 527 U.S. 581 (1999).

14. Ibid.

15. Ibid.

16. For an interesting examination of these issues, see Mary C. Cerreto, "Olmstead: The Brown v. Board of Education for Disability Rights—Promises, Limits, and Issues," *Loyola Journal of Public Interest Law* 3, no. 1 (Fall 2001): 47–78.

17. Henry, "Elaine Wilson."

18. Olmstead Rights, "Sue Jamieson's Story Continued."

19. Vicki Gaylord et al., eds, *Impact: Feature Issue on the ADA and People with Intellectual, Developmental, and Other Disabilities* 28, no. 1, Institute on Community Integration (UCEDD) and the Research and Training Center on Community Living, College of Education and Human Development, University of Minnesota, Winter 2015.

20. Henry, "Elaine Wilson."

21. Olmstead Rights, "I Am Olmstead," https://www.olmsteadrights.org/iamolmstead/.

6. Early Adopters and Tearing Down Assumptions

1. Context in segregated programs, whether in the institution or sheltered workshop, is often not considered. More often, the person who is "having behaviors" is simply viewed through the lens of the deleterious conduct that needs to be ameliorated rather than those actions being seen and interpreted as the communication of a need.

2. Several YouTube videos show Gold speaking and using the "Try Another Way" approach with people considered "profoundly" intellectually disabled.

3. Rehabilitation Act Amendments of 1986, S. 2515, 99th Cong. (1986).

4. Rehabilitation Act Amendments of 1992, Pub. L. No. 102–569, 102nd Cong. (1992).

5. Known simply by policy makers as the "DD Act," the legislation in its first iteration in 1963 focused on the scientific understanding of DD (which includes the labels of intellectual disability, autism, cerebral palsy, and brain injuries prior to age twenty-one). The DD Act has been amended several times, most fundamentally in the Developmental Disabilities Assistance and Bill of Rights Act of 2000, Pub. L. No. 106–402, 106th Cong. (2000).

6. Administration for Community Living, "The Developmental Disabilities Assistance and Bill of Rights Act of 2000," 2017, https://acl.gov/about-acl/authorizing-statutes/developmental-disabilities-assistance-and-bill-rights-act-2000.

7. An interviewee was granted anonymity, if requested.

8. National Council on Disability, "National Disability Employment Policy, From the New Deal to the Real Deal: Joining the Industries of the Future" (Washington, DC, 2018), https://ncd.gov/sites/default/files/Documents/NCD_Deal_Report_508.pdf.

9. Ibid.

10. P. Rogan, M. Held, and S. Rinne, "Organizational Change from Sheltered to Integrated Employment for Adults with Disabilities," in *Supported Employment in Business: Expanding the Capacity of Workers with Disabilities*, edited by P. Wehman (St. Augustine, FL: TRN, 2001).

11. Gordon C. Shen and Lonnie R. Snowden, "Institutionalization of Deinstitutionalization: A Cross-National Analysis of Mental Health System Reform," *International Journal of Mental Health Systems* 8, no. 1 (2014), https://doi.org/10.1186/1752-4458-8-47.

7. Federal Policy as Catalyst, Barrier, and Duality

1. Internal Revenue Service, "Work Opportunity Tax Credit," https://www.irs.gov/businesses/small-businesses-self-employed/work-opportunity-tax-credit.

2. Lila MacLellan, "German Attitudes about Disability Disclosure Are Shaped by a Nazi Past," Quartz at Work, 2017, https://qz.com/work/1110806/german-attitudes-about-disability-disclosure-in-the-workplace-are-shaped-by-a-nazi-past/.

N3. Corada, "Department of Labor, Office of Disability Employment Policy (ODEP)," https://www.corada.com/links/department-of-labor-office-of-disability-employment-policy-odep.

4. Ibid.

5. Ibid.

6. PACER, "Video Series: Work Early, Work Often," 2015, https://www.pacer.org/transition/video/series.asp?se=40.

7. Angela Montgomery, "How to Overcome Resistance to Change—A Systemic Approach," Intelligent Management, June 17, 2020, https://www.intelligentmanagement.ws/how-to-overcome-resistance-to-change/.

8. *Making A Difference Magazine*, Fall 2005, https://gcdd.org/archived-making-a-difference-magazine/2367-making-a-difference-magazine-fall-2005.html.

9. Tod Citron et al., "A Revolution in the Employment Process of Individuals with Disabilities: Customized Employment as the Catalyst for System Change," *Journal of Vocational Rehabilitation* 28, no. 3 (2008): 169–179.

10. Gov Info, "Federal Register," https://www.govinfo.gov/app/collection/FR.

11. For examples, see "Customized Employment Makes Dreams Come True," *Making a Difference*, Summer 2004, 18–21, http://dlg.galileo.usg.edu/ggpd/docs/2004/ga/g630_pd4/p1/m3/summer/2004/elec_p_btext.con/1.pdf.

12. Cary Griffin, David Hammis, and Tammara Geary, *The Job Developer's Handbook*, 1st ed. (Baltimore, MD: Paul H. Brookes, 2007).

13. Samantha Crane, "New CMS Regulation on HCBS Settings: Implications for Employment Services," (LEAD Center, June 25, 2014), http://leadcenter.org/webinars/new-cms-regulation-hcbs-settings-implications-employment-services.

14. Chai R. Feldblum, Dexter Brooks, Aaron Konopasky, and Jennifer Sheehy, "Federal Government as a Model Employer: Understanding Changes to Section 501 of the Rehabilitation Act" (EARN, January 23, 2017), https://askearn.org/event/federal-government-as-a-model-employer-understanding-changes-to-section-501-of-the-rehabilitation-act/.

15. Mustafa Karakus, William Frey, Howard Goldman, Suzanne Fields, and Robert Drake, *Federal Financing of Supported Employment and Customized Employment for People with Mental Illnesses: Final Report* (US Department of Health and Human Services, February 2011), https://aspe.hhs.gov/system/files/pdf/76216/supempFR.pdf.

16. Jean Winsor et al., "StateData: The National Report on Employment Services and Outcomes through 2016" (Boston: Institute for Community Inclusion (UCEDD) University of Massachusetts, 2018), https://www.statedata.info/sites/statedata.info/files/files/statedata2018_web_F.pdf.

17. Ibid.

8. The Nightmare in Atalissa

1. David Weil, "Field Assistance Bulletin No. 2015–1" (Washington, DC: US Department of Labor, Wage & Hour Division, 2015).
2. UCLA Labor Center, "The Bracero Program," https://www.labor.ucla.edu/what-we-do/research-tools/the-bracero-program/.
3. Dan Barry, *The Boys in The Bunkhouse* (New York: Harper Perennial, 2017).
4. Sue Gant, Final Expert Report on Equal Employment Opportunity Commission v. Hill Country Farms, Inc., d/b/a Henry's Turkey Service (Gant, Yackel and Associates, 2013).
5. Shantha Rau Barriga, "We Need to Stop Treating People with Disabilities as Less Than Human," *Guardian*, June 20, 2016, https://www.theguardian.com/global-development-professionals-network/2016/jun/20/we-need-to-stop-treating-people-with-disabilities-as-less-than-human.
6. Raymond Lemay, "Social Role Valorization and the Principle of Normalization as Guides for Social Contexts and Human Services for People at Risk of Societal Devaluation," in *Encyclopedia of Disability and Rehabilitation*, ed. Arthur E. Dell Orto and Robert P. Marinelli (New York: Simon & Schuster Macmillan, 1995), 515–521.
7. *New York Times*, "Broken Trust: A Cycle of Abuse", in *The Weekly*, produced by Sweta Vohra, February 21, 2020, https://www.nytimes.com/2020/02/21/the-weekly/child-abuse-willowbrook-union-ave-bronx-si.html.
8. Gant, Expert Report.
9. Rita Price, "Workshops Still Get Most Federal Funds for Disabled", Inde Online, April 3, 2012, https://www.indeonline.com/article/20120403/NEWS/304039709?template=ampart.
10. US Equal Employment Opportunity Commission, "Henry's Turkey Service, Heirs Must Turn over Almost $600,000 Owed to Disabled Workers" (Washington, DC, 2015), https://www.eeoc.gov/newsroom/henrys-turkey-service-heirs-must-turn-over-almost-600000-owed-disabled-workers.
11. Brian Wellner, "Bunkhouse Demo Closes Chapter for Atalissa," *Quad-City Times*, https://qctimes.com/news/local/bunkhouse-demo-closes-chapter-for-atalissa/article_390eda30-9eed-5e69-a67d-7f371c082083.html.
12. Dan Barry, "Bias Suit Filed on Behalf of Disabled Men in South Carolina Meat Plant," *New York Times*, September 30, 2016, https://www.nytimes.com/2016/10/01/us/bias-suit-disabled-workers-meat-plant.html.
13. Clark Kauffman, "Echoes of Atalissa: Federal Agency Sues Bunkhouse Owner for Exploiting Mentally Disabled Workers," *Des Moines Register*, https://www.desmoinesregister.com/story/news/2017/12/11/atalissa-echoes-federal-agency-sues-bunkhouse-owner-exploiting-mentally-disabled-workers/924471001/.

9. Boycotting Goodwill

1. Goodwill, "Goodwill Industries: 100 Years of the Power of Work," https://www.goodwill.org/wp-content/uploads/2011/01/First_100_Years_Timeline.pdf.
2. Nelson, *Workshops for the Handicapped*, 38–39.
3. Goodwill, "Morgan Memorial Goodwill Industries," https://www.goodwillmass.org/.
4. National Federation of the Blind, "Marc Maurer," https://www.nfb.org/about-us/leadership/presidents-corner/past-presidents/marc-maurer.
5. DC Advocacy Partners, "An Analysis of and Recommendations regarding Disability Employment Issues that Include Center-Based Employment and Section 14(c) of the Fair Labor Standards Act," http://dcpartners.iel.org/sites/default/files/sub%20minimum%20wage%20silverstein.pdf.

6. Change.org, "Goodwill Industries International: Pay Disabled Workers A Real Wage," 2013, https://www.change.org/p/goodwill-industries-international-pay-disabled-workers-a-real-wage.

7. Ibid.

8. In 1976 author and historian James Weinstein founded *In These Times* with the mission to "identify and clarify the struggles against corporate power now multiplying in American society."

9. Change.org.

10. Aimee Christian, "My Disabled Daughter Isn't Your Inspiration Porn," *Washington Post*, February 19, 2020, https://www.washingtonpost.com/lifestyle/2020/02/19/my-disabled-daughter-isnt-your-inspiration-porn/.

11. The Arc, "Self Determination," https://thearc.org/position-statements/self-determination/.

12. J. David Smith and Michael L. Wehmeyer, *Good Blood, Bad Blood: Science, Nature, and the Myth of the Kallikaks*, 1st ed. (Washington, DC: American Association on Intellectual and Developmental Disabilities, 2012).

13. Arc, "Self Determination."

14. National Federation of the Blind, "Groups Urge End to Subminimum Wages for Disabled Workers," https://nfb.org/index.php/about-us/press-room/cross-disability-groups-join-national-federation-blind-protests.

15. Ibid.

10. Oregon, Rhode Island, and the Promise of a Way Forward

1. Wikileaks, "The SourceAmerica Tapes—Background," November 16, 2015, https://wikileaks.org/sourceamerica-tapes/background.html.

2. SourceAmerica, "Statement on CNN Story," https://www.sourceamerica.org/newsroom/press-releases/statement-cnn-story.

3. US Department of Labor, "Customized Employment," https://www.dol.gov/agencies/odep/topics/customized-employment.

4. Kristin Andrews, "What Were the Top Outcomes of State Medicaid Infrastructure (MIG) Grants?" (Washington, DC: Mathematica Policy Research, 2013), https://www.mathematica.org/our-publications-and-findings/publications/what-were-the-top-outcomes-of-state-medicaid-infrastructure-mig-grants.

5. Ibid.

6. ADA, "State and Local Governments (Title II)," https://www.ada.gov/ada_title_II.htm.

7. Camilli, Danielle. "State Saves Sheltered Workshops for Adults with Developmentally Disabilities," *Burlington County Times*, July 29, 2013, https://www.burlingtoncountytimes.com/article/20130729/NEWS/307299778.

8. Ibid.

11. A Legislative Fix Was In

1. *Lane v. Kitzhaber*, 841 F.Supp.2d 1199 (D. Oregon, 2012), 27.

2. Institute for Community Inclusion, "National Core Indicators: Employment Trends for Adults with ID/DD and Suggestions for Policy Development," http://www.nationalcoreindicators.org/upload/presentation/ASPE_Presentation_060914FINAL_1.pdf.

3. *Lane*, 841 F.Supp.2d 1199 at 1.

4. *Huffington Post*, "How Some Charter Schools Leave Special Needs Students Behind: Students with 'Fairly Substantial Special Education Needs' Are Not Faring Well in Some

Charter Environments," June 1, 2016, https://www.huffpost.com/entry/charter-schools-special-needs_n_574f0be2e4b0ed593f12e8a4.

5. National Technical Assistance Center on Transition, "Evidence-Based Practices," https://www.transitionta.org/evidencepractices.

6. Loretta Kalb, "Special-Needs Students Pick up Trash at School: It's 'Demeaning,' Says One Teen," *Sacramento Bee*, July 6, 2016, https://www.sacbee.com/news/local/education/article87652802.html#storylink=cpy.

7. Amy Silverman, "Food, Flowers, and Filth," *Phoenix Magazine*, December 1, 2018, https://www.phoenixmag.com/2018/12/01/food-flowers-and-filth/.

8. Ibid.

9. US Department of Labor, *Fact Sheet #39H: The Workforce Innovation and Opportunity Act and Limitations on Payment of Subminimum Wages under Section 14(c) of the Fair Labor Standards Act*, February 2019, https://www.dol.gov/agencies/whd/fact-sheets/39h-14c-WIOA.

10. *Denoewer v. UCO Industries*, 2:17-CV-660 (S.D. Ohio, April 18, 2018), https://www.leagle.com/decision/infdco20180418f70.

11. Kathryn Watson, "Trump Wants to Bring Back Mental Institutions to Address Mass Shootings," *CBS News*, August 16, 2019, https://www.cbsnews.com/news/trump-wants-to-bring-back-mental-institutions-to-address-mass-shootings/.

12. Brown Goldstein & Levy, "Disability Consulting," https://browngold.com/practice-areas/disability-consulting/.

12. Ohio and the Future of Subminimum Wages

1. John H. Cushman, Jr., "International Business; Nike Pledges to End Child Labor and Apply U.S. Rules Abroad," *New York Times*, May 13, 1998, https://www.nytimes.com/1998/05/13/business/international-business-nike-pledges-to-end-child-labor-and-apply-us-rules-abroad.html.

2. UCO Industries, "Welcome to UCO Industries, Inc," https://ucoindustries.com/.

3. *Smith v. Chrysler Corp.*, 155 F.3d 799 (6th Cir., 1998), https://www.casemine.com/judgement/us/5914805eadd7b04934471e50.

4. Hillel Aron, "Lawsuit Takes Aim at Sheltered Workshops, Where Disabled Workers Make Far Less than Minimum Wage," *Fair Warning*, September 18, 2019, https://www.fairwarning.org/2019/09/hundreds-of-thousands-of-disabled-workers-still-make-less-than-minimum-wage/.

5. State of Rhode Island General Assembly, "House Votes to Repeal Bill Allowing Subminimum Wages for Disabled Workers." February 25, 2020, http://www.rilin.state.ri.us/pressrelease/_layouts/RIL.PressRelease.ListStructure/Forms/DisplayForm.aspx?List=c8baae31-3c10-431c-8dcd-9dbbe21ce3e9&ID=370788.

6. National Council on Disability, "2018 National Disability Employment Policy, From the New Deal to the Real Deal: Joining the Industries of the Future" (Washington, DC: National Council on Disability, 2018), https://ncd.gov/publications/2018/new-deal-real-deal.

7. Jean Winsor et al., "StateData: The National Report on Employment Services and Outcomes through 2017," (Boston: Institute for Community Inclusion (UCEDD) University of Massachusetts 2019), 21–27, https://www.thinkwork.org/sites/default/files/files/bluebook2019_Final.pdf.

8. Ibid.

9. National Council on Disability, "2018 National Disability Employment Policy."

10. Corlyn Voorhees, "A Maine Nonprofit Paid Its Disabled Workers Less than Minimum Wage, While Its Executives Got Six Figures," *Bangor Daily News*, July 12, 2017,

https://bangordailynews.com/2017/07/12/mainefocus/a-maine-nonprofit-paid-its-disabled-workers-less-than-minimum-wage-while-its-executives-got-six-figures/.

11. Ri'Shawn Bassette, "Lowndes Co. Non-profit to Pay More Than $150k in Back Pay," *WALB News 10*, July 23, 2019, https://www.walb.com/2019/07/23/lowndes-co-non-profit-pay-more-than-k-back-pay/.

12. US Department of Labor, "U.S. Department of Labor Acts to Protect Individuals with Disabilities from Workplace Exploitation" (Washington, DC, 2018), https://www.dol.gov/newsroom/releases/whd/whd20180423.

13. Mark Maxwell, "Goodwill Pulls Paychecks from Disabled Workers," *WCIA 3 News*, July 16, 2019, https://www.wcia.com/news/local-news/goodwill-pulls-paychecks-from-disabled-workers/.

14. NPR, *Abused And Betrayed*, 2018, https://www.npr.org/series/575502633/abused-and-betrayed.

15. NPR, "NPR Investigation Finds Hidden Epidemic of Sexual Assault," hosted by Joseph Shapiro, *Abused And Betrayed*, January 8, 2018, https://www.npr.org/2018/01/08/576428410/npr-investigation-finds-hidden-epidemic-of-sexual-assault.

16. Erika Harrell, "Crime against Persons with Disabilities, 2009–2015—Statistical Tables," Bureau of Justice Statistics, 2017, https://www.bjs.gov/index.cfm?ty=pbdetail&iid=5986.

17. US Commission on Civil Rights, "U.S. Commission on Civil Rights Releases Report: Subminimum Wages: Impacts on The Civil Rights of People with Disabilities" (Washington, DC, 2020), https://www.usccr.gov/files/2020-09-17-Subminimum-Wages-Report-PR.pdf.

18. Zack Budryk, "Commission on Civil Rights Calls for End to Subminimum Wage for Disabled People," *Hill*, September 17, 2020, https://thehill.com/regulation/labor/516869-commission-on-civil-rights-calls-for-end-to-subminimum-wage-for-disabled.

19. An adaption of the Maya Angelou quote, "When someone shows you who they are, believe them the first time."

INDEX

9 781501 762628